Macroeconomics
and the
Environment

Macroeconomics
and the
Environment

*Proceedings of a Seminar
May 1995*

editor
Ved P. Gandhi

International Monetary Fund

© 1996 International Monetary Fund

Design and production: IMF Graphics Section

Library of Congress Cataloging-in Publication Data

Macroeconomics and the enviroment / edited by Ved P. Gandhi
   p. cm.
   Includes bibiographical references.

   ISBN 1-55775-536-1

   1. Enviromental economics—Congresses. 2. Macroeconomics—Congresses.
   3. Economic policy—Congresses. I. Gandhi, Ved P. (Ved Parkash)
   II. International Monetary Fund.
   HC79.E5M323   1996
   333.7—dc20   96-8789
                                           CIP

Price: $22.50

Address orders to:
External Relations Department, Publication Services
International Monetary Fund, Washington D.C. 20431
Telephone: (202) 623-7430; Telefax: (202) 623-7201
Internet: publications@imf.org

Contents

v

Session 3. Experience

Session 4. Looking Ahead

Preface

The International Monetary Fund (henceforth, the Fund) staff's official interest in the environment, and the issues relating to it, began in early 1991. At that time, the Executive Board asked the staff to study the interactions between macroeconomics and the environment and, wherever important, keep them in mind when conducting policy dialogues with Fund member countries. An early search of the available literature revealed that, while environmental economics was a reasonably well-developed discipline, little work had been done on the impact of macroeconomic policies on the environment and the impact of environmental policies on the macroeconomy.

In order to improve its understanding of the interrelationships between macroeconomics and the environment, the Fund held its first seminar in May 1993, inviting many nongovernmental organizations (NGOs) dealing with the environment to share with it their views and concerns. At a second seminar, held in May 1995, recognized experts shared with Fund staff the results of their thinking and research on the interrelationships between macroeconomics and the environment. This volume contains the papers and proceedings of this second seminar.

The seminar was held with four specific objectives in mind: (1) to make the Fund staff aware of the current research on macroeconomics and the environment; (2) to present work being done on the environment by Fund staff in support of the mandate and primary functions of the organization; (3) to assess the feasibility of integrating macroeconomic and environmental policy formulation in the Fund's member countries at different stages of development; and (4) to identify the main elements of work that the Fund staff should undertake in the future, including finding ways of incorporating environmental concerns into the staff's policy dialogue with national authorities whenever warranted and desired by the authorities.

The seminar was held over a two-day period (May 10–11, 1995), and participants included experts from academic and research institutions, NGOs, the World Bank, and the Fund (including representatives from Executive Directors' offices, as well as staff economists working on operations, policy development, and research). The participants were welcomed by the Deputy Director of the External Relations Department, Margaret Kelly, who provided the welcoming remarks, and the seminar was closed by the Director of the Fiscal Affairs Department, Vito Tanzi, who offered the concluding remarks. In between, participants had open, frank, and intensive discussions on the interplay between macroeconomics and the environment. These discussions were enriched by many constructive and provocative comments from the floor. The First Deputy Managing Director of the Fund, Stanley Fischer, gave a luncheon speech entitled "What Is Reasonable to Expect of the IMF on the Environment?"

In preparing this volume, much gratitude is owed to outside experts, including paper writers (Knut Alfsen, Peter Bartelmus, Wilfrido Cruz, Kirk Hamilton, Stein Hansen, Mohan Munasinghe, and David Pearce), discussants (Cielito Habito, Kirit Parikh, Andrew Steer, and Michael Ward), and others who participated actively from the floor (Phil Bagnoli, Herman Daly, Salah El Serafy, Ian Johnson, Jim MacNeill, and David Reed). From the Fund, active participation was provided by the paper writers (Adriaan Bloem, Ved Gandhi, Ronald McMorran, and Ethan Weisman), session chairs, moderators, and discussants (Peter Clark, Mohammed El-Erian, Margaret Kelly, Naheed Kirmani, Malcolm Knight, and Vito Tanzi), and others who made useful contributions from the floor (Benedicte Christensen, Paul Cotterell, Nuri Erbas, David Nellor, Ganga Ramdas, and Emilio Sacerdoti).

Many Fund staff members helped in organizing the seminar (here Laura Wallace, David Nellor, and Ronald McMorran need special mention) while others (including Dale Chua) assisted during the seminar. The recorded proceedings were ably transcribed by Audrey Gross, Tammie Leedham, and Meike Gretemann. Ms. Gretemann also typed the first draft of the manuscript while Ms. Nezha Karkas helped with all later drafts and David Driscoll provided expert editorial assistance.

The editor is particularly thankful to all the people named above who have contributed significantly to the successful conduct of the seminar and producing this volume in record time.

1

Macroeconomics and the Environment: Summary and Conclusions

Ved P. Gandhi

Two themes dominated the discussions at the seminar. How do macroeconomic policies and the environment interact? How important is it that the Fund staff become aware of this interaction and take it into account in dealing with member countries?

Sessions 1, 2, and 3 of the seminar were devoted mainly to the first theme, while Session 4 focused primarily on the second theme. The seminar opened with welcoming remarks, which provided to the participants the background of Fund work on the environment, and closed with concluding remarks, which, among other things, looked forward to establishing priorities for Fund work on the environment.

In her welcoming remarks, Margaret Kelly reminded participants that the primary mandate of the Fund is to promote international monetary cooperation and exchange rate stability and to help member countries solve their balance of payments problems. Nevertheless, should resource depletion or environmental damage in a country be so severe as to affect seriously the longer-term viability of its balance of payments, the IMF staff cannot but be involved. Kelly described how Fund staff work on the environment has so far focused on monitoring the research of other specialized institutions and developing an understanding of the links between macroeconomic policies and conditions and the environment—thereby enabling the staff to design sound macroeconomic policies.

Interrelationships Between Macroeconomics and the Environment

In dealing with links between macroeconomics and the environment, the first three sessions of the seminar reviewed the conclusions of read-

1

ily available studies using alternative analytical frameworks (Session 1), the urgency and feasibility of integrating the environment into national accounts (Session 2), and case studies of the possible impact on the economy of integrating environmental objectives into macroeconomic policymaking (Session 3).

Impact of Macroeconomics on the Environment

The Ved Gandhi and Ronald McMorran paper highlighted four conclusions that have been reached by the analyses carried out in the partial equilibrium framework. First, macroeconomic stability is a minimum and necessary condition for preserving the environment. Second, environmental degradation is generally caused by market, policy, and institutional failures relating to the use of environmental resources. Third, macroeconomic policies can have an adverse impact on the environment but only when market, policy, and institutional failures exist, although it is difficult in advance to judge how serious these impacts will be. Fourth, macroeconomic policies are inefficient and blunt instruments for mitigating environmental degradation, for which appropriate environmental policies are the most efficient and direct instruments. The authors conclude that only general equilibrium analyses, carried out with the help of computable general equilibrium (CGE) models, can help one reach country-specific conclusions on how the country's macroeconomic policies, or their reform, are likely to affect the environment.

The Stein Hansen paper begins where the Gandhi and McMorran paper leaves off. Using examples of the research work done in Norway and in the United States, it highlights many advantages of CGE modeling, which, among other things, can help to (1) establish the loss of GDP and the reduction in its growth rate owing to environmental policies aimed at reducing CO_2 and SO_2 emissions, (2) permit policymakers see the direct and indirect consequences for the macroeconomy of alternative uses of revenues from environmental taxes, such as a CO_2 stabilizing gasoline tax, and (3) bring together policymakers (from ministries of finance and economy and the ministry of environment) for a professional and political dialogue and make them recognize the tradeoffs between pursuing alternative macroeconomic and environmental objectives. Hansen also shows (giving the examples of higher stumpage fees and raising the wage rate in Costa Rica) how sometimes general equilibrium results can be quite opposite from the partial equilibrium results. He recognizes that CGE models require lots of reliable data and assumptions, which not all countries have, and certainly most developing countries do not have.

Much like the Gandhi and McMorran conclusions, Hansen points out partial equilibrium impacts of fiscal discipline, exchange rate and trade liberalization, interest rate and credit policy reform, and external debt relief, especially in developing countries. These can be both negative and positive at the same time, depending upon environmental policies, and can in the end yield "uncertain" final outcomes. Nonetheless, he suggests that macroeconomic policies of developing countries would greatly improve the environment if the following measures were undertaken: (1) avoid reducing small and fragile environmental and health care budgets, (2) curtail fertilizer, pesticide, water, and energy subsidies, (3) restructure health budgets from capital-intensive curative hospitalization to labor-intensive preventive primary health care, (4) include land-reform and property-right measures in the reform program in order to facilitate internalizing the environmental externalities resulting from malfunctioning land markets, (5) increase taxes and lower subsidies that affect forests and other natural resources, and (6) ensure that external debt relief is not used to finance environmentally harmful projects.

Andrew Steer, in commenting on both papers, agreed with their overall conclusions that the impact of macroeconomic policy reforms on the environment is generally positive. He highlighted the four paths through which this comes about. First, macroeconomic instability promotes high discount rates and short-term calculations, guaranteeing environmental destruction through excessive natural resource exploitation and deforestation, while macroeconomic stabilization encourages environmentally sound decisions by economic agents. Second, although a curtailment of aggregate demand in theory helps the environment through less consumption, less depletion, and less waste, cuts in environmental public expenditures (as a part of a reduction in public expenditures to reduce fiscal imbalances) in certain cases may be detrimental to protecting the environment. Third, macroeconomic policy reforms affect the environment through relative price shifts. Most of these impacts, especially those which move the economy from subsidized input prices toward world prices, help improve the quality of the environment. However, as Hansen and Gandhi and McMorran point out, the impact will also depend on a number of features of the economy, especially whether or not complementary "first-best" environmental policies exist. Fourth, structural reforms relating to financial sector, accountability of state-owned enterprises, property rights, and the like, often associated with macroeconomic adjustment programs, also promote economic efficiency and reduce waste. As with relative price shifts, for structural reforms to work for sustainable development and not against it, certain preconditions must exist. As an illustration, privatization can easily become a cause for air and water pollution if environmental policies are absent or civil society is weak and lacks empowerment.

Steer also agreed with Hansen that, based on the simulations of CGE models in Norway and the United States, radical environmental policies may not greatly reduce the rate of economic growth in industrial countries. Whether or not the public is ready and willing to accept even that much reduction is another matter.

In the discussion that followed, there was support for the general equilibrium approach and CGE modeling. It was pointed out, however, that with a suitable choice of parameters one can get any result that one wants, and that these models were less useful in generating specific numbers and more useful in supplementing other tools to develop broad trends. On the whole, development of CGE models was not seen as a priority for the use of limited resources in developing countries.

Developing sectoral policies and implementing them effectively were recognized as important for the overall impact of macroeconomic policies on the environment. Given that these sectoral policies had significant feedbacks, a commentator argued that the Fund cannot absolve itself of the responsibility of taking these policies into account. However, there was also a consensus that macroeconomic policy reform was too critical to wait until sectoral policies have been properly designed or effectively implemented.

Ecotaxes were underscored as an important element of environmental policies. The scope for such taxes to replace distortionary income taxes and regressive value-added taxes was explored. Because a tax system must meet the criteria of efficiency, equity, and revenue productivity, it was felt that ecotaxes should supplement, rather than replace, existing broad-based taxes.

One participant stressed the importance of social structures to the environment and the impact of macroeconomic policies on social structures. Although it was argued that the Fund should recognize the importance of social structures in its operational work, the consensus was that because the World Bank had the necessary expertise in matters relating to social structures, the Fund should utilize the knowledge and expertise of the Bank staff in this regard.

It was emphasized that natural resources in many developing countries were exploited excessively because of a nontransparent system of rent-seeking by vested groups and that the Fund staff should therefore encourage a greater transparency in leasing of exploitation rights.

Finally, it was questioned whether strong environmental policies were compatible with an acceptable level of macroeconomic performance.

Here, the general feeling was that reasonably (but not excessively) strong environmental policies may mean some reduction in the level and growth rate of GDP, conventionally measured, but that outcome should not be considered intolerable. The Norwegian simulations, given as major evidence of this conclusion, had broad support.

Impact of the Environment on Macroeconomy

David Pearce and Kirk Hamilton stressed the impact of pollution and environmental degradation on the macroeconomy, in the first instance through its impact on human capital. They argued and provided evidence that air pollution, caused mainly by a weak transportation policy for fuel conservation and vehicular traffic, often resulted in ill health and premature mortality. Similarly, they argued that a lack of water-treatment facilities led to contamination of water and caused many waterborne diseases.

They further argued that investments in environmental protection, which often had high rates of return and benefits even in terms of conventionally measured GNP, are often ignored in macroeconomic analysis. An example of such investments was afforestation, which could help improve soil fertility and crop yields, increase timber production and other tree products, and produce forest fodder. Such investments, of course, will also have nonmarket returns in the form of biological diversity and carbon storage.

Pearce and Hamilton then took up the issue of depletion of natural resources and degradation of the natural environment (or natural capital) which can have a significant impact on economic welfare and macroeconomy through erosion of what they call the "genuine savings rate." They felt that the concept of "genuine savings rate," defined as [GNP-Consumption-Depreciation of produced capital] – [value of "net" depletion of natural resources] – [marginal social cost of "net" accumulation of pollution], is the most relevant way to assess the impact of depletion of natural resources and pollution of the environment on economic welfare and the sustainability of the macroeconomy. In fact, they showed that an economy can have a positive conventionally measured savings rate, derived from conventionally measured national accounts under the system of national accounts (SNA), but a negative genuine savings rate. They emphasized that an economy will be unsustainable and economic welfare will eventually decline, if a negative genuine savings rate persists. Hence, they suggested that only those policy reforms should be implemented that will not only enhance the SNA-based savings rate but will curtail losses resulting from natural resource depletion and environmental pollution.

The authors made heroic attempts to estimate the genuine savings rates for various parts of the world. These estimates reveal that the Middle East and North Africa have negative genuine savings rates; in Latin America and the Caribbean, they have turned from positive to negative in recent years; and in most sub-Saharan African countries, they are consistently negative, holding a serious potential for the unsustainability of their economies.

Pearce and Hamilton therefore concluded with a call for revised economic accounting, for the development of better valuation techniques of nonmarketed natural and environmental resources, and for the Fund in particular to revise its savings and other macroeconomic indicators to incorporate sustainability considerations.

Kirit Parikh, who commented on the Pearce-Hamilton paper, had little difficulty with the authors' urging that the countries should have a proper transport policy (to curb air pollution) and investments in water treatment (to improve water quality), but found three major flaws in the concept of genuine savings rate. First, in adding man-made physical capital to natural capital, the authors assume a one-to-one substitutability between the two, which is inappropriate. Second, the concept of a genuine savings rate refers strictly to the domestic economy and ignores the environmental damage done elsewhere when a country imports pollution—and natural—resource-intensive products from elsewhere. Third, the authors do not deduct the losses of global commons caused by the lifestyle of a country; as a result, the U.S. economy, for example, comes out being "sustainable" by their criteria.

In the discussion that ensued, the participants noted alternative approaches to the concern for the environment—an all-out approach of the Norwegian kind, in which environmental targets are agreed to with the NGOs and macroeconomic policies are made subject to those constraints, and an incremental approach along the Pearce-Hamilton lines, under which the negative impact of macroeconomic policies on the environment is measured through some index, like the genuine savings rate. Which approach is more suitable for the Fund staff to pursue? While not fully resolved, the latter approach appeared pragmatic and feasible at this stage, since it essentially required the Fund staff to focus on how macroeconomic adjustment was achieved and what its effect was on some index of sustainability.

One participant reminded the seminar that the Fund staff, which did medium-term balance of payments projections, did consider the longer-term sustainability of natural resources, to the extent that the impact of the exhaustion of exportable resources on the medium-term macroeconomic outlook was of serious concern to the Fund. However, environmental economists present wanted the Fund staff to go even further

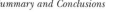

and start looking at the erosion of soil and other environmental re-sources, which may not necessarily affect the medium-term outlook of exports, but were important to the sustainability of macroeconomic per-formance, economic welfare, and quality of life.

Another participant reminded the seminar that the concept of sus-tainability was still not fully defined. What the policymakers should aim at was unclear. Was it sustainability? Over what period? Would environ-mental damage over the short to medium term be acceptable if it was reversible and helped countries improve their financial and economic situation in the short run, which provided resources to pay for the cost of reversing the damage in the medium to long run? The answer seemed to be yes.

A question was whether there were trade-offs between the rate of macroeconomic adjustment (macroeconomic objectives) and the rate of environmental protection (environmental objectives). Here, the answer was probably yes. However, it was not clear how far macroeconomic ad-justment should be forgone in the interest of environmental protection.

Feasibility of Environmentally Adjusted National Accounts

The Adriaan Bloem and Ethan Weisman paper, as presented by Paul Cotterell, recognized the importance of "green" and "brown" accounts for raising public awareness of environmental issues and toward an un-derstanding of interrelationships between macroeconomy and the en-vironment. However, of the two possible approaches—the physical ap-proach (which would involve the measurement of physical data on natural resources and pollution) and the monetary approach (which would require monetary values associated with the physical data)—they preferred the physical approach as the first step. In their opinion, this approach abstracts from "correct" prices while the monetary approach would require valuations and estimations based upon a variety of sensi-tive assumptions and modeling of economic behavior.

Bloem and Weisman pointed out that the traditional measures of na-tional accounts aggregates should not be replaced by green national ac-counts, but that a supplementary set of satellite accounts should be de-veloped as recognized by the 1993 SNA. However, Bloem and Weisman also recognized that the satellite accounts were "a work-in-progress" and that further research and experience would be needed to develop fully these satellite accounts to integrate the entire financial accounts, the rest of the world account, and the balance sheets. Practical experience with this approach in the United States and the Netherlands provided adequate support for staying with this approach at this stage. Even this approach would require physical data on the environment, which were not always available and whose generation in itself would represent substantial progress.

Peter Bartelmus in emphasized his paper the significance and need for environmentally adjusted national accounts. He quoted the studies on Mexico and Papua New Guinea to show how results and conclusions on growth rates of the economy can vary significantly whether unadjusted or adjusted national accounts were used. He stressed how environmentally adjusted national accounts can facilitate modeling and creation of data relevant for policy analysis for sustainable development. Finally, he suggested that "valuation" of natural resources, notably through maintenance costing of the use of environmental assets can help in full-cost pricing and therefore in the internalization of environmental costs. But he also recognized the many problems and limitations of developing environmentally adjusted national accounts and using them to assess sustainability in growth and development. There are conceptual and statistical difficulties in defining and measuring social (human and institutional) capital. Even with respect to environmental capital, serious problems exist in relation to valuing the environmental services or estimating the depletion and depreciation of environmental assets. Bartelmus, however, felt that techniques designed to overcome data and definitional problems did exist and had been successfully applied in several country case studies.

Bartelmus also argued that integrated environmental-economic accounts can help see the sustainability of economic growth in terms of positive trends of environmentally adjusted net domestic product (EDP). The definition and measurement of a broader concept of sustainable development, on the other hand, would require supplementary physical indicators as, for instance, developed in Frameworks for Indicators of Sustainable Development.

The System of integrated Environmental and Economic Accounting (SEEA), proposed by the United Nations, is based on the revised 1993 SNA. It attempts to measure the sustainability of economic growth in terms of the costs of maintaining both produced and natural assets. Welfare-oriented approaches to national accounts would require the removal from GDP of the so-called "defensive expenditures," needed to mitigate the effects of pollution. However, both the definition and the elimination of defensive expenditure from accounting aggregates are controversial and inconsistent with conventional economic indicators. The SEEA, therefore, identifies environmental protection expenditures as part of intermediate and final use and only by appropriate classifications.

Bartelmus concluded that the macroeconomy-environment interactions can be studied at this stage by means of "satellite" accounts, parallel to conventional national accounts, without replacing the core accounts of the SNA by environmental ones. He also described the advantages of an integrated information system such as the SEEA. In this context, he indicated a number of direct policy uses of the results of integrated accounting, notably the setting of economic instruments at maintenance cost levels (at the microeconomic level), and the use of environmentally adjusted indicators such as capital (including natural capital), capital accumulation, environmental cost of depletion and degradation, and adjusted aggregates of final consumption and trade (at the macroeconomic level). Bartelmus pleaded for international cooperation to standardize concepts and methods of environmental accounting for worldwide use and application.

Michael Ward, who commented on both papers, noted that neither Bloem and Weisman nor Bartelmus showed exuberance for a fully integrated and comprehensive environmental accounting system. The former take this position because such accounts have many intractable and systemic measurement problems with limited relevance to fiscal and monetary management and the development of overall macroeconomic strategy. The latter believes that the ultimate objective of sustainability should be sustainability of people and their welfare rather than of the economy alone. Ward recapitulated two serious difficulties with an integrated accounting framework. First, there was the issue relating to the quantities—industrial production generates environmentally degrading outputs, such as polluting effluents, wastes, and energy losses, but technological changes can convert such "dirty" residual outputs into "clean" outputs. It was unclear how one should take account of such quantities. Second, there were many issues relating to valuation and pollution. What were the "appropriate" prices, given the ill-conceived interventions by governments, income and wealth inequalities, and intergenerational factors that shape social and economic policies? How should one "price" cross-border environmental externalities? How should one deal with different "valuations" that countries at different stages of development are bound to apply to environmental damage? How to "value" a natural resource being exploited by a multinational monopoly for which competitive markets did not exist? How to know that external costs have not been internalized already into "prices"? Thus, Ward also considered integrated environmental accounting unachievable until the relevant conceptual, methodological, and statistical issues had been resolved.

Nevertheless, he advised that policy practitioners at the Fund and the World Bank can still take certain initiatives. The Fund can remain a macroeconomic organization but can ensure sustainability through an insistence on "green taxes" in its operational work, so that countries achieve a more balanced and rational pattern of progress. The World Bank, on the other hand, should ensure that, at a minimum, all countries have an adequate provision of safe water, solid waste disposal, and clean sanitation, which are the key environmental issues everywhere. The Fund staff could then ensure that government expenditures and investments in these services would be protected from cuts in public outlays following a fiscal stringency. Ward also called on the World Bank to help enhance institutional capacity for environmental protection and, as a start, assess the importance to future development of "big ticket" items of resource depletion and ecological deterioration in a dozen selected developing countries.

The discussion that followed supported the general conclusion that while it would be desirable to have environmentally integrated national accounts, for short-term macroeconomic policy formulation conventional national accounts would suffice. Only one discussant felt that conventional national accounts, especially in economies heavily dependent on natural resources, would send out wrong signals on savings, investments, and balance of payments.

There was also a general agreement, that given serious conceptual and methodological issues, the approach that the 1993 SNA has taken, of creating satellite accounts, was quite acceptable at this stage. Efforts to resolve the serious outstanding issues must nevertheless continue.

Integrating Macroeconomics and the Environment— Industrial Country Experience

Knut Alfsen describes in his paper how Norway, a small industrial country, has attempted to integrate environmental concerns into its macroeconomic policymaking.

Historically, because natural resources have been important to the Norwegian economy (most important among all OECD countries except for Ireland) natural resource accounting (for energy, fishing, land use, sand, and gravel) was the first step the authorities took, some 20 years ago, primarily to improve long-term conservation and resource management. The accounts consisted of reserves, extraction rates, and domestic end uses, and, in the context of energy accounts, air pollution emission. However, the authorities used only energy accounts information actively (as energy was an input into production and energy output was important to the economy) and integrated this information into macroeconomic modeling.

More recently, however, the coverage of resource and environmental accounts has been broadened. In addition, environmental assets and environmental degradation have been linked to the economic productivity of capital and labor; as a result, the macroeconomic model used in policy formulation has become more versatile. It now contains energy use and associated emissions of nine polluting compounds, generation of various types of wastes, physical effects of air pollution and waste generation, and economic valuation of environmental degradation based on shadow prices of capital and labor. Alfsen pointed out the many questions the authorities have sought to answer with the help of the integrated model. These have included determining the costs in GDP terms (net of indirect gains to the GDP) of meeting targets set in international treaties and protocols and comparing costs in GDP terms associated with meeting environmental targets (i.e., increase in pollution) with those that would accrue if no environmental targets were set. Alfsen admits, however, that the Norwegian model depends heavily on many assumptions and ignores the links between employment and the environment.

Alfsen describes how the model has been used in Norway to identify the economic and environmental effects of introduction of carbon taxes, the decline in emissions (or emission elasticity) when fuel and electricity prices are raised, and the costs to specific sectors of the economy of specific environmental policies.

According to Alfsen, important policy conclusions have been derived from such analyses. *On carbon taxes:* (1) These are not the most efficient means of reducing NO_x emissions. (2) Since national targets of emissions and pollution are unachievable even with high carbon taxes, other measures need to be taken as well. (3) Secondary economic effects of introducing carbon taxes are highly uncertain. (4) Loss of GDP estimates owing to carbon taxes vary with varying assumptions. *On emission elasticity:* (1) Elasticities depend greatly on the assumptions made. (2) Transport activities have the greatest impact on pollution and the greatest sensitivity for emissions. (3) Energy and capital are complementary inputs and taxation of sulphur emissions reduces long-term economic growth. As to the *impact on individual sectors*, taxation is found to be the most cost-effective means in Norway for lowering emissions from polluting sectors.

In analyzing why Norway has been successful in integrating environmental concerns into macroeconomic policy formulation, Alfsen could provide only a tentative answer: because of economic, political, and institutional factors. The main economic factor is the importance of natural resources to the society and how they are managed. The main political factor is that organized political groups, including the NGOs, that depend on government funds have supported politicians responding to their needs and objectives. The long experience of Statistics Norway, first with natural resource accounting and later with modeling integrated national accounts for policy formulation purposes, has encouraged dialogue between relevant institutions and actors in the debate. In addition, the Ministry of Finance has come to see environmental taxes as a way of expanding the tax base. These are the peculiar institutional factors. Alfsen is not sure if the Norwegian experience with integrating environmental considerations into macroeconomic policymaking can be replicated in other countries, but he believes that, if properly carried out, it can help break the power of vested interest groups.

Peter Clark, commenting on the Alfsen paper, drew from the Norwegian experience four lessons that he thought could be useful to other industrial countries. First, a model-based integration of environmental and macroeconomic policies facilitates consensus building by resolving differences in opinions and preconceived notions. Second, it places environmental concerns at the center of macroeconomic policymaking. Third, it helps analyze the feasibility of applying major environment policy shocks to the economy. Fourth, it helps identify both direct and indirect effects and nets them out.

Clark also had a few specific questions on Alfsen's paper: Are there any alternatives to carbon taxes if they are considered inefficient means of reducing NO_x? By assuming that technology is exogenous, thereby denying technological progress, and by assuming that an energy tax is basically a tax on capital, does the model exaggerate the output losses owing to CO_2 taxes? How serious are the employment effects of environmental policies, such as the carbon tax? While Clark agreed that the production of power through hydroelectricity results in little pollution, it does make the country vulnerable to shocks in world prices of oil, which is the alternative form of fuel for energy production. Have the authorities paid attention to these consequences? All in all, Clark believed that that country's experience held the prospects of wider applicability.

Alfsen's paper generated much enthusiastic discussion among participants and raised several questions. Must conventional GDP losses result from environmental policies and can they be offset? What are the economic and distributional consequences of carbon taxes and other green taxes? How does the Norwegian CGE model integrate natural resources into the macroeconomy? Are integrated national accounts appropriate for international comparability? Has the monopoly in modeling by Statistics Norway in any way been hazardous, and has it done any damage to policymaking in Norway?

In his reply, Alfsen agreed that there are bound to be, and have been in Norway's case, some costs to the economy of environmental policies and nobody can foresee whether technological changes will help to reduce these costs. In fact, nobody can foresee the nature and direction of technological change over time. Environmental policies, including ecotaxes, need not have crushing effects on economies, if their revenues are utilized wisely. The distributional consequences of such taxes and policies, however, may not be positive, especially in developing countries where income and wealth distribution is already heavily skewed.

Alfsen agreed that modeling oil and gas is not easy and, in the Norwegian CGE model, the natural resources are largely treated exogenously. He also agreed that integrated national accounts are necessary for international comparability, but not necessarily for the conduct of a domestic policy dialogue. As to the final question, Norway does have a Model Forum, where the shortcomings of various models are continuously discussed, so that the model of Statistics Norway is used after a consensus has been reached. In fact, it is because of the CGE model that the preconceived notion of the NGOs, that all economic growth is bad for the environment, has been corrected.

In connection with environmental taxes, a discussant made the point that, in addition to being supportive of environmental objectives, such taxes can provide finances for reducing the distortionary taxes on labor and capital and can help improve economic efficiency and prospects for economic growth. Environmental taxes were therefore seen as a true win-win policy for the environment as well as the macroeconomy.

Integrating Macroeconomics and the Environment— Developing Countries

Few developing countries have integrated their environmental objectives and policies with their macroeconomic objectives and policies; many still do not have clear-cut objectives and strategies for environmental protection. Therefore, little is known by way of experience. The country case studies carried out in the World Bank, however, throw much light on what would happen in developing countries if macroeconomics and the environment were integrated.

Mohan Munasinghe and Wilfrido Cruz summarized the main conclusions of recent World Bank case studies. These conclusions are in line with those in the Gandhi and McMorran paper, but the World Bank authors provide abundant evidence for their conclusions. For example, exchange rate reform is seen to be helpful to the environment by correcting the prices of tradables, encouraging wildlife protection and discouraging cattle ranching (in Zimbabwe and Zambia), providing incentives to protect nature preserves and game parks (in Tanzania), and helping expand the forests, and reduce land degradation and losses from floods (in Vietnam).

Pricing and subsidy reform in relation to electricity is shown to have a favorable impact on the environment because of energy conservation and improvements in air quality resulting from a reduction of electricity subsidies (in Sri Lanka) and rangeland improvement resulting from the reduction of livestock subsidies (in Tunisia). Reduction of price distortions and corrections of price signals are shown by the authors as creating significant benefits for the macroeconomy as well as for the environment.

High and unstable interest rates are shown to be detrimental to farm productivity over the longer run (in Brazil), while low and stable interest rates have had a welcome positive influence in curtailing the rate of logging (in Costa Rica).

The case studies also reveal how the beneficial effects of macroeconomic policy changes would have been much greater if complementary environmental policies had been in place. Munasinghe and Cruz emphasize that while the overall benefits of trade liberalization were positive—by promoting exports and encouraging industrialization—they were eroded in certain countries because the relative price changes brought about changes in the structure of production that had undesired side effects on the environment and that were not corrected by appropriate environmental policies. For example, trade liberalization promoted a water-intensive crop, such as sugarcane (in Morocco), that should have been discouraged by raising water charges. It encouraged a surge of (dirty) processing industries (in Indonesia) that could have been curbed by pollution regulations. It encouraged pressure on land resources and increased encroachment on marginal land as well as soil erosion (in Ghana) that could have been constrained by establishing property rights. The case studies of Mexico, Poland, and Thailand were mentioned as evidence of the extreme importance of building institutional capacity in developing countries that would help authorities foresee the undesired effects of macroeconomic reform and adopt appropriate corrective environmental measures.

Basing their arguments on the case studies, Munasinghe and Cruz point to the potential of fiscal cutbacks to damage the environment. Cutbacks in environmental expenditures, though insignificant to begin with, were shown to be environmentally unfriendly (in Thailand, Mexico, Cameroon, Zambia, and Tanzania) while cutbacks in the purchasing power, coupled with population growth, led to deforestation and cultivation of marginal lands (in the Philippines and Cameroon and certain other countries of sub-Saharan Africa).

The point made earlier by Hansen that partial equilibrium results can be misleading in certain circumstances is reconfirmed by Munasinghe and Cruz. In Costa Rica's case, an increase in minimum wages was found to increase deforestation. Directly, it encouraged unskilled workers to move to cities (thus reducing deforestation), but indirectly investors found minimum wage legislation binding in the industrial sector and sought refuge in the agricultural sector (thereby increasing deforestation). The net result was increased conversion of forest land to farming.

Munasinghe and Cruz conclude from the World Bank case studies that economy-wide policies tend to have significant and important effects, but if environmental policies do not exist, there is no assurance that efficiency-oriented economic reforms will be beneficial to the environment. They believe that developing countries have substantial scope for implementing the right environmental policies and suggest a step-by-step approach to integrate the environment into macroeconomic policy formulation at the country level. Toward this, they regard the Action Impact Matrix proposed by them as a versatile analytical tool.

Cielito Habito, in commenting on the paper, agreed with Munasinghe and Cruz that the impact of macroeconomic reforms (and structural adjustment programs) was generally beneficial for the environment and that complementary environmental policies were needed to guard against or mitigate their adverse effects on the environment.

Taking the case of the Philippines, Habito illustrated how the economy-wide policies adversely affected the environment as the environmental policy framework was weak to nonexistent. There was a depletion of forest resources (and soil erosion owing to deforestation), as well as depletion of fisheries, as macroeconomic reforms turned the terms of trade against agriculture and farmers resorted to extensive farming and engaged in overfishing to make up for the loss of income. This process was facilitated by unduly low stumpage fees and liberal licensing rules. The air pollution also grew, owing to the anti-agriculture and pro-industry bias of macroeconomic reforms, as industries enjoyed excessive industrial protection provided by the Government. Water pollution became a serious problem, especially in cities, as public spending on water and sanitation facilities and garbage collection services was grossly inadequate. This pollution was exacerbated by migration from the country to the cities. In the Philippine case, Habito considers the anti-agriculture and pro-industry bias of macroeconomic reforms to be the major culprit.

But he also recognizes that the Philippines needs jobs, incomes, and industries to support her growing population, and that polluting industries may have been accepted because of their backward linkages with agriculture. Habito thus brought forth the trade-off between incomes and jobs and environmental concerns that the authorities of developing countries often face and for which the adoption of complementary environmental policies are absolutely indispensable. Once implemented, these policies have feedback effects on the economy and the prospects of economic growth that should also be taken into account.

Finally, Habito questioned the usefulness of the Action Impact Matrix proposed by Munasinghe and Cruz. Where conditions are changing rapidly and many factors and policies simultaneously affect the environment, he argued that the Matrix is bound to have an extremely limited usefulness. It will also be difficult to use it in practice owing to various constraints, including the paucity of data and analytical tools to balance the conflicting impacts.

In the discussion that followed, one discussant asked if, by stressing the importance of complementary policies, the World Bank and the Fund simply wish to treat the environmental protection as an add-on objective instead of fully integrating it into macroeconomic policy formulation. Another discussant asked Cielito Habito if it were at all possible that the staff of international organizations would ever be able to convince the authorities of developing countries to adopt politically sensitive environmental policies. Another question that was raised related to the emphasis on win-win policies resulting from subsidy reductions and price reforms. Munasinghe and Cruz were asked whether the effects of such reforms were overstated since much of the environmental damage in countries with structural adjustment programs resulted from their social impacts and effects on social structures. At least one participant argued that ignoring the social impacts of adjustment and the role of social structures in environmental damage was shortsighted on the part of the Fund and the Bank.

A participant wanted to know how feasible it was to design and implement environmental taxes in the context of developing countries. Another participant wanted to know if the World Bank had done studies on how the levels and patterns of environmental expenditures of the governments have been affected in countries undergoing severe fiscal stringency.

In response, Munasinghe argued that ensuring that desirable environmental policies will all be in place before macroeconomic reforms are implemented may not always be possible. When macroeconomic reforms cannot wait, it would seem necessary to have complementary policies, at least as add-ons, instead of completely ignoring them. As to the relevance of social structures to the environment, both Munasinghe and Cruz agreed that they were important, although they stressed that little analytical work had been done until now in the Bank as well as elsewhere that would facilitate its integration into the operational work of the Bank and the Fund.

Munasinghe gave many reasons why it is difficult to design adequate environmental taxes. It is not easy to decide who should be made to bear the tax or even determine its level. (Should it be based on the extent of damage, the level of emissions, or the size of the particulate matter that is causing the damage in the first place?) Regarding the impact of structural adjustment programs and fiscal stringency on environmental expenditures, the participants were informed that some work has been done at the World Bank. Another participant pointed out that a recent study of eight countries with structural adjustment programs in recent years showed no decline (as a proportion of GDP) in social expenditures (health and education).

Cielito Habito, responding to a question, thought that, at least in the Philippines, the authorities are now convinced of the urgent need for environmental policies to address the short-term negative impacts of macroeconomic adjustment on the environment.

One Fund staff member reminded the participants that, as a prior step, a synthesis of macroeconomic and environment objectives must take place in the member countries themselves, if the Fund staff is to design macroeconomic reform packages that would be fully supportive of the country's environmental objectives. Most participants seemed to agree to the urgent need for a coordination of economic and environmental work at the country level itself.

The Fund and the Environment

The last session of the seminar focused on the Fund and the environment.

Stanley Fischer, in his luncheon remarks on what is reasonable to expect of the Fund in the environment area, stated that the work of the Fund and its staff is guided by the Articles of Agreement, which discourage member countries from resorting to macroeconomic policies "destructive of national and international prosperity" and in fact encourage them to adopt macroeconomic policies which would achieve monetary and financial stability and "contribute thereby . . . to the development of productive resources." He argued that although the environment is not referred to in the Articles of Agreement, excessive exploitation of natural resources and increased deforestation, which can occur particularly when appropriate environmental policies are lacking, cannot be ignored because they can give rise to structural balance of payments problems and can reduce economic growth prospects.

He indicated that the Fund's advice on public policy reforms is generally supportive of the environment; besides, the Fund, working closely with the World Bank, helps countries prepare Policy Framework Papers, which often include plans for addressing environmental problems. The Fund has been also supporting the work on environmental or "green" accounting being carried out by the United Nations, the World Bank, and others.

Finally, environmental issues tend to show up in Fund dealings with member countries in a number of ways. Developing countries, for example, whose economic growth strategy relies heavily on depletable resources are advised to use such resources at an optimal rate. Countries whose economies are still in transition are advised to remove price distortions and subsidies (e.g., for energy) and to eliminate soft budget constraints for state-owned enterprises. Industrial countries, which may already be paying attention to environmental issues, could consider the results of analytical research on the impact of environmental policies and conditions on the macroeconomy and incorporate them in policy formulation.

David Pearce, who initiated the panel discussion on the subject, was of the view that the Fund staff must take the environment into account because it makes little sense to revitalize the economy or bring about macroeconomic stability if it is at the expense of the resource base of the economy on which economic growth ultimately depends. Macroeconomic stability without care for the environment will not be sustainable, and, in his opinion, the Articles of Agreement of the Fund do invite the staff to be concerned with sustainability. He argued that the fear that environment was a complex and multifaceted subject for which the Fund economists were not adequately trained was unfounded because the staff of the World Bank and the World Trade Organization have acquired the necessary environmental skills without much difficulty. The fact that the Fund staff already looks at the stock of mineral resource base in economies dependent on minerals, or the stock of oil in economies dependent on oil, or the stock of forests in economies dependent on timber, is already a good beginning. Such work should now be extended to other elements bearing on the environment, for example, soil base for productive agriculture, or the quality of air and water for human health and labor productivity. In his opinion, it will not be too difficult for Fund staff, who are well trained in economics, to acquire the relevant knowledge about the environment and to incorporate environmental concerns in their policy dialogues with the authorities of member countries.

Cielito Habito, the second panel discussant, reemphasized the need for the Fund to take environmental sustainability seriously for it is environmental sustainability that will ensure sustainability of economic growth in the longer run. In his opinion, integrating the environment into the design of macroeconomic programs should be relatively easy and can be done primarily through the design of the fiscal content of the program. On the public expenditure side, every attempt should be made to insulate environmental programs and projects from budgetary cutbacks, or at least prevent such programs and projects from becoming the first to suffer as a result of austerity measures. On the revenue side, the Fund staff could highlight environment-friendly tax measures, such as taxes on petroleum, pollution taxes, and forestry charges, in designing fiscal reform programs. Even in terms of other policy reforms, there was scope for structural adjustment programs to incorporate market-based incentive measures for encouraging the adoption of environmentally sound practices in the productive sectors of the economy, including appropriate pricing of natural resources and environmental charges. Habito was of the firm opinion that developing country policymakers are ready for policies that would support the objective of sustainable development and that environmental considerations are increasingly being woven into overall economic policymaking.

Andrew Steer, the third panel discussant, argued that, even with the knowledge that they currently have, Fund and Bank economists can do at least five things in support of the environment. First, they should be able to assess the first-order impacts of macroeconomic policy reforms on the environment in a more systematic manner. It should not be too difficult for them to prepare environmental impact statements covering, for example, the impact of devaluation and trade liberalization on the exportable extractive sector and on cropping patterns in the agricultural sector, the potential impact of budget cutbacks on public expenditures for environmental protection, and the potential impact of austerity on activity patterns among the poor. Second, having established these first-order impacts and identified the potential adverse effects, if any, they should be able to help countries design "first-best" environmental policies to mitigate such effects and, at the same time, integrate them into adjustment programs. It does not matter whether these policies are actually woven into the adjustment programs or are implemented in parallel; what does matter is that macroeconomic and environmental reforms get implemented simultaneously and effectively. Third, Fund and Bank economists should make every effort to incorporate environmental concerns into calculations of national income and other macroeconomic aggregates. Without this, one will never know if the nations are saving enough for the future. The present focus of Fund and Bank staff on man-made and produced assets only, to the complete neglect of natural assets and human assets, is shortsighted. Fourth, the Fund and Bank economists simply have to gain a better understanding of the impacts that structural reforms have on the environment, via their effects on informal traditional mechanisms, such as water and forest users associations, traditional communal management mechanisms, business-led self-enforcement schemes, voluntary conservation organizations. In Steer's opinion, they, even more than governments, are the most effective mechanisms for the protection of the environment, especially in a developing country. Fifth, the staff of the two Bretton Woods institutions must build the support for macroeconomic stability and macroeconomic policy reforms within the environmental community, especially the mainstream analytical and professional NGOs. Steer thus saw ample scope for Fund and Bank staff to internalize environmental objectives into macroeconomic policy work even with the current state of knowledge.

Ved Gandhi, acting as the final panel discussant, highlighted what he considered to be the major conclusions of the seminar for the Fund staff. First, ignoring environmental degradation means ignoring its impact on human capital, natural capital, and output, all of which have a bearing on the sustainability of macroeconomic stability and economic growth. The Fund staff is therefore ill advised to ignore instances of serious environmental degradation or depletion of natural resources. Second, green national accounts are not absolutely essential for formulating appropriate short-term financial and macroeconomic policies. The Fund staff need not wait until environmentally adjusted national accounts become ready; until that occurs, they can take into account the most important environmental indicators, including the need for maintaining the basic social services, in designing macroeconomic and fiscal programs. Third, in some industrial countries where computable general equilibrium modeling is prevalent and the authorities have started using this tool in pursuing their economic objectives consistent with environmental targets, the Fund staff can bring this work to bear on their policy dialogues with the authorities. Fourth, the Fund staff can help countries exploit the very many win-win possibilities, giving greater attention to the removal of subsidies on environmentally damaging inputs, adjustment of utility and energy prices, levying or raising of stumpage fees, levying or increasing of environmental taxes, users' fees, and other measures, and, at the same time, protecting crucial and essential environmental expenditures and investments from budgetary cuts. Fifth, the Fund staff can start examining the National Environmental Action Plans, wherever they exist, and start to bring the economic and environmental ministries together to identify the interest of the authorities in pursuing them. The staff can, then, help the authorities work out the financial and fiscal implications of such plans, if this has not already been done.

Vito Tanzi, in making his concluding remarks, pursued the question of the future involvement of the Fund staff with the environment. He admitted that knowledge about the extent of environmental degradation and the analytical tools readily available to deal with the subject are far from perfect and that prescriptions about environmental problems cannot be made with a great deal of confidence. Besides, one cannot foresee the role of technological change in presenting solutions that may be easier to adopt.

Nonetheless, Tanzi stressed that there are a few things that the Fund staff can do even without necessarily changing the mandate of the institution. They can make themselves aware of environmental concerns of the countries they work on. They can make these concerns enter into macroeconomic policy dialogues with the authorities of all countries, including countries not seeking financial support, to the extent that the authorities wish them to do so. Where the Fund is providing balance of payments support, they can encourage the country authorities to exploit various win-win opportunities highlighted again and again in the seminar. The Fund staff could also encourage developing countries with serious environmental problems and without institutional capabilities to seek assistance from the World Bank to develop appropriate complementary environmental policies for the short run as well as for the long run. Finally, Tanzi emphasized that the pace at which the Fund staff can act on the environment would depend upon the pace at which the countries themselves integrate their environmental concerns into their macroeconomic policymaking.

2

Welcoming Remarks

Margaret Kelly

It is a great pleasure for me to welcome you to the IMF Seminar on Macroeconomics and the Environment. Most of you are from Washington, but some guests have come from as far away as Canada, England, India, Norway, and the Philippines. As we received your responses to the invitations, we also received a number of expressions of curiosity—even surprise—that the IMF would be holding an academic seminar on environmental issues. To some extent the curiosity is understandable. We are a *monetary* institution, not an environmental one. Our basic mandate, as spelled out in Article I of the IMF Articles of Agreement, is to promote international monetary cooperation and exchange rate stability and to help member countries solve their balance of payments problems. Moreover, the timeframe for our work—whether surveillance or programs—is typically short term, while environmental problems, unlike exchange-rate and balance of payments crises, tend to be long term.

But the matter of the Fund's involvement with the environment is not quite so clear cut. For example, a member country that exhausts its natural resources may become a prolonged user of Fund resources. The country, therefore, must make every attempt to develop a sustainable development strategy, including a strategy to have a viable balance of payments in the longer run.

By way of background, the IMF began its examination of environmental issues in November 1990 when the staff presented a paper on the topic to the Executive Board, asking its guidance on how to respond to growing environmental concerns at the national and international level. The Board held a number of discussions on the topic in early 1991. It decided that the Fund should not ignore environmental preservation in promoting balanced and sustainable growth. It also stressed the need to develop a better understanding of the links between macroeconomics and the environment. Toward this end, the Board charged the staff with

- monitoring the environmental research of other specialized organizations, such as the World Bank and the OECD
- developing an understanding of how public policy instruments, especially tax and public expenditure policies, affect the environment.

In 1992, worldwide interest in the concept of sustainable development was stimulated by the Earth Summit in Rio de Janeiro. At the Summit, IMF Managing Director Michel Camdessus referred to high-quality growth as the Fund's ultimate objective. He also met with leaders of environmental nongovernmental organizations, promising them that the Fund would continue the dialogue back in Washington. The Fund followed through on this promise, when it invited 20 leading environmentalists in May 1993 to a seminar with staff members.

What does the Managing Director mean by high-quality growth? He has defined this term to cover "growth that is sustainable, growth that reduces poverty and distributional inequalities, that respects human freedom and national cultures, and protects the environment." And, of course, monetary stability provides part of the foundation for this high-quality growth.

In keeping with the wishes of the Executive Board, the Fund staff has worked to increase their awareness of environmental issues in a number of ways. The Fund continues to examine the links between macroeconomics and the environment. It is ready to integrate the financial and fiscal implications of National Environment Action Plans and Sustainable Development Strategies into policy discussions. It actively participates in a number of multilateral fora on the environment, including the United Nations Commission on Sustainable Development, which is responsible for monitoring the implementation of the agreements reached at the Earth Summit, the Inter-Agency Task Force on Environment Statistics, and the World Trade Organization, which has a committee on trade and the environment.

However, I should also add a note of caution. Given the competence of the World Bank and other specialized agencies dealing with the environment, the Executive Board and many Fund staff members worry that the Fund's active pursuit of environmental objectives would overlap with that of other agencies. Moreover, if it spread itself too thin, the Fund may even dilute its efforts in the area of its primary mandate—monetary and exchange stability—where it has comparative advantage.

We would like to continue the dialogue and the education process that was begun at the seminar in 1993, which is why the External Relations Department and Fiscal Affairs Department have decided to hold this seminar. Our objective is to improve staff understanding of the links between macroeconomic policy instruments and conditions and the environment in the hope of enabling the most effective design of macroeconomic policies. We are inviting you to join us in a frank exchange of views and a sharing of experiences.

In the four sessions of the seminar over the next day and a half, we hope to touch on a number of vital questions. Let me just mention a few of them. In Session 1, we look at the two-way relationships between the macroeconomy and the environment.

- How, and under what conditions do macroeconomic policy instruments, particularly those related to monetary, fiscal, and exchange rate policies, have an impact on the environment?
- How, and to what extent, do deteriorating environmental conditions influence macroeconomic conditions? This would include the impact of pollution on labor productivity, or the depletion of the natural capital base on the development of some economies.
- How far are we from quantitative models that can estimate and explain changes in environmentally adjusted economic activity as a result of changes in macroeconomic policies? And how essential are these models for policymaking?
- How much of a toll in human terms has environmental degradation taken through ill health and premature mortality, forgone GNP, and the erosion of the natural capital base on which the development of many economies depends?

In Session 2, we look at green accounting.

- How far are we from integrated environmental and economic accounts, given the remaining methodological and measurement difficulties? This question arises both in developed countries, with their strong databases, and developing countries, many of which are still struggling with providing basic national income account data.

In Session 3, we focus less on theory and more on country experiences.

- What are the *practical* difficulties of integrating macroeconomic and environmental policies? For the developed countries, we look to lessons from Norway—a pioneer on this front. For the developing countries, we must look at the case studies of over a dozen countries carried out at the World Bank.

Finally, in Session 4, we try to draw conclusions and lessons that are relevant to the work of the Fund.

Session 1

Analytics

Issues of Interest

Session 1 was intended to address the issues relating to
1. the impact of macroeconomic policy reforms on the environment, and
2. the impact of environmental conditions on the macroeconomy.

Addressing the former required dealing with the following questions.
- How do macroeconomic policy instruments (monetary, credit, interest-rate, fiscal, and exchange-rate policies) affect the environment?
- How do macroeconomic stabilization efforts (implemented through a combination of monetary stringency, fiscal discipline, trade and exchange-rate liberalization, price and other structural reforms) affect the environment?
- Under what conditions and circumstances are the effects of macroeconomic stabilization efforts likely to be positive? When would they likely be negative? And when are they likely to be benign?
- Which approach—partial equilibrium approach or general equilibrium approach—is most appropriate in assessing the impact of macroeconomic policies on the environment?

The papers by Ved P. Gandhi and Ronald T. McMorran and by Stein Hansen attempt to answer these questions. Andrew Steer commented on both papers.

Addressing the latter meant answering the following questions.
- How does environmental degradation affect the prospects of economic growth, and does it affect the rates of savings or the returns to investments?
- When does the depletion of natural resources affect macroeconomic balances, both external and domestic (fiscal as well as nonfiscal), and become a drag on achieving macroeconomic stability?
- Are there any countries of the world whose economic prospects are suffering owing to excessive depletion of natural resources or severe environmental degradation?

The paper by David Pearce and Kirk Hamilton attempts to answer these questions. Kirit Parikh commented on the paper.

3

How Macroeconomic Policies Affect the Environment: What Do We Know?

Ved P. Gandhi and Ronald T. McMorran

The International Monetary Fund is a monetary institution charged with the responsibility of promoting international financial and exchange stability through the adoption of sound macroeconomic policies in its member countries (see Annex 1, and IMF, 1993). It is not an environmental institution and is not concerned with the environment per se. Fund work on the environment is therefore related to its primary mandate of helping member countries achieve economic stability through reform of macroeconomic policies.

Interest of the Fund staff in the subject arose soon after the Executive Board's discussion of the environment in late 1990 and early 1991 when the Board directed the staff to develop a better understanding of the interplay among macroeconomic policies, economic activity, and the environment.[1] Toward developing this understanding of the possible impact of macroeconomic policies on the environment, the Fund staff has, over the last four years, done some work (see Annex 2) and has studied and reviewed the work done by academics and researchers at the World Bank, the OECD, and other specialized governmental and nongovernmental institutions. Although many of the conclusions reached by the Fund staff have been confirmed and reinforced by those reached by others, we continue our studies on how macroeconomic policies affect

Note: The authors are Assistant Director and Economist, respectively, in the Fiscal Affairs Department. The opinions expressed in this paper are those of the authors and not necessarily those of the International Monetary Fund. They would like to thank David Nellor and Dale Chua for their helpful comments on an earlier draft.

[1]See IMF, 1991.

the environment and how the environmental conditions and policies affect the macroeconomic situation.

This paper describes the major conclusions that the Fund staff has reached on how macroeconomic policies and their reform affect the environment. It also identifies the reasons why the impact of macroeconomic policies on the environment remains a difficult area of study and research.

Conclusions

Drawing clear-cut conclusions about the direct impact of macroeconomic policies on the environment is not easy because environmental problems are generally sectoral and are often a result of microeconomic policies (pricing and institutional), while macroeconomic policies normally affect relative prices at the economy-wide level. Reaching conclusions on the subject is further hampered by the lack of a well-developed theoretical framework to explain the interrelationships between macroeconomic policies and the environment.[2] Finally, the environment has not yet been fully integrated into computable general equilibrium models that alone can help generate meaningful empirical results and that are readily accepted.[3]

Nevertheless, four conclusions, which enjoy broad agreement, seem to have emerged from recent studies regarding the effect of macroeconomic policies on the environment.[4]

- Macroeconomic stability is a minimum and necessary condition for preserving the environment.
- Environmental degradation is caused primarily by market and policy failures at the sectoral level.
- Macroeconomic policies can sometimes harm the environment but only indirectly and only when serious market and policy failures exist.
- Macroeconomic policies are inefficient instruments for mitigating environmental degradation; appropriate environmental policies are more efficient and effective.

These conclusions are more fully described now.

---

[2]A recent paper by Girma, 1992, is a worthy attempt in this regard.

[3]See Panayotou and Hupe, 1995.

[4]See, among others, Cruz and Repetto, 1992; Mason, 1995; Munasinghe and Cruz, 1995; Nellor, 1993; Panayotou and Hupe, 1995; Reed, 1992; World Bank, 1994; Dasgupta and Maler, 1993; Markandya, 1992; Pearce and others, 1989; and World Commission on Environment and Development, 1987.

Macroeconomic stability is a minimum and necessary condition for preserving the environment.

Macroeconomic instability is often characterized by high and variable inflation, serious balance of payments problems, large fiscal deficits, low or negative output growth, and high and growing unemployment. Together these have a serious impact on the environment through their influence on incentives to preserve environmental resources or to invest in environmental protection.

High rates of inflation, for example, frequently distort intertemporal choices concerning the use of forests, mines, and other natural resources, reducing the incentive to preserve resources as producers and consumers act as if they were facing high discount rates.[5] To the extent that macroeconomic policies help control inflation, lower discount rates, and create stable macroeconomic conditions, they encourage "a longer term view on the part of decision-makers at all levels, and lower inflation rates lead to clearer pricing signals and better investment decisions by economic agents."[6]

Sound macroeconomic management creates conditions for environmental protection in other ways as well:

- Demand management (controlling aggregate demand to match aggregate supply) also means better management (or control) of demand for natural resources.
- Exchange rate reform and trade liberalization raise the costs of environmentally damaging inputs and outputs (fertilizers, pesticides, insecticides, petroleum products) and improve the capacity of exporters to use environmental investments (in controlling soil erosion and other land improvements, if they are in farming, and in pollution-curbing technologies, if they are in manufacturing).[7]
- Interest rate reforms reduce implicit subsidies to capital and encourage employment, thereby discouraging deforestation and other damage to the environment that would otherwise have been caused by the unemployed.

---

[5]See Nellor, 1993, p. 12, and the World Bank, 1994, p. 33.

[6]Munasinghe and Cruz, 1995.

[7]As noted in IMF, 1995, p.13, the large majority of the population and the poor in many sub-Saharan African countries live in rural areas and their incomes depend on exports while their expenditures are largely made on domestic goods. In these circumstances, a more realistic exchange rate, accompanied by sound macroeconomic policies, helps improve real output, employment, and incomes in rural areas, laying the basis of poverty alleviation and environmental preservation.

- Reduction of fiscal deficits and improvements in revenue buoyancy enhance the capacity of the government to undertake and support environmental protection programs.
- Sound macroeconomic policies encourage larger external capital flows and facilitate external debt rescheduling and relief, some of which may be specifically dedicated to improving environmental conditions.

Macroeconomic stability is thus a prerequisite for the preservation of the environment.

Environmental degradation is caused primarily by market and policy failures at the sectoral level.

Economic theory suggests that environmental degradation is the consequence of economic agents—firms and households—not taking into account social costs associated with their consumption and production decisions. This may be because of market failures or of policy failures. Market failures can arise when no mechanism exists for making economic agents aware of the social costs of their actions or forcing them to internalize these costs into their private decision-making. It may also be the case that such mechanisms do exist but are simply inadequate or ineffective. Policy failures, on the other hand, exist when the government fails to charge adequately for the exploitation or use of mining, forestry, fishery, and other natural and environmental resources. They also exist if the government provides price subsidies to environmentally damaging inputs or outputs in the name of economic or social objectives. Environmental degradation, in fact, tends to be compounded when policy failures exist simultaneously with market failures.

Industrial and developing countries differ somewhat in respect of market failures but not necessarily in respect of policy failures. Industrial countries generally have relatively well-functioning markets, adequate environmental infrastructure and institutions, relatively well-defined and secure property rights over communal resources, and well-structured and enforced environmental standards and regulations. They even tend to have environmental taxes (though not always adequate) for internalizing environmental costs, and their public utility prices normally reflect long-term private (though not necessarily social) costs. Developing countries, on the other hand, have nonexistent, thin, or uncompetitive markets, inadequate environmental infrastructure and institutions, poorly defined and insecure property rights (with large open-access resources), poorly designed or enforced environmental standards and regulations, few (if any) environmental taxes, and prices for public utility services that do not reflect even the long-run private costs. In developing countries, therefore, prices of resource- and environment-intensive goods and services rarely reflect environmental costs.

Environmental degradation in both developed and developing countries, for the most part, is thus the result of market or policy failures at the sectoral level rather than of macroeconomic policies or their reforms.

Macroeconomic policies can sometimes harm the environment but only indirectly and only when serious market or policy failures exist.

In the first-best world, where environmental resources are priced to reflect social costs and private decisions are based on social costs, macroeconomic policymakers need to worry little about the environment, except to the extent macroeconomic policy changes may call for some adjustments in the levels of environmental taxes or subsidies to ensure their intended effect on the behavior of economic agents.

As noted above, however, in practice policymakers operate in a second-best world, where market or policy failures are present and even pervasive. This is especially so in developing countries, but developed countries are not immune to these failures either. Where such failures are present, macroeconomic policy reform can have an adverse impact on the environment, although this impact tends to be indirect. Besides, how adverse this impact will likely be is extremely difficult to determine without reference to the structure and effectiveness of environmental policies of the country and whether or not the adverse effects are partially or fully offset by some positive effects. A few examples in support of this conclusion will suffice.

Monetary stringency may form an important element of the macroeconomic reform package aimed at reducing domestic absorption. This may be implemented, in part, through tight credit policy that may curtail the availability of credit to farmers (much like other borrowers) and may reduce their capacity to purchase agricultural inputs or invest in land improvements. This, in turn, may encourage an environmentally undesirable shift by them to extensive farming in the presence of an open-access land policy. However, the same monetary stringency may have a positive impact on the environment if increases in real interest rates limit borrowings by farmers who might have had plans to invest in environmentally damaging crops or sectors of the economy. The net outcome may therefore be difficult to determine.

Reducing the fiscal deficit, as another example, may be a second major element of the demand restraint package to help reduce public sector absorption of output. Among other things, this may be accomplished through a reduction in public sector employment. Laid-off staff, who may be unable to find alternative employment in cities, may be compelled to move to the country and engage in clearing land, which might contribute to deforestation. This would occur provided marginal lands have open access. However, the same fiscal deficit reduction strategy may have a positive impact on the environment if price subsidies for fertilizers and petroleum products are sharply curtailed. Once again, the net impact would be hard to determine.

Exchange rate reform can be taken as yet another and final example. It may encourage the rate of depletion of nonrenewable natural resources, as their value grows with devaluation and their exports are encouraged. The extent to which this will occur will depend upon the existence of user charges, royalties, and the like. While exchange rate reform in this way may be seen as having an adverse impact on the sustainability of certain natural resources, it may, at the same time, raise the domestic prices of certain environmentally damaging imports, such as fertilizers and pesticides, and curtail their use, which would help protect the environment. Thus, the net impact of this macroeconomic reform also is not that clear cut.[8]

Only a computable general equilibrium model of an economy, which incorporates macroeconomic variables as well as environmental variables and policies, can help determine the net impacts of macroeconomic policies on the environment.

Macroeconomic policies are inefficient instruments for mitigating environmental degradation; appropriate environmental policies are more efficient and effective.

Given the lack of clear and direct links between macroeconomic policies and the environment, as noted above, the role of macroeconomic policies as instruments of solving environmental problems cannot but be limited; in any case they cannot be efficient. Furthermore, given that market policy failures are the primary causes of environmental degradation everywhere, the most efficient and effective instruments simply have to be the environmental policies of the country.

---

[8]In fact, three country studies, sponsored by the World Wide Fund for Nature, provide adequate evidence that the environmental impact of an exchange rate devaluation is inconclusive. In the case of Thailand and Côte d'Ivoire, an exchange rate devaluation was found to have a negligible or benign impact on the environment while in the case of Mexico, it proved to be somewhat harmful to the environment as it encouraged firms to establish in a region with weak enforcement of environmental laws (see Reed, 1992).

Macroeconomic policies are inadequate and inefficient instruments of environmental protection because they change the relative prices of broad categories of goods and services and not the prices of specific environmental goods and services whose underpricing or easy access may have been the major cause of environmental degradation to begin with. Protecting the environment would, therefore, require the adoption of appropriate environmental policy instruments.

A number of environmental policy instruments can be employed: Pigouvian taxes, indirect environment taxes, land (property tax) reform, pricing reform for products linked to environmental damage, pollution standards and other regulatory policies, and tradable permits. An efficient environmental policy for a given environmental problem would encourage socially optimal behavior at least social cost.

Much in the literature suggests that one of the most efficient environment policies is the Pigouvian tax, a specific rate tax on units of emissions or damage.[9] Two distinctive features of Pigouvian taxes make them attractive as efficient environmental policy. First, the costs of achieving a given environmental objective may be lower with taxes because they rely on the price system in contrast to the administrative costs of command and control policies. Second, Pigouvian taxes reduce pollution in the least-cost manner by encouraging the greatest pollution abatement by firms able to adjust at lowest cost and least cost abatement by each firm.

As regards other environmental policies, they, unlike Pigouvian taxes, may not encourage abatement of environmental damage along all possible abatement margins at the least social cost unless there is an identifiable functional relationship between the policy instrument and the environmental damage. Because identifiable functional relationships are rare, these other environment policy instruments may end up imposing greater costs than a Pigouvian tax in efficiently mitigating environmental damage.

Environmental policies, if efficiently designed and effectively implemented, can help not only to achieve environmental objectives, but also to address one or more macroeconomic imbalances. As an example, eliminating subsidies on environmentally damaging products and imposing environmental user charges and fees can bring about proper pricing of environmental resources and thus help mitigate environmental degradation. In addition, these policies can help raise revenue for investing in environmental protection and at the same time reduce overall fiscal imbalance. Such policies can be considered win-win

---

[9]McMorran and Nellor, 1994.

policies for macroeconomic improvement as well as environmental protection.

Before closing this lengthy section on major conclusions, it is worth repeating that these conclusions are in the nature of broad generalizations and only a general equilibrium approach can help us understand how macroeconomic policies of a country interact with its environment. To integrate environmental objectives of a country into macroeconomic policy calls for the development and adoption of a new analytical framework.[10] How easy or difficult that task may be at this stage is described in the next section.

Integrating Environment into Macroeconomic Policy

The growing body of literature referred to earlier has greatly improved our understanding of the links between macroeconomic policies and the environment. A common feature of these studies, however, has been the assessment of the environmental impact of macroeconomic policies undertaken in a second-best world where substantial market or policy failures are prevalent. As a result, definitive conclusions concerning the environmental impact of macroeconomic policies have proven difficult to draw and, more often than not, the researchers have tended to attribute environmental degradation to macroeconomic policies, although it should properly have been attributed to a failure of environmental policies or institutions.

In our opinion, the analytics of integrating the environment into a macroeconomic policy framework still remains to be developed, and this work continues to be hindered by three factors.

First, integrated environmental and economic accounts are presently lacking in most countries. While considerable effort has gone into developing a methodology for taking into account the environment in national accounts,[11] environmentally adjusted national accounts have been developed only for a few countries and often only in an exploratory and experimental way.[12] To date, few governments have actively pursued the development of or produced environmentally adjusted national accounts.

---

[10]The framework underlying the Fund macroeconomic advice is described in IMF, 1987 and 1992.

[11]See, for example, United Nations, 1993a, p. 508, and United Nations, 1993b.

[12]See, for example, Repetto and others, 1989, for Indonesia; Solorzano and others, 1991, for Costa Rica; van Tongeren and others, 1993, for Mexico; Bartelmus and others, 1993, for Papua New Guinea; and Giannone and Carlucci, 1993, for Italy.

Second, we still know very little about the functional relationships between macroeconomic policies and the environment. As Warford has pointed out, "Long-term impacts are difficult to predict in the best of circumstances, and in the environmental area there are special problems: behavioral and physical linkages are poorly understood, [and] many of the effects are long-term. . . ."[13] While environmentally adjusted national accounts can provide a basis for determining the level of economic activity, quantitative models would be needed for estimating and explaining changes in environmentally adjusted economic activity as a result of changes in macroeconomic and, for that matter, any other economic policies. Environment economics being a relatively new discipline, few quantitative models are presently available.

Third, as the environment is a multifaceted subject and many macroeconomic policies may be simultaneously affecting the net outcome (sometimes positive impacts may cancel out or outweigh the negative impacts while other times they may be reinforced by other positive impacts), a computable general equilibrium model of the economy is necessary to assess the impact of the macroeconomic policies of the government on the country's environment. Unfortunately, not many countries at present have such models that can be considered reliable. Even where they exist (in some industrial countries they do), the models do not always incorporate environmental variables.

For the time being, therefore, it appears that we will have to be satisfied with the broad generalizations noted above, however inadequate or partial they might be. Nevertheless, the work on developing environmentally adjusted national accounts, as well as other elements of the analytics for integrating the environment into macroeconomic policy framework, must continue and even accelerate.

References

Bartelmus, Peter, and others, 1993, "Integrated Environmental and Economic Accounting: A Case Study for Papua New Guinea," in *Toward Improved Accounting for the Environment*, ed. by Ernst Lutz (Washington: World Bank).

Cruz, Wilfrido, and Robert Repetto, 1992, *The Environmental Effects of Stabilization and Structural Adjustment Programs: The Philippines Case* (Washington: World Resources Institute).

Dasgupta, Partha, and Karl-Goran Maler, 1993, "Poverty, Institutions, and the Environmental-Resource Base," The Development Economics Research Program Working Paper No. 48 (London: London School of Economics).

---

[13]See Warford and others, 1994, p. 4.

Giannone, A., and M. Carlucci, 1993, "Environmental Variables in National Accounts: A Case Study for Italy," in *Approaches to Environmental Accounting*, ed. by Alfred Franz and Carstens Stahner (Proceedings of the I.A.R.I.W. Conference on Environmental Accounting, Baden, Austria, May 27–29, 1991, Physica Verlag).

Girma, Messaye, 1992, "Macropolicy and the Environment: A Framework for Analysis," *World Development*, Vol. 20, No. 4, pp. 531–40.

International Monetary Fund, 1987, *Theoretical Aspects of the Design of Fund-Supported Adjustment Programs*, Occasional Paper 55 (Washington: International Monetary Fund).

———, 1991, "IMF Reviews Its Approach to Environmental Issues," *IMF Survey*, Vol. 20, April 15, 1991.

———, 1992, *Financial Programming and Policy: The Case of Hungary*, ed. by Karen Swiderski (Washington: International Monetary Fund).

———, 1993, *Articles of Agreement* (Washington, International Monetary Fund).

———, 1995, *Social Dimensions of the IMF's Policy Dialogue*, IMF Pamphlet Series, No. 47 (Washington: International Monetary Fund).

Markandya, Anil, 1992, "Criteria for Sustainable Agricultural Development," in *Environmental Economics: A Reader*, ed. by Anil Markandya and Julie Richardson (New York: St. Martin's Press).

Mason, Jocelyn, 1995, "Notes on Economic Policy Instruments at the Macroeconomic and Sectoral Level and Their Application to Environmentally Sustainable Development," Environment Department (Washington: World Bank).

McMorran, Ronald T., and David C.L. Nellor, 1994, "Tax Policy and the Environment: Theory and Practice," IMF Working Paper 94/106 (Washington: International Monetary Fund)

Munasinghe, Mohan, and Wilfrido Cruz, 1995, *Economy-Wide Policies and the Environment: Lessons from Experience* (Washington: World Bank).

Nellor, David C.L., 1993, "Economic Adjustment Policies and the Environment," International Monetary Fund Fiscal Affairs Department Working Paper 93/2 (Washington: International Monetary Fund).

Panayotou, Theodore, and Kurt Hupe, 1995, *Environmental Impacts of Structural Adjustment Programs* (Cambridge, Massachusetts: Harvard Institute for International Development).

Pearce, David W., Anil Markandya, and Edward Barbier, 1989, *Blueprint for a Green Economy* (London: Earthscan Publications).

Reed, David, ed., 1992, *Structural Adjustment and the Environment* (Boulder: World-Wide Fund for Nature).

Repetto, Robert, and others, 1989, *Wasting Assets: National Resources in the National Income Accounts* (Washington: World Resources Institute).

Solorzano, Raul, and others, 1991, *Accounts Overdue: National Resource Depreciation in Costa Rica* (Washington: World Resources Institute).

United Nations, 1993a, *System of National Accounts 1993* (New York: United Nations).

———, 1993b, *Integrated Environmental and Economic Accounting* (New York: United Nations).

van Tongeren, Jan, and others, 1993, "Integrated Environmental and Economic Accounting: A Case Study for Mexico," in *Toward Improved Accounting for the Environment*, ed. by Ernst Lutz (Washington: World Bank).

Warford, Jeremy, and others, 1994, "The Evolution of Environmental Concerns in Adjustment Lending: A Review," Environment Working Paper No. 65 (Washington: World Bank).

World Bank, 1994, *Economy-Wide Policies and the Environment: Emerging Lessons from Experience* (Washington: World Bank).

World Commission on Environment and Development, 1987, *Our Common Future* (Oxford: Oxford University Press).

Annex 1

Purposes of the Fund from Article I of Its Articles of Agreement

(1) To promote international monetary cooperation through a permanent institution which provides machinery for consultation and collaboration on international monetary problems.

(2) To facilitate the expansion and balanced growth of international trade, and to contribute thereby to the promotion and maintenance of high levels of employment and real income and to the development of the production resources of all members as primary objectives of economic policy.

(3) To promote exchange stability, to maintain orderly exchange arrangements among members, and to avoid competitive exchange depreciation.

(4) To assist in the establishment of a multilateral system of payments in respect of current transactions between members and in the elimination of foreign exchange restrictions which hamper growth of world trade.

(5) To give confidence to members by making the general resources of the Fund temporarily available to them under adequate safeguards, thus providing them with opportunity to correct maladjustments in their balance of payments without resorting to measures destructive of national or international prosperity.

(6) In accordance with the above, to shorten the duration and lessen the degree of disequilibrium in the international balances of payments of members.

The Fund shall be guided in all its policies and decisions by the purposes set forth in this Article.

Annex 2

Papers Prepared by International Monetary Fund Staff

Chua, Dale, 1996, "The Scope for Economic Instruments for Mitigating Global Environmental Problems," presented at the Third Expert Group Meeting on Financial Issues of Agenda 21 on 6–8 February 1996 in Manila, Philippines.

Clark, Peter, 1994, "Sustainable Economic Growth: An Essential Precondition for Environmental Protection," paper presented at the Conference on Structural Adjustment in the North—Strategies for the Sustainable World Economy held in Germany, November 11–13, 1994.

Clements, Benedict, 1995, "Public Expenditure Policy and the Environment: A Review and Synthesis," Proceedings of the Workshop on Economic Instruments for Sustainable Development held in Pruhonice, Czech Republic, January 12–14, 1995 (Praha: Ministry of the Environment of the Czech Republic, 1995).

Development Committee, 1992a, "The Interaction of Environment and Development Policies," prepared by staff of the World Bank in consultation with staff of the International Monetary Fund (Washington: The World Bank).

———, 1992b, "Outcome of the United Nations Conference on Environment and Development," prepared by staff of the World Bank in consultation with staff of the International Monetary Fund (Washington: The World Bank).

Gandhi, Ved P., 1992, "Macroeconomic Adjustment and the Environment: A Personal View," paper presented at International Round Table on Structural Adjustment and the Environment, German Foundation for International Development, held in Berlin, Germany, November 10–13, 1992.

———, 1995, "The International Monetary Fund [and the Environment]," in *The Halifax Summit, Sustainable Development, and International Institutional Reform*, ed. by John Kirton and Sara Richardson (Ottawa: Canadian National Round Table on the Environment and the Economy, March 1995).

———, and David C.L. Nellor, 1991, "Financing Instruments and Conditions for Environmental Protection in Developing Countries," paper presented at Malente Symposium IX of the Dräger Foundation, held in Timmendorfer Strand, Germany, November 18–20, 1991.

Gupta, Sanjeev, Kenneth Miranda, and Ian Parry, 1995, "Public Expenditure Policy and the Environment: A Review and Synthesis," *World Development*, Vol. 23, No. 3, pp. 515–28.

Hemming, Richard, and Kenneth Miranda, 1991, "Public Expenditure and the Environment," in *Public Expenditure Handbook: A Guide to Public Policy Issues in Developing Countries* (Washington: International Monetary Fund).

Herber, Bernard, 1993, "International Environmental Taxation in the Absence of Sovereignty," IMF Working Paper 92/104, International Monetary Fund (Washington).

International Monetary Fund, 1993, "Seminar Explores Links Between Macro Policy and the Environment," *IMF Survey*, International Monetary Fund (Washington), Vol. 22, No. 2.

Levin, Jonathan, 1990, "The Economy and the Environment: Revising the National Accounts," *IMF Survey*, International Monetary Fund (Washington), Vol. 19, No. 2.

———, 1991, "Valuation and Treatment of Depletable Resources in the National Accounts," IMF Working Paper 91/73, International Monetary Fund (Washington).

———, 1993, "An Analytical Framework of Environmental Issues," IMF Working Paper 93/53, International Monetary Fund (Washington).

McMorran, Ronald T., 1996, "The Scope for Fiscal Instruments for Mitigating Domestic Environmental Problems," presented at the Third Expert Group Meeting on Financial Issues of Agenda 21 on 6–8 February 1996 in Manila, Philippines.

———, and David C. L. Nellor, 1994, "Tax Policy and the Environment: Theory and Practice," IMF Working Paper 94/106, International Monetary Fund, (Washington).

Miranda, Kenneth, and Timothy Muzondo, 1991, "Public Policy and the Environment," *Finance and Development*, International Monetary Fund (Washington), Vol. 28, No. 2, pp. 25–7.

Muzondo, Timothy R., 1992, "Environmental and Macroeconomic Effects of Military Conversion," paper presented at the UN Conference on Conversion—Opportunities for Development and Environment, held in Düsseldorf, Germany.

———, 1993, "Alternative Forms of Mineral Taxation, Market Failure, and the Environment," *Staff Papers*, International Monetary Fund (Washington), Vol. 40, No. 1, pp. 152–77.

———, Kenneth M. Miranda, and A. Lans Bovenberg, 1990, "Public Policy and the Environment: A Survey of the Literature," IMF Working Paper 90/56, International Monetary Fund (Washington).

Nellor, David C.L., 1992a, "Structural Adjustment and Sustainable Development in the Philippines: A Comment" (unpublished, Washington: International Monetary Fund)

———, 1992b, "The United Nations Conference on Environment and Development" (unpublished, Washington: International Monetary Fund).

———, 1992c, "Carbon Taxation: Tax Policy Issues and European Carbon Taxation" (unpublished, Washington: International Monetary Fund).

———, 1992d, "Comments on Country Case Studies," in *Structural Adjustment and the Environment*, ed. by David Reed (London: Earthscan Publications).

————, 1992e, "A Survey of Carbon Taxes and Global Warming" (unpublished, Washington: International Monetary Fund).

————, 1993, "Economic Adjustment Policies and the Environment," Fiscal Affairs Department Working Paper 93/2, International Monetary Fund (Washington).

————, 1994, "Energy Taxes and Macroeconomic Policy," IMF Paper on Policy Analysis and Assessment 94/9, International Monetary Fund (Washington).

————, and Emil M. Sunley, 1994, "Fiscal Regimes for Natural Resource Producing Developing Countries," IMF Paper on Policy Analysis and Assessment 94/24, International Monetary Fund (Washington).

Sorsa, Piritta, 1995, "Environmental Protectionism, North-South Trade, and the Uruguay Round," IMF Working Paper 95/6, International Monetary Fund (Washington).

Subramanian, Arvind, and Peter Uimonen, 1994, "Trade and the Environment," *International Trade Policies: The Uruguay Round and Beyond,* Vol. II, International Monetary Fund (Washington).

Summers, Victoria P., 1994, "Tax Treatment of Pollution Control in the European and Central Asian Economies in Transition," paper presented at the Conference of the American Council for Capital Formation on U.S. Environmental Policies: Are We Barking up the Wrong Tree?, held in Washington, D.C., on November 16, 1994.

Uimonen, Peter, 1992, "Trade Policies and the Environment," *Finance and Development,* International Monetary Fund and World Bank (Washington), June 1992.

Wallace, Laura, 1995, "Linking Macroeconomics and the Environment," *IMF Survey,* International Monetary Fund (Washington), Vol. 24, No. 11.

————, and Ronald T. McMorran, 1995, "Why Macroeconomists and Environmentalists Need Each Other," *Finance and Development,* International Monetary Fund and World Bank (Washington), December 1995.

4

Macroeconomic Policies and the Environment

Stein Hansen

Summary of Findings and Conclusions

It is by now widely agreed that links between the environment and the economy are too important to be ignored. This holds true for all countries, industrial and developing. And yet there is persistent asymmetry in the way governments treat environmental costs and benefits as compared with more tangible market-based realities. This asymmetry is illustrated by the widespread focus on the economic costs in terms of reduced GDP growth rate from stricter environmental requirements, coupled with equally widespread ignorance about the benefits from environmental improvements and costs imposed on society by increased pollution and resource degradation.

This paper reviews a study of the United States and one of Norway, both adopting computable economy-wide general equilibrium models to establish the joint economic and environmental impact of comprehensive policy packages addressing issues related to sustainable development. Such issues include adequate resource management to maintain sufficient savings for securing options for future generations at least as good as we have enjoyed. Policy measures aim at securing safe environmental standards, as well as healthy public budgets and current account balance.

Note: Stein Hansen is the Director of the Project for a Sustainable Economy, Norway, Partner of the Nordic Consulting Group A.S., and Senior Fellow of the Fridtjof Nansen Institute in Norway. The author is heavily indebted to Knut H. Alfsen, Pål Føyn Jespersen, Bodil M. Larsen, Ingeborg Rasmussen, and Haakon Vennemo for comments and assistance in preparation of this paper, but the author is solely responsible for conclusions and interpretations.

Taking a perspective of several decades and comparing alternative combinations of macroeconomic and environmental policies, this paper concludes that substantial environmental improvements are within reach at modest cost in terms of sectoral adjustments and reduced overall growth rates. Although the paper is unable to establish whether the changes resulting from the simulations are sufficient to divert the economy onto a sustainable development path, to the extent that continuing on the "business as usual" path will lead toward an increasingly difficult and possibly irreversible situation, the options examined in this paper suggest that the insurance premium in terms of reduced growth and structural adjustments is modest considering the already high level of material consumption in rich countries. Cost-effectiveness figures from the Norwegian simulations provide instructive illustrations of how such information can be presented to guide decision-makers in such a complex and uncertain trade-off.

In developing countries the setting is quite different and the policy choices much more limited, but clearly there is great scope for adjustment reforms with apparent win-win outcomes in many cases. And still influential parties can prevent the implementation of such options in order to continue harvesting the resource rent.

In addition, a number of myths about economy-environment links need to be exposed. These concern the links between indebtedness and environmental management, the environmental impact of agricultural and trade liberalization, as well as the environmental impact of public budget strengthening and more generally economic and political stabilization. By and large, sound economic advice placed in a broader policy context tends to be environmentally benign. Also, one should apply economy-wide analytic tools to capture the impact of links sometimes lost in partial or ad hoc analyses, and thus capture a larger range of possible policy outcomes.

Introduction

It is increasingly recognized that macroeconomics via its impacts on the level and structure of economic activities in a region, a country, and the world at large has a multitude of direct and indirect environmental impacts. In response to this recognition, a series of studies of possible links between economy-wide policies and the environment has been conducted for different countries, both developed and developing.

Studies of this kind in developed countries have been undertaken because of a genuine concern that important links between the ecosystem and the economic system (both the market and the institutional setting) need to be understood as a basis for designing policies that will sustain today's welfare options for future generations. Such studies have focused on the economic policy impact on pollution and environmental quality indicators and on the losses or gains in economic performance criteria, that is, growth in GDP, employment, current accounts, budget balance, inflation, and interest rates, resulting from stricter environmental controls. Some studies have even attempted to incorporate the estimated benefits of reduced environmental damage so that these can be traded against the direct economic losses resulting from the initial environmental policies. Typically, such studies in developed countries are based on countrywide single- or multi-sectoral growth models.[1]

The setting for such studies in developing countries has been quite different. Since the late 1970s, stabilization and structural and sectoral adjustment programs have been adopted by developing countries to maintain a viable balance of payments consistent with the inflows of foreign exchange to allow policies of economic modernization and growth to continue.

Stabilization programs are likely to encompass demand management policies, such as fiscal policy measures that control the domestic budget balance and improve the balance of payments. Devaluation of national currency, real wage reductions, and measures to ensure a positive real rate of interest are typical elements of these programs. Such measures are first of all aimed at restoring macroeconomic stability.

To complement these macroeconomic measures a typical structural adjustment program, as well as sector development program, includes measures to improve the incentive system, increase the market efficiency of the price mechanism, and restore investments and growth over the medium and long term. In addition, building or strengthening institutions required to implement the adjustment reforms, is included or attached (piggy-backed). The main macroeconomic policy measures might include

• trade liberalization
• financial liberalization, including credit market reforms
• public sector reforms
• tax, price control, and subsidy reforms
• monetary reforms
• exchange rate adjustments (unification and devaluation)
• complementary institutional reforms and capacity strengthening.

---

[1]See, for example, Lars Bergman and Øystein Olsen, eds., 1992, *Economic Modeling in the Nordic Countries* (Amsterdam: North-Holland).

Such policy reforms have come under increasingly severe criticism for failing to deliver the projected improvements, for failing to recognize the social and environmental adjustment costs, and for failing to assess realistically the time required and political obstacles to be overcome in order to implement the proposed programs.[2] As a result, studies were initiated in the late 1980s by UNEP, the World Bank, and the Asian Development Bank to look more closely at the validity of the very vocal accusations that such policies were indeed environmentally devastating.[3]

Early studies of the effects of adjustment policies on the environment undertaken in developing countries were dominated by partial ad hoc analyses of the environmental impact of one or more economic policy reforms undertaken as part of stabilization and structural or sectoral adjustment programs to which the World Bank (the Bank) or the International Monetary Fund (the Fund) have provided credits or technical advice to smooth the policy reform.[4] In recent years, computable general equilibrium models have also been adopted for studies of developing countries to trace the environmental and economy-wide impact of such reforms. These studies have led to more comprehensive and often surprising conclusions as regards the primary and secondary environmental impacts of such programs. Thus, macroeconomic stabilization and adjustment efforts must be implemented through a carefully tailored combination of economic and institutional policy measures addressing monetary, fiscal, and sectoral issues, and their combined effects on the environment must be measured rather than measuring such policy's partial environment impact.[5]

It is against this background that the present paper sets out to establish the circumstances under which the environmental effects of macroeconomic policy reforms are likely to be benign and under which the effects are likely to be adverse. The question of win-win possibilities and why they are so hard to pursue will be discussed, as well as what to do

---

[2]See, for example, G.A. Cornia, R. Jolly, and F. Stewart, eds., 1987, *Adjustment with a Human Face: Protecting the Vulnerable and Promoting Growth* (Oxford: Clarendon Press), and Susan George, 1988, *A Fate Worse than Debt* (London: Penguin Books).

[3]See, for example, Stein Hansen, 1988, "Structural Adjustment Programs and Sustainable Development," Nairobi, Papers and Proceedings from the Annual Session of the Committee of International Development Institutions (CIDIE); Stein Hansen, 1989, "Debt for Nature Swaps: Overview and Discussion of Key Issues," *Ecological Economics*, Vol. 1; and Stein Hansen, 1990, "Macroeconomic Policies and Sustainable Development in the Third World," *Journal of International Development*, October 1990.

[4]Stein Hansen, 1988 and 1990.

[5]World Bank, 1994, *Economy-Wide Policies and the Environment: Emerging Lessons from Experience* (Washington: World Bank).

when, for political or other reasons, one cannot pursue a first-best solution. Depending on the policy issue in focus, some studies address the environmental impacts of specific policy changes, while others start from set environmental targets and derive policy options that will achieve these targets, but at the same time will yield different economy-wide repercussions.

Industrial Countries: Macroeconomic Costs of Achieving Environmental Targets

Most macroeconomic studies of environmental impacts in industrial countries have emerged from political pressure for improved environmental protection. Some such studies have taken on a global scope owing to the concerns of natural scientists and environmental pressure groups over global warming impacts. They have focused, for example, on the GDP impacts of introducing carbon taxes to reduce fossil energy use and gas concentrations in the atmosphere. Climate-cost models used in this context have been crude, but have established increasing marginal cost curves (in terms of GDP loss) as a function of increasing CO_2 taxes.[6] These models will not be discussed because their main use has been to determine the GDP impact of different levels of CO_2 taxes, with little or no focus on the impact of changes in the conventional macroeconomic instruments that constitute the topic of this paper.

The focus of this paper is on macroeconomic country studies of interaction between the economy and environment. Two categories of industrial countries are singled out for closer examination: a large, resource-rich economy with chronic budget deficits and international trade modest relative to GDP, and a small, open, resource-rich economy with strong foreign trade and a public budget more or less in balance.

United States

The United States represents the first country category. Many studies have addressed environment-economy links such as the cost of environmental controls on economic growth. This paper will not review the findings of such studies, but will summarize one study which focused on alternative macroeconomic policy options to reach an environmental target.

---

[6]For a recent overview, see A.S. Manne and R.G. Richels, 1994, "The Costs of Stabilizing Global CO_2 Emissions: A Probabilistic Analysis Based on Expert Judgements," *The Energy Journal*, Vol. 15, No. 1., pp. 31–56.

A few years ago, the Environmental Protection Agency commissioned a macroeconomic study of policy options for reducing gasoline consumption and the resulting CO_2 emissions. (The ancillary benefits of reducing other adverse environmental and health externalities that are highly correlated to gasoline consumption and traffic volume were not explicitly addressed.) The study concentrated on the level of gasoline tax necessary for stabilizing CO_2 emissions from a light vehicle fleet over a 20-year period and the impact of such a tax on a set of macroeconomic indicators.[7]

What makes this study particularly interesting is its discussion of how different recycling and other fiscal uses for the gasoline tax revenue affect the performance of the economy. Which macroeconomic policy package will be most benign to the economy in achieving the stated environmental goal? The study focused on a gasoline tax increase (revenue raising) that can help reduce the federal budget deficit or help finance a simultaneous reduction in personal and corporate income taxes or a reduction in the employer-paid portion of payroll taxes (both revenue neutral). The first option is revenue raising in the sense that gasoline tax revenues are applied to federal deficit reduction. The other two options are deficit neutral. To define the impact of the proposed environmental policy (the CO_2-stabilizing gasoline tax), it is necessary to neutralize its impact on federal finances by offsetting it with other fiscal policies. This is done by establishing the difference between government expenditures and revenues that would obtain if the economy operated at full employment.

Not surprisingly, each of the three options would result in a different level of economic performance. The revenue-raising scenario is shown to have adverse short-term macroeconomic impacts, because the gasoline tax raises inflation and reduces after-tax household income. If monetary policies curtail the inflation, the recessionary impulse of the policy would strengthen. After ten years this recessionary burden eases, however, and benefits begin to appear. The lower budget deficit enhances national savings, implying lower real credit costs and higher investment. After 16 years it is suggested that GDP performance will be back to normal, and in addition, the underlying strength of the economy developed during this adjustment period will contribute to a faster growth in the following years, in spite of the stabilized CO_2 emissions.

The two revenue recycling policies are shown to have quite different impacts on the economy. The income tax cut replaces most of the direct

---

[7]Roger E. Brinner, Michael G. Shelby, Joyce M. Yanchar, and Alex Cristofaro, 1991, "Optimizing Tax Strategies to Reduce Greenhouse Gases Without Curtailing Growth," *The Energy Journal*, Vol. 12, No. 4, pp. 1–14.

purchasing power drained by the gasoline tax, thus eliminating the short-term recessionary burden. On the other hand, the increased income enhances the inflationary pressure of the overall policy, because neither theory nor empirical experience supports an assumption that personal and corporate income tax cuts lead to lower wages and prices. It is therefore expected that this policy will induce the Federal Reserve to tighten credit policies and raise nominal interest rates. Because the primary short-term determinant of inflation is the level of economic activity under a full employment, targeting inflation is nearly equivalent to targeting real GDP during the first ten years of the simulation. As a consequence, the revenue-raising and tax-cut scenarios yield very similar growth rates for the first ten years. As regards sustainability, however, the two policy strategies differ fundamentally. The real GDP composition is critically different and this takes effect on GDP growth after ten years, because personal income tax reductions help support consumption at the expense of lower business investments, which are curtailed by the higher interest rates. After ten years this reduces the productive capital stock and the economy's growth potential so that GDP losses are magnified.

The second revenue-recycling policy generates a much more favorable development path because it is both deficit and inflation neutral. The gasoline tax revenue is offset by a reduction in the employer-paid portion of payroll taxes. Such a policy has only a slight recessionary impact after five years, and national income losses over the long run are virtually eliminated. Prices of gasoline intensive goods rise (and gasoline consumption falls, as intended), while prices of labor-intensive goods and services decline (and consumption of these goods and services rise). Changes in inflation, interest rates, and the distribution of national income between households and businesses are minimal, and this overall policy package maintains the level of national income while achieving the environmental target. In the case of the United States, this study appears to suggest that there is scope for double dividend in the form of improved environmental quality and enhanced demand for labor while the level of key macroeconomic indicators remains steady.

Norway

In Norway, a unique study was commissioned in 1993 by the ministries of Finance and Environment and the National Research Council, based on initiatives taken by the Friends of the Earth and Project Alternative Futures of Norway at the time of UNCED in 1992. The project challenges the long-term (1990–2030) scenarios of the official governmental four-year plan, which portrays a near doubling of most per capita economic indicators by 2030 and a continued increase in CO_2 emissions.[8]

This project brings the environmental demands of the Friends of the Earth of Norway to the macroeconomic models routinely used by the central government for national planning and budgetary purposes. The idea is to simulate the long-term environmental and economic impact of imposing such environmental demands on a small, open economy as a basis for an expanded dialogue on the feasibility of the various policy choices with long-term impacts. The project has established a close professional and political dialogue involving both the Ministry of Finance and the Ministry of Environment. This has been possible because Norway has a long tradition in the integrated use of macroeconomic policy modeling.[9] It has been further facilitated because Statistics Norway pioneered the field of resource accounting in the 1970s and gradually expanded the coverage of environmental satellite accounts for use in the routine planning and budget work along with national income accounting. Gradually, this framework was expanded for integration in applied macroeconomic modeling with particular focus on environmental impact assessment of alternative paths of macroeconomic development. Such analyses are now part and parcel of the budgetary process of the central government, and both the Ministry of Finance and the sectoral ministries (including the Ministry of Environment) develop scenarios by means, for example, of multi-sectoral long-term computable equilibrium models or medium-term disequilibrium models to test the macroeconomic and environmental impacts of their respective policy proposals.

The study enters this dialogue by adopting the same macroeconomic models and by contracting the Research Department of Statistics Norway to incorporate the various environmental demands of the Friends of the Earth, and to simulate Norway's environmental and economic development outlook for the next 40 years as a basis for comparison with the official government perspectives. This has been no small order. The Friends of the Earth posed some 54 environmental demands to be taken into account by the macro-modelers. To determine how these demands could be met in the project, a forum was established and met regularly for almost a year, gradually establishing that out of the 54 environmental demands, 26 could be incorporated in the macroeconomic models. Some were incorporated directly as exogenous constraints/variables, while others took the form of goals to be met en-

---

[8]Ministry of Finance, 1993, "St. meld. nr. 4 (1992–93): Langtidsprogrammet 1994–97" ("Long-Term Program, 1994–97"), Oslo.

[9]See Bergman and Olsen, 1992.

dogenously as a result of explicit macroeconomic or sectoral policy choices, a few of which are drastic compared with what is envisaged in the government's official long-term perspective. The remaining 28 demands could not be met in any meaningful way within the existing macroeconomic models, either because they were of a local nature or because they reflected issues not presently covered by the national-income or satellite-resources accounts. The project therefore initiated a series of parallel partial studies (both theoretical and empirical) to try to shed some light on these environmental concerns.[10]

The models have been calibrated on the basis of historical data, putting certain constraints on how far one can deviate from historical developments and still retain some faith in the usefulness of the simulations. The initial CO_2 requirement of the Friends of the Earth serves to illustrate this problem. Referring to the scientific reports from the UN Intergovernmental Panel for Climate Change (IPCC), they required 60 percent annual reduction in CO_2 emissions from Norway as Norway's fair contribution to stabilize global CO_2 concentrations. However, both CO_2 and emissions of several air pollutants are endogenously determined in the models. Economic and regulatory policies needed to achieve a reduction of this magnitude were considered too far removed from anything the models could cope with and retain some validity. It was therefore decided to strike a compromise and impose strong policy measures that would result in significant reductions in CO_2 emissions compared both with the official government scenario for 2030 and the actual 1989 emissions, but admittedly not meeting Norway's share of the IPCC goal of stabilizing CO_2 concentrations or other output goals suggested by the Friends of the Earth. The simulations, as presented, are therefore meant to illustrate possible long-term environmental and economic impacts if Norway embarks on drastic policy commitments today and sticks to gradually introducing stiffer economic and regulatory measures related to energy production and use, while at the same time preserving the current account balance and attempting to maintain a balanced public budget.

The main regulatory measure adopted in the simulations was a reduction in the extraction of oil and gas and associated investment activities, compared with what was assumed in the official long-term perspective plan. This involved stopping or postponing most further

---

[10]The book with detailed documentation of this project is so far available in Norwegian only from Ad Notam Gyldendal Pub., Oslo, 1995, titled *Barekvaftig Dkonomi* by Stein Hansen, Pål Føyn Jespersen, and Ingeborg Rasmussen. An English edition of the book is planned for publication in 1996, and several working papers have been issued in Norwegian.

developments of oil and gas fields. The main economic instrument adopted in the simulations is an isolated Norwegian CO_2 tax, which is gradually increased annually for all sectors of the economy until 2015 and from then on kept constant in current prices, with some energy-intensive industries exempted in one of the simulations. The first simulation applied regulations only, the second applied the CO_2 tax only, and the third combined the two and thus allowed for more moderate growth in the CO_2 tax. A fourth simulation exempts energy-intensive industries from the CO_2 tax, but is otherwise equal to the third simulation.

The findings are interesting. The simulations suggest substantial resilience in the economy when one has 40 years to adjust gradually to new conditions for production and consumption. The simulations suggest considerable—albeit significantly less—growth in per capita GDP and private consumption, but the consumption pattern turns drastically away from fossil-fuel-intensive activities, such as gasoline consumption, which is reduced by around 65 percent in the various CO_2 tax simulations. The simulations adopt the same technological improvement assumptions for each and every sector (for example, specific gasoline consumption of the future car) as does in the official perspective plan. The change in consumption is primarily due to people buying cars that are much less fuel intensive than what they would buy without these CO_2 tax increases. The number of cars purchased is hardly changed at all.

Full employment is implicitly assumed in all the simulations with the long-term multi-sectoral growth (MSG) model. In the medium-term models (MODAG and MISMOD), on the other hand, unemployment and adjustment costs are explicitly modeled. The adjustments are significant. The sectoral composition of production and employment changes significantly away from sectors dependent on energy and fossil fuel. On the other hand, overall employment impacts are less dramatic, and although there is increased unemployment for the first few years as a result of the policy changes, this effect tapers off gradually (with MODAG when applied to the first set of policy assumptions, that is, regulatory measures only). With the alternative MISMOD model, a double dividend emerges after ten years in the form of increased overall employment and reduced emissions to air, when the CO_2 tax is increased to stabilize CO_2 emissions at the 1989 level.

The modeling requirement to close the model can be done in different ways, with different results. In the present simulation, by reducing oil and gas investments, overall investments are reduced, leading to reduced savings (private and overall). Since private income is initially fixed, this opens the way for increased private consumption (but over time reduced output will also reduce the level of consumption). Alternatively, one could have decided to close the model via the level of total

Table 1. *MSG Simulation Results*
(Government base case scenario, percentage deviation from the 2030 results)

Impact Indicator	Simulation 1	Simulation 2	Simulation 3	Simulation 4
GDP	–5	–4	–8	–7
Private consumption	–9	–2	–10	–10
Exports	–1	–9	–7	–4
Imports	–3	–5	–6	–5
CO_2 emissions	–15	–30	–35	–26
NMVOC	–30	–15	–40	–40
NOx	–10	–15	–20	–17
SO_2	+2	–40	–32	–12

Source: *MSG Simulations for Project for a Sustainable Economy, Norway,* carried out by Statistics Norway, March 1995.

private investments. In that case, as a result of reduced oil and gas investments, on-shore investments would increase because private savings are fixed as long as private income is fixed. In other words, the model can be closed in a way that leads to increased on-shore investments or in another way that leads to increased private consumption.

The long-term simulations also assume a fixed current account balance. When a deficit in the commodity and services trade arises, the balance as regards payments of interest, dividends, and foreign aid must be improved. To the extent that interest and dividends payments are fixed, foreign aid grants must be reduced (quite substantially in some simulations) to meet the current account balance requirement. Subjecting the simulations to such current account constraints implicitly stabilizes the foreign exchange and interest rates. At the same time the budget balance is quite well maintained over the 40-year period. Indicators from the four long-term simulations are compared in Table 1.

In the second simulation, a rapidly increasing CO_2 tax on top of the CO_2 tax already in place in Norway is the sole policy instrument in use (other than measures to stabilize the current account and to keep an eye on the government budget so that the exchange rate and interest rates remain stable). This appears to provide the most cost-effective way of achieving the emission reductions. (See Figure 1 for a comparison of the cost effectiveness of the four alternatives.)

As far as emission reductions are concerned, Figures 2 and 3 show that major improvements are within reach relative to both the base scenario in the government's long-term perspective plan and the levels in 1989. CO_2 emissions are reduced by 26–35 percent relative to the 2030 scenario in the three simulations in which a CO_2 tax is applied. As regards non-methane volatile organic compounds (NMVOC), since emissions originate to a large extent from oil and gas field operations, re-

Figure 1. *Percent Reduction in Emissions Divided by Percent Reduction in GDP for the Alternative Scenarios*

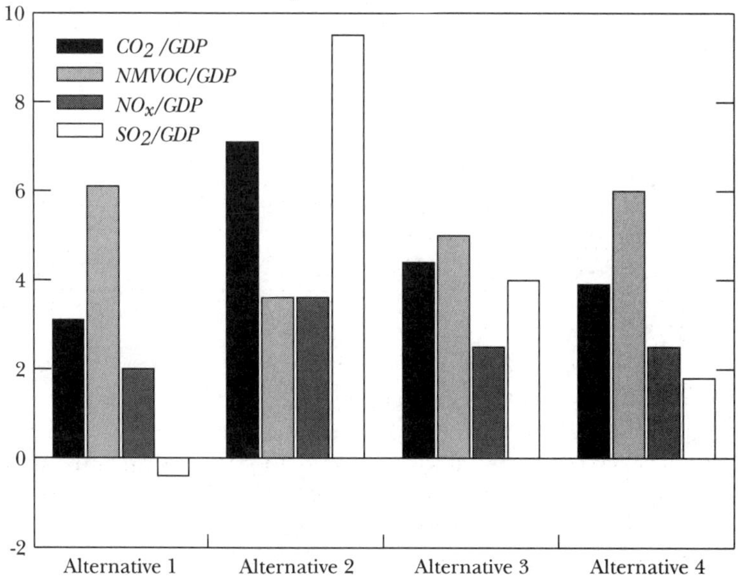

Source: MSG Simulations for Project Sustainable Economy, Norway.

ductions are greatest in the three simulations that involve direct regulation of the activity level in these sectors. SO_2 emissions, on the other hand, increase slightly relative to the government base case, if no CO_2 tax is introduced, but decrease significantly in the other scenarios, except when energy-intensive industries are exempted from the CO_2 tax.

In Table 2, changes in the 2030 consumption pattern compared with that of the government base case simulation are presented for the regulation/CO_2 tax combination (third simulation).

The project does not settle for only the macroeconomic costs (i.e., GDP and consumption losses) of reducing the various emissions. It also uses dose response information and best available environmental and health value estimates to determine the benefits from reduced emissions and reduced traffic. When such benefits are included in the overall macroeconomic impact assessment, the loss of GDP is reduced by 0.5–1 percentage point. Since direct GDP losses range from 4 percent (alternative 2) to 8 percent (alternative 3), these benefits improve the overall picture only marginally, but should nevertheless be included for completeness.

Sustainable development implies providing future consumption choice opportunities that are no less than those of the present. Such

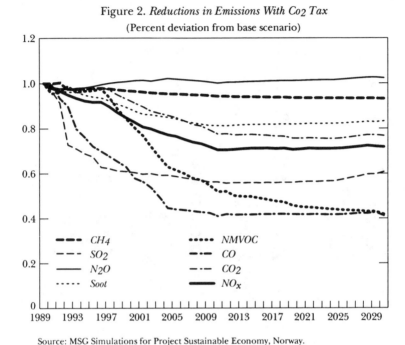

Figure 2. *Reductions in Emissions With Co₂ Tax*
(Percent deviation from base scenario)

Source: MSG Simulations for Project Sustainable Economy, Norway.

choices depend to large extent on the value of the national wealth in the future, that is, on the management of human capital, natural capital, man-made capital, institutional capital, and financial assets and debts to other countries. The simulations calculate the resilience to policy change for the part of this wealth that is easiest measure: the sum of man-made capital, petroleum wealth, and net assets on other countries. Table 3 shows that national wealth almost doubles even when the environmental austerity measures are introduced. Man-made capital dominates overwhelmingly (almost 90 percent of total), but is reduced when less petroleum revenue becomes available for on-shore investments. Petroleum wealth, however, increases when it is stored for future use. Foreign assets are scenario insensitive.

Developing Countries: Environmental Impact of Macroeconomic Reform

This section is limited to the environmental impact of "pure" macroeconomic policy instruments, that is, adjustments in the exchange rate,

Figure 3. *Reductions in Emissions with CO2 Tax*
(Percent deviation from 1989 levels)

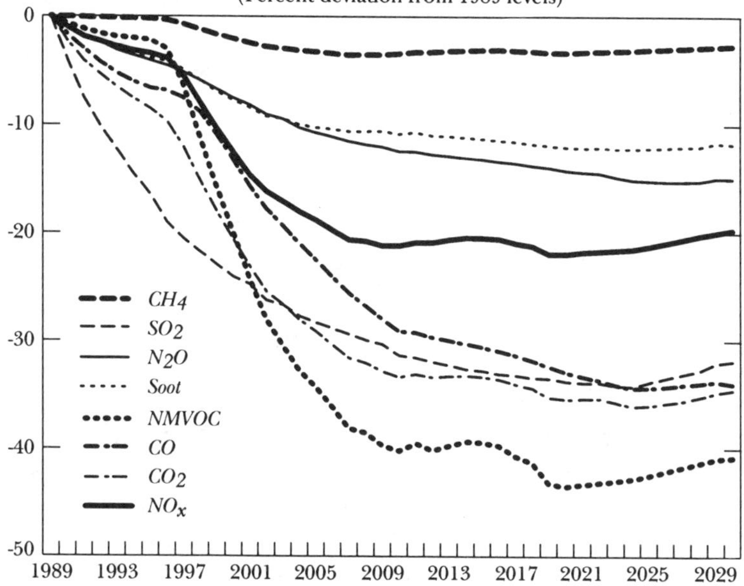

Source: MSG Simulations for Project Sustainable Economy, Norway.

monetary policy, interest rates, and fiscal and current account balances. To a much lesser degree, the section also focuses on sectoral policy measures, such as social-cost pricing and related tax issues, even though in many countries (both industrial and developing), the removal of such market distortions and policy rigidities may be welcome from the macroeconomic point of view.

In the context of developing countries, however, it is not possible to isolate pure macroeconomic policy variables from sectoral ones, because adjustment very often focuses on sectoral policy as a major component of an integrated macroeconomic reform program. To leave out sectoral reform would render the remaining part of the program worthless, because without sectoral reform, such as the removal of price distortions and subsidies, much of the basis for the design of fiscal and monetary reforms would vanish.

It has become popular to apply computable general equilibrium (CGE) models to analyze the results of economy-wide policy reform, including environmental results. There is no denying of the usefulness of this approach, as has been convincingly documented in the literature.[11] Often, however, lack of data poses a real obstacle to the meaningful use

Table 2. *Deviation in Private Consumption from 2030 Base Scenario*
(In percent)

Consumption Category	Change
Electricity	+2
Stationary use of oil	−36
Gasoline	−63
Car purchases	−10
Public transport	−9
Food	−5
Beverages	−10
Other goods	−9
Clothing and footwear	−9
Furniture	−11
Housing	−13
Other services	−7
Tourism abroad	−14
Total private consumption	−10.4

Source: *MSG Simulations for Project for a Sustainable Economy, Norway,* Simulation 3.

of CGE models although such models seem to have an advantage (if data are available) in studies of trade-offs between stricter pollution control and economic growth (as was discussed in the industrial country cases above), and in studies having to do with the lack of property rights, such as deforestation and soil erosion, that is, areas of market failure.

Many environmental impact assessments related to macroeconomic policy measures can—at least initially—be addressed without the use of sophisticated computable general equilibrium models, as discussed in the following sections.

Fiscal Discipline and the Environment

A widely believed myth is that improved fiscal discipline is environmentally harmful. This belief is based on the observation that when a fiscal deficit reduction is sought, governments start cutting where resistance is weakest, and environment ministries and agencies are generally the youngest and least-established governmental agencies. Budget reductions for such small and weak agencies, yet to establish their position and identity, can be a hard blow, and certainly damaging for the environmental awareness work in the country.

---

[11]Shantayanan Devarajan, 1993, "Can Computable General Equilibrium Models Shed Light on the Environmental Problems of Developing Countries?" Revised version of paper presented at a WIDER Conference, Helsinki, September 3–7, 1990.

Table 3. *National Wealth, 1989 and 2030*
(1989 prices; in thousands of Norwegian crowns per capita)

Wealth Component	1989	Base Case	Simulation 1	Simulation 2	Simulation 3	Simulation 4
Man-made	545	1,021	961	971	924	940
Net foreign assets	31	113	115	113	115	114
Petroleum	200	33	58	33	58	58
Leisure	—	—	—	—	—	—
Total wealth	776	1,167	1,134	1,117	1,097	1,112

Source: *MSG Simulations for Project for a Sustainable Economy, Norway.*

However, such fiscal disciplining measures tend to require far larger expenditure reductions than what the cuts in environment budgets can offer. Cuts have to be made in other areas as well. Even if the military budget is protected by influential ministers, infrastructure sectors will likely be hard hit as well. Typically, during periods of austerity, projects requiring large public transfers are also shelved or postponed. In many cases such projects have an environmental and cultural dimension, for example, hydroelectric power projects, power transmission lines, and transnational highways. The resulting investment inaction could therefore be environmentally benign. Not only that, the environmental damages avoided by not implementing these projects as a result of budgetary discipline would likely far exceed any environmental gains that a small, powerless, and probably ineffective and understaffed environment agency could have achieved. Therefore, while it is sad to see a fragile and enthusiastic environment agency crumble, there could be some comfort in the sobering observation that the much larger (but probably much smaller in terms of percentage point change) cuts in other budget components more than compensate for the loss of environmental protection capability. Suffice it to say that overall sustainability would of course be further enhanced if reallocations secured the survival and strengthening of the infant environment agencies.

Criticism of stabilization and structural adjustment programs by environmentally and socially concerned groups should, however, not at all be dismissed as a result of the above conclusion. Much more economic and environmental improvement could be achieved from stabilization and adjustment, provided there is political will to implement the proposed reform. The question of incidence is at the core of obstacles to improvements. Asymmetry of political power and information among affected parties tends to prevent the simultaneous implementation of apparent win-win reforms. One could in most cases easily avoid reducing small and fragile environmental and primary health care budgets, by savings on budget drains caused by, for example, fertilizer, pesticide, water, and energy subsidies, most of which accrue to the well-to-do, rather than to the poor and vulnerable. The health budget could be restructured from capital-intensive curative hospitals to labor-intensive preventive health care, which typically is enhanced by simple pollution prevention in residential areas. A lot of environment-related health damage is avoided when fewer pesticides are used. Because such broader reform packages are frequently proposed, it is important to trace their economic and environmental repercussions in order to devise compensatory measures to reduce the political obstacles to implementation.

Debt Service and the Environment

Along the same line of reasoning, it is frequently asserted that heavy foreign debt is destructive to the environment. The reasoning is that in order to service the foreign debt, the country must earn foreign exchange, which means, in the case of natural resource-based economies, cutting down the forests, overfishing, engaging in excessive mining, and planting erosive export crops. Empirical correlations notwithstanding,[12] the reality of the matter is less clear and requires a situation specific analysis.

Assume for a start that some kindly donor comes along and offers to forgive, reduce, or postpone debt servicing. This is equivalent to an immediate improvement in the current account and a reduced pressure on the public budget for interest and principal payments. Assume further that the government, prior to the debt crisis, had ambitious development plans for the country's fragile land and vulnerable rain forests. The debt crisis has quite possibly increased the political risk to foreigners of investing in the country and undermined domestic ability and willingness to mobilize savings for these investments. As a result, the environmental resources threatened by these projects are saved for the time being.

With a sudden debt relief measure, the fiscal situation improves, political stability is regained, and the government may decide it is time to implement the environmentally harmful projects it had to shelve while it was short on funds and creditworthiness. Unless strict environmental conditionality—or better yet, strong domestic ownership of environmental policy measures—is attached to the debt relief measure, it is un-

[12]James R. Kahn, and Judith A. McDonald, 1995, "Third World Debt and Tropical Deforestation," *Ecological Economics*, Vol. 12, No. 2, pp. 107–23.

likely that self imposed discipline will take charge and put the country on a sustainable development path.

What happens if the debt-ridden country is experiencing rapid population growth, high unemployment and underemployment among unskilled workers, a large landless workforce, and unclear and poorly monitored property rights in forested areas? It may well happen that the unemployed will end up as squatters in the forests and thus increase deforestation. Debt relief could reduce this pressure by providing more jobs, but considering the complexity of the setting and the capital intensity of most foreign-investment projects, politically difficult and time-consuming reforms independent of the debt problems will be needed to counter the immediate pressure on resources of the infrastructure projects inaugurated by the debt relief.

It has been suggested that so-called debt-for-nature swaps could create a double dividend in the sense that the fiscal burden is relieved simultaneously with the enhancement of environmental management capacity. Nevertheless, fiscal relief may have a much faster multiplier effect in the form of environmentally harmful investments and polluting operations than the institution building that the proceeds on the local currency bonds from the swap can mobilize.

Clearly, the above pessimistic conclusions are not at all synonymous with saying that to keep the people poor is to protect the environment. The conclusions merely establish the simple fact that whenever funds are suddenly available for investment on attractive terms, investment will happen and, unless one can assure against market and policy failures, there is no guarantee that the investment will be environmentally benign.

Exchange Rate Reform and the Environment

When stabilization and adjustment programs become necessary, local currencies are usually overvalued. As imports are too cheap and exports noncompetitive, the balance of payments pressure is obvious. Devaluation is therefore a typical ingredient of reform, but when a government has sustained this policy failure for a long time, it is likely that related distortions have established themselves as well. Such distortions typically interfere in the market for exportables (export licenses and taxes) and for imports (special exemptions from customs duties for capital imports and other capital subsidies), as well as food subsidies for urban dwellers and taxes on the farm output. Detailed marketing regulations often eliminate competition, so that the export sectors are poorly prepared for reaping the benefits from devaluation and the accompanying trade liberalization. In such circumstances the supply-side response is poor and slow, and strong technical support for the institutional reha-bilitation is needed for the supply side to respond.

The effect of devaluation and trade liberalization on the environment cannot, however, be predicted in any generalized way, even with a CGE model. Each country is different, and even the world market, to which the country's export sector adjusts, keeps changing. For a developing country it is sufficient to study the effects by means of a country model that assumes exogenous world market prices, even if several small developing economies succeed with their supply-side efforts simultaneously. (Occasionally, a few countries have such a large market share of supplies that their joint action will influence world prices, but those few occurrences can be dealt with as special cases.)

The environmental impact of the above measures then depends on the products, inputs, and production methods encouraged or discouraged by the policies. As regards the product mix, it is well known that growing certain export and local food crops causes erosion, while growing others retains the soil very well. One needs to know not only which crops will be phased in or out, but also the growing conditions, because some crops may be environmentally acceptable on certain soils, but destructive on others.

The reform is likely to raise the price of imported inputs and make some domestic inputs more competitive. If fertilizer and pesticide subsidies are removed at the same time, less of these inputs will be used, but the final environmental impact could be quite different from the direct impact on the soils and waters affected by fertilizer and pesticides, thus requiring a CGE modeling approach for a complete impact analysis. One needs to determine the availability and cost of labor when additional labor is needed to substitute for (say) pesticides and imported farm machinery, and one needs to know whether the increased cost of fertilizer stimulates more land clearing as opposed to the more intensive land use encouraged by low fertilizer and pesticide costs. In other words, what may be environmentally benign for cultivated areas, may be offset by increased land clearing and deforestation, which may be accelerated if the forest land to which the marginal farmers migrate is open-access land. This calls for the expansion of the reform program to include land and property-rights reform as well as internalization of the environmental externalities resulting from a malfunctioning land market.[13]

---

[13]David Reed, ed., 1992, *Structural Adjustment and the Environment* (London: Earthscan Publications).

Interest Rate Reforms and the Environment

The impact of interest rate changes has been addressed in the context of a CGE model for studying deforestation in Costa Rica. The model explicitly simulates the effects of introducing property rights to forest resources and includes a market for logs and a market for cleared land (in demand by the squatters). The rate of land clearing depends on the definition of property rights as well as on taxes or subsidies that affect the forest and agricultural sectors. The study finds that establishing property rights tends to decrease deforestation, because both the loggers and the squatters internalize losses associated with deforestation. The simulation further shows that higher interest rates promote deforestation while lower interest rates contribute to conservation. To the extent this observation is transferable among developing countries, one would expect credit market reforms, leading to increased credit supply at lower interest rates, to enhance environmentally more benign natural-resource management among borrowers.

What Do CGE Models Contribute?

The Costa Rica study illustrates how the direct impact of sector-specific policies are modified once the indirect effects arising from intersectoral links are accounted for. Two effects illustrate how the CGE approach can help diagnose and prescribe solutions in the form of alternative policy mixes for better overall results.

The first is the effect of increased stumpage fees on logging. Partial equilibrium analysis predicts reduced logging from such a measure, but once the relationship between loggers and squatters is properly identified in the model, deforestation spreads. While logging will indeed decline, total deforestation nevertheless increases because the contraction of logging and forest industries shifts resources toward agriculture. As agriculture expands, so does deforestation.

The second effect pertains to an increase in the wage rate in the same economy. Owing to specified intersectoral resource flows, the effects of wage changes in the CGE model could be very different from those stemming from partial equilibrium analysis. If the wages of unskilled labor were increased by, say, minimum industrial wage legislation, the model predicts that deforestation could worsen instead of declining. Logging declines as a result of the increased labor costs, but so do other industrial activities in the economy. As a result, labor and capital tend to flow to agriculture, leading to conversion of open-access forest land for farming, as long as alternative employment opportunities are absent.

Clearly one should not accept CGE simulation results without reservations. Such models designed to address simultaneously economic and environmental issues in developing countries that have inadequate and unreliable statistics are at best speculative, and their econometric basis is generally poor if at all present. Nevertheless, the important lesson learnt from comparing partial equilibrium conclusions with CGE model simulations is that intersectoral links matter in industrial and developing countries alike and to ignore the environmental dimension can lead to costly and damaging policies.

Discussion

Discussant's Comments

Andrew Steer

These papers shed interesting insights into the links among economy-wide policy reform, the natural environment, and economic growth. Stein Hansen examines the issue from both sides, discussing first the impact on the path of economic growth of radical environmental policies and then the impact on the environment of macroeconomic policy reforms. Ved Gandhi and Ronald McMorran focus exclusively on the second of the two issues.

Hansen's conclusion to the first question—can we survive radical environmental policies?—is encouraging. It seems we certainly can survive such policies. Economies are, it appears, remarkably robust. The commonly expressed view that economies would collapse in the event that radical green advice is followed is, according to the Norwegian study, not correct. Of course, the cost is not trivial. The results of the Norwegian modeling exercise suggest that GDP would be lower by 4–5 percentage points from what it would otherwise be. At one level this is small—perhaps two years growth over a 30-year period. At another it is very large. While many contingent-valuation studies suggest that citizens would be willing to pay this much for a radically cleaner and more pristine environment, revealed preference indicates that no electorate in the world (not even in Norway) is willing to pay anything close to this amount.

Hansen's conclusions are, I believe, correct and largely consistent with other studies. A few of the model's detailed predictions are surprising, and I suspect wrong, and some of the elasticities will probably need some checking. (For example, public transportation is predicted in equilibrium after the new policies are in place to be down by 9 percentage points—surely surprising given that a number of the policies are designed to shift travelers toward public transport.) But for the most part the results are persuasive.

Many other studies have looked at similar questions, although none has assumed such a wholesale restructuring of incentive structures within the economy. Some studies of the likely impact of adjustments to

---

Note: The discussion was chaired and moderated by Malcolm Knight.

energy use, in the context of climate-change abatement, have concluded that a major transition toward renewable energy would be possible. Even a radical shift from today's 80 percent dependence on fossil fuels for electricity generation toward, say, 30 percent by the middle of the next century, would, it seems, cost only 1–2 percentage points of GDP. While most citizens would regard this as a reasonable price to pay, it is important to remember that for the United States, for example, this would amount to US$100 billion per year, or seven times America's foreign assistance program.[14]

Other studies have examined the impact of environmental regulations on economic growth over the past two decades. The best of such analysis has been undertaken by Jorgenson and Wilcoxen for the United States. Using a general equilibrium model, with carefully estimated elasticities of substitution, they show that today's GDP is around 2–3 percent lower than it would have been had there been no environmental regulations. Absent such regulations, there would have been a much worse environment, of course, which may have had a negative impact on economic productivity, so the cost of regulation may even be smaller. Most people would regard this price well worth paying for a cleaner environment. (Incidentally had more cost-effective environmental policies been followed, the cost would have been much smaller—but this is a subject for another day.)

An interesting question is whether the impact on developing countries would be greater or less than for industrial countries. Here the evidence is weak since little research has been done. My hypothesis is that the answer depends on the speed with which radical environmental policies are adopted. My guess would be that many developing countries would be less flexible (than industrial countries) in responding in the short term (costs in lost growth would be greater), but more able to adjust with a more gradual phase-in of such policies. Work by Blitzer and Eckaus on Egypt and India, respectively, in the context of the World Bank's 1992 World Development Report (p. 164) on environment and development, would seem to support this view.

Turning now to the second question—the impact of macroeconomic reforms on the environment—both papers make useful points. Essentially there are four paths by which such impacts might be effected:

- the impact of stabilization (lower rates of inflation and reduced macroeconomic imbalances)

---

[14]For a discussion of the issues, see William R. Cline, *The Economics of Global Warming* (Institute for International Economics), 1992; and articles by Birdsall and Steer, Cline, and Wallace in *Finance and Development*, March 1993.

- the impact of associated levels of aggregate demand in the economy
- the impact of relative price shifts
- the impact of associated institutional reforms (e.g., financial sector).

Stabilization, once completed, surely has an unambiguously positive impact on the environment. Instability promotes high discount rates and short-term calculations, which are anathema to longer-term sustainability. Gandhi and McMorran make this point effectively. Unfortunately, we have failed to make this point successfully to the bulk of the environmental critics of structural adjustment programs, many of whom, if given the option, would prefer the pre-adjustment instability, which would usually guarantee environmental destruction. The clearest empirical evidence of the impact of high inflation on natural resource exploitation has been provided by the work of Bob Schneider on deforestation in the Amazon. The work shows clearly that slash and burn (swidden) agriculture is the rational thing to do in the presence of macroeconomic instability and associated high interest and discount rates, while even poor farmers can be expected to be encouraged to make the investments required for more environmentally sound agriculture in a stable macroeconomic context.

Unfortunately, to get to this environmentally benign stability may require reduced aggregate demand. In the abstract this might be thought to help the environment (on the grounds that less consumption implies less "throughput," less depletion, and less waste). But since the instability is more often than not caused by public budget imbalances, it is often necessary to cut public expenditures. And, given the relative weakness of the constituency for environmental public expenditure, it is likely that this category of public expenditure may be cut as much or more than other categories of expenditure. To be truthful, there is still no systematic evidence for this proposition, but it has anecdotal support.

The most important impact of policy reform on the environment is through the third path—relative price shifts. A good number of such impacts—those that move the economy away from subsidized input prices toward world prices—will help improve the quality of the environment. Studies carried out at the World Bank show that full-cost pricing would cut air pollution in Eastern Europe by half, and would dramatically reduce water shortages around the world. It would also help bring sanitation to the two billion people currently lacking it and would reduce pesticide poisoning. But not all relative price shifts would be benign. As both Hansen and Gandhi and McMorran point out, the impact will depend on a number of features. The World Bank has done substantial analysis of this issue (see Munasinghe and Cruz in this volume) as have the World Resources Institute (WRI) and The Worldwide Fund for Nature (WWF). At the Bank we are encouraging our task managers working on policy reform programs to cooperate with governments and local research institutes in assessing the potential impact of the proposed reforms, with the purpose of countering any such pressure with complementary "first-best" environmental policies.

A final route is through institutional reforms associated with the overall reform programs. I am not sure these get classified as macroeconomic policies, but they are often a point toward a stable growth path. They include financial reform, the introduction of financial accountability in state-owned enterprises, improved property rights management, and the like. Most of these, by promoting improved efficiency and the reduction of waste, benefit the environment and should be wholeheartedly supported by those of us concerned about environmental sustainability. But, again, as in the case of relative price shifts, not all reforms might be environmentally benign. It is vital therefore that we do our homework so that these reforms work for sustainable development rather than against it. An example here is privatization. Where done right, the new private owners can be encouraged to reduce environmental damage. Done wrong—that is, where enterprises are privatized in the absence of environmental policies or the absence of a strong civil society empowered by information and by its right to demand improvements—the quality of air and water may deteriorate further.

Other Discussion

Peter Bartelmus: Just two short observations. The first one concerns survival of the economy if we followed the advice of the green lobby. The clear answer given by the speakers is that the economy will survive. To me the answer is not so clear because the question has not been clearly formulated. The question should be: can we survive *tough* environmental policy advice? What is tough? Tough does not mean a few percentage points of reduction of physical indicators of pollutants or emissions, but reduction in the actual damage done, not in emissions alone, but in the whole chain of ambient contamination and health effects. We should discuss damage values.

My second observation. I fully agree with the view that there is a need to link the microeconomic and macroeconomic aspects of economic and environmental policymaking, and the general equilibrium models are one way. These models and the assumptions behind them range from utility measurements to cost and production functions. Is the general equilibrium approach applicable in the case of markets that are noncompetitive and that lack transparency? Has any study looked seriously into this issue in the context of the environment?

Knut Alfsen: It is fairly easy to criticize the assumptions behind CGE models on the data quality, as Peter has done. In doing so, we are focusing on the wrong part of CGE modeling; we are focusing on the equations and the mathematics. An advantage of CGE models in Norway has been to bring together the Ministry of Finance, the Ministry of Environment, environmentalists, and those concerned with monetary issues, and provide them with a common framework for fruitful discussions. I would like to fight for CGE modeling on that basis alone.

I also have a comment about the relation of macroeconomic and sectoral policy to the environment. The playing field is very often tilted in favor of economic growth and against the environment. There is need to level the playing field in a way that makes environmental concerns count just as much as economic and other concerns. Macroeconomic policy can contribute to this just as much as sectoral policies can.

Phil Bagnoli: The Gandhi and McMorran paper focuses on sectoral failures. I wonder if these sectoral failures could be dealt with even if markets were functioning and social costs were internalized into the private markets. I am inclined to think that such failures would continue because these countries have a high discount rate, as their governments and economies are liquidity constrained. A high premium is put on investing and giving resources to these countries, and even if they could borrow against their future incomes, their future incomes are not going to be all that high. This leads me to ask whether the Western nations want these countries to protect their environmental resources, whether there is some sort of mechanism for transferring resources to these countries for purchasing those resources, and whether these mechanisms can be formalized so that the richer nations can identify environmental resources that they may want to purchase in these countries?

Kirit Parikh: About general equilibrium modeling, I agree with Knut Alfsen that the most important part of general equilibrium modeling is the feedback and the interrelationship it brings into the forefront and how it makes it easier to communicate across different disciplines. It is, of course, true that with the general equilibrium model and with a suitable choice of parameters you can get any result that you want. But I think the choice of parameters is not for the model to make—the parameters are in the system. You should estimate the parameters from the system and once you estimated them then you have no choice. So I think the criticism that Peter Bartelmus made is valid, but that is not to say that you do not need a good general equilibrium model.

As has been pointed out, even macroeconomic policies have sectoral outcomes, for the environment, so I think the Fund cannot really absolve itself of the responsibility of at least thinking about the consequences of macroeconomic policies on the environment. Let me give the example of removing a fertilizer subsidy. A study we did in India found that removing fertilizer subsidies would encourage the use of cow dung as fertilizer, and as cow dung is also used as fuel, this would create a fuel shortage and result in more deforestation. There are feedbacks and interactions that ought to be taken into account.

Nuri Erbas: Both papers lacked emphasis on privatization and the issues of private property. Given that environmental degradation is often a direct result of lack of private property, or the lack of enforcement of property rights, I wonder if the speakers would comment on the effect of privatization on the environment. I also have a question about external financing for environmental protection in a developing country. I would like to know if rich countries would be willing to form a trust to buy or lease, for instance, a national park in Kenya, make it private property, and pay for the preservation of the black rhino, which Kenya cannot afford.

Jim MacNeill: I was puzzled by the insistence of Ved Gandhi and Ronald McMorran that the IMF is not an environmental agency, and I would like to ask why this insistence? I suppose if you define an environment agency as an agency with a mandate for environmental protection or resource management, then clearly the IMF is not an environmental agency. But if you define an environment agency as an agency whose policies, expenditures, and programs have an impact on the environment, then the IMF, by the evidence of the Fund staff's own paper, is an environment agency. It is certainly an agency that should have a vital interest in the promotion of sustainable development and in deploying macroeconomic policies, to the extent that they have an effect, in support of more sustainable forms of development. So I would like to query the Fund staff on their insistence that IMF is not an environment agency.

Ganga Ramdas: I have a question regarding the implementation of sectoral policies. I will briefly outline a scenario. Suppose we have an identified polluter, say, a coal-mining company, and we want to curb pollution. The obvious possible solution might be to tax the polluter. However, the tax-to-GDP ratio in the country might already be very high; besides, this solution might be too slow to prevent the damage. Is there a quasi-fiscal method to deal with this? Is it possible, for example, to insist on the polluter to escrow a part of his export receipts and use it to clean up the environment or reverse the damage that was done?

Herman Daly: One macroeconomic policy in support of environmental improvement is ecologically oriented tax reform—to shift the entire tax base gradually away from taxes on incomes and value added to taxes on resource depletion and pollution. The idea, of course, is not to tax what you want more of—value added and incomes—but tax what you want less of—depletion and pollution. I wonder if the general equilibrium model that Stein Hansen talked about could be used to test the implications of such a policy and also if the IMF considers this to be within its purview in relation to its work on the effects of macroeconomic reforms on the environment.

David Reed: We have been discussing at length the relationship between relative price changes and the environment. In this connection I would like to point out that we have just concluded a series of studies on the impact of structural adjustment on the environment in nine developing countries and have seen that the impact of price changes on the environment is uniformly insignificant relative to the impact of structural adjustment on social structures and institutions. In my opinion, we need to broaden our discussion and begin looking at these issues—that is, not just focus on the direct links between one instrument (or a package of instruments) and a particular environmental problem, but to understand how the effects of these instruments are transmitted to social structures and institutions and, as a consequence, how they fundamentally alter the rate and composition of natural resource use in developing countries.

Responses

Stein Hansen: There have been a lot of good and relevant questions. I do not have anything to say about Andrew Steer's comment because by and large we are in agreement.

An important part of the project in Norway—this dialogue between the NGO community, on the one hand, and us economists, on the other—has been to identify precisely the issues of concern to the NGOs that can be meaningfully addressed in the CGE model. Some issues are on the priority list of the NGOs that we feel we cannot meaningfully address within the kind of CGE model at our disposal. We therefore had to commission parallel studies of a partial microeconomic framework, sometimes with a model, sometimes without a model. So we are quite sober about what we can use the CGE model for, and this has been a valuable exercise for us. This takes care of part of the comment of Peter Bartelmus on the macro-micro links within the CGE models.

Kirit Parikh posed the interesting question of a second-best world, where removal of a chemical fertilizer subsidy in India might have an unexpected impact on deforestation. The question then, of course, arises about how you manage your forests in order to counter that secondary and indirect impact. This may call for some massive interference with regard to property rights and free access, and shows how complicated these issues are.

A question was asked if richer countries can form some kind of trust or fund and offer the proceeds to low-income countries to lease protected areas. The answer in theory is yes, but the annual leasing fee may be so high that it cannot be easily afforded. In this regard, an ecologically unique area could be looked upon as an exportable to those who can afford it and who would be prepared to pay for it, but how do you organize such a trust or fund? How would it work? Some attempts, like debt-for-nature swaps, have worked in a few small countries and have created all sorts of emotions.

In response to Herman Daly, in Norway we have a Green Tax Commission to look into the scope of ecotax reform. We can give some answers in the context of our CGE model, for example, what happens to the public budget (that is a sum of the state budgets and the municipal budgets in Norway), if we could replace payroll taxes, for example, by ecological taxes. CO_2 tax is one tax that could provide a fairly stable revenue for the government, but that does not seem to be true of the other environmental taxes.

Ved Gandhi: Three or four questions were directed at the IMF and I will try to answer them. The first question was by Jim MacNeill who said that IMF is an environmental agency because somewhere along its policy advice has some indirect effects on the environment. As all of us know that every institution, every organization, has a primary objective. The IMF has the primary objective of ensuring exchange stability and macroeconomic stability in member countries. If somewhere along the line, because of lack of sectoral and environmental policies or inadequacies of relevant institutions, there are environmental effects, must one "correct" them before proceeding with macroeconomic policy reforms? This may not always be possible in the time available, and macroeconomic stability, which is a primary objective of the Fund and which is also generally good for the environment, cannot always wait, certainly not in every situation.

Herman Daly raised an issue that environmentalists have been pleading and rightly so. Why do we not replace income taxes and value-added taxes by ecotaxes? Replace? It is not so easy nor is it desirable. This is because tax policy has three objectives—efficiency, revenue, and equity—and ecotaxes do not achieve all of them. Ecotaxes may be efficient because they achieve social efficiency, but they often fail on revenue and equity grounds. If ecotaxes were perfectly tailored, there could be zero revenue, as everybody would behave and meet the environmental objectives! About their equity, everybody knows how regressive some of the ecotaxes can be. In fact, one of the reasons why value-added taxes exist in most countries is revenues and why income taxes exist in every country of the world, including the very poor countries, is equity. So, in my opinion, ecotaxes can supplement income and value-added taxes but cannot replace them. This is also another reason: the political powers that be will not allow you to have adequate levels of ecotaxes anyway!

David Reed noted that structural adjustment programs have affected social structures and institutions and, through them, the natural resources and the environment. In the Fund, unfortunately, we do not have social scientists who can understand the social and cultural environment of each country to the depth that will be needed to tailor structural adjustment programs of a country to such an extent that its social structures will not be affected in any way. Perhaps we can rely on the World Bank for this assistance.

Andrew Steer: Peter Bartelmus asked if we can survive tough green policies. The right question should be how tough is tough. If an environmentalist says we do not want any of the land to be used for agriculture, that is very tough indeed, and the costs would be very high according to how big agriculture is. When I said earlier that we can tolerate radical policies, I was referring to reasonably tough policies, such as not overexploiting certain oil fields, or whatever else seemed reasonable to me. Clearly, if we got tougher than that, then the costs would be much higher.

Regarding the comment by Knut Alfsen, I certainly do not wish to discourage those who are involved in CGE modeling and I agree very much with him that the process of putting the whole thing together is most useful. If I were allocating resources, I would rather do more analysis on the actual coefficients—at the microeconomic level—than build comprehensive CGE models.

Kirit Parikh raised a related point about the use of fertilizer, the cow dung-deforestation link. That is the level of analysis, a sort of microeconomic level of interaction, that I would want to study. I do not think an economy-wide CGE model of India would shed a whole lot of light beyond what a serious analysis of the interactions in rural areas would do.

Nuri Erbas raised the issue of privatization. Privatization generally, I think, will be beneficial for the environment, but it depends on what you privatize.

David Reed raised what I think is a fascinating issue—the importance of the intermediary institutions and social structures. It is because of this that the Environment Department of the World Bank has a large staff of anthropologists and sociologists. In the Bank we came to the conclusion we could not do our work without this expertise. I do not think the IMF necessarily needs to hire a lot of sociologists and anthropologists, however.

Additional Comments

Malcolm Knight: A point was made in the Gandhi and McMorran paper that environmental degradation is generally caused by market and policy failures, which are sectoral issues. One can question this point. Suppose you have a stabilization program that resulted in a stabilization of the general price level, but that also raised the rate of exploitation of, say, a renewable resource? Is that a sectoral-level issue, or is it a macroeconomic issue as well? Our speakers have placed a lot of stress on macroeconomic policy as demand-management policy. But, of course, supply management can be an important aspect of macroeconomic policy as well.

Mohan Munasinghe: I personally would come out in the middle of the spectrum of opinions expressed on CGE modeling. I would certainly not go so far as Ved Gandhi and Ronald McMorran have and assert that CGE models are the only way in which you can look at the net effects. But, at the same time, the work we have done on about three or four developing countries now shows that this is a very useful tool to supplement all the other ways of looking at these links. So, what we are looking for in our CGE work are the broad trends, not specific numbers, and also some hidden links that may not have emerged from the partial approach. The CGE approach can also be used to check results from partial equilibrium or traditional approaches. So we feel CGE models are a useful tool, but they do not give you a complete picture and they certainly are not that good for detailing numbers.

David Reed: I would like to reemphasize the impact of macroeconomic changes and reforms on the consumption of renewable resources. This is very much at the forefront of our concerns because, as we in the WWF have documented through our studies on macroeconomic stabilization and adjustment in nine countries, extractive economies react differently from manufacturing economies, as they undergo adjustment. It is quite simple. As extraction increases, there is a drawing down, at ever greater rates, of natural capital and, over time, economies become unsustainable. This is a fundamental issue. We have similar conclusions regarding agricultural-based economies, which have responded differently from, say, Mexico, Thailand, and other manufacturing economies, where as the pressure on the agricultural base expands—whether it is the production of tradables, or the production of nontradables—and they lead to unsustainable changes in those societies.

Malcolm Knight: This is an issue that I am sure will receive much more discussion in the course of this seminar. It may well be that the rate of exploitation of renewable resources is excessive. One of the reasons that happens is because the rights to exploit those resources are provided through a system of nontransparent rent seeking. Making that process much more transparent by, for example, auctioning the rights to exploit the resource, would have two advantages: first, it reduces the degree to which rent seeking results in an excessive rate of exploitation of the resource, and, second, it gives an opportunity for groups opposed to a higher rate of exploitation to present their views. So one should aim at making the process much more transparent.

5

How the Environment Affects the Macroeconomy

David Pearce and Kirk Hamilton

Standard texts in economic development have little or nothing to say about the natural or non-built environment. A well-known review of the state of development economics, for example, contains neither an essay on nor mention of the environment-development link (Ranis and Schultz, 1988). The same is true of more recent surveys (e.g., Balasubramanian and Lall, 1991). Those texts that have taken the environment on board provide a welcome relief to the general picture, but even here the analysis tends to be confined to descriptive issues (e.g., Hogendorn, 1992). In contrast, officially sponsored documentation on the environment-development interface, such as that from the World Bank, the United Nations, or Organization for Economic Cooperation and Development, has increased dramatically in recent years (Pearce and Warford, 1993; Eröcal, 1991; Bartelmus, 1986; Pearce, Whittington, and Georgiou, 1994), not to mention the ever-growing number of texts specifically on economics and the environment. All this suggests that, despite the efforts of those who have sought to uncover the environment-development-environment interactions, much of this work has still to filter down to those who effectively provide introductions to development planning, and, perhaps more seriously, to those who define the cutting edge of development economics.

This past neglect of the environment in development economics has a human cost. We argue below that this cost shows up as the deteriora-

Note: The authors are respectively Director and Senior Fellow, Centre for Social and Economic Research on the Global Environment, University College London and University of East Anglia, United Kingdom.

tion of human capital through ill health and premature mortality arising from environmental risks, as forgone GNP because of the failure to
recognize the high economic rate of return to many environmental investments, and as the erosion of the natural capital base on which the
development of many economies depends.

Environmental Deterioration and Erosion of Human Capital

A growing body of epidemiological studies is identifying substantial
economic costs from urban air pollution in the developing world.
Table 1 assembles results from several city studies of health damage
from air pollution. A UK national damage estimate is shown for reference. Valuing health symptoms and risks of mortality in economic terms
is controversial and has additional complications in developing country
contexts. Essentially, if life and health appear to have a low value generally, this will show up in the economic magnitudes and may give rise
to the view that one developing country resident is worth less than one
industrial country resident. But as proportions of available income,
there is no reason to suppose that willingness to pay for avoiding ill
health is less in a low-income country than in a high-income country.
Moreover, what matters in most policy decisions is the set of priorities
for action determined by the country in question. A willingness to pay
offers one way of setting such priorities.

Table 1 suggests several conclusions about priorities in air pollution
control. First, two air pollutants, particulate matter and lead, are especially damaging. The exact manner in which particulate matter may
cause health damage is not known with certainty, but statistical associations with respiratory illness and premature death are strong. Because
the studies tend to use consensus dose-response functions, overall damage costs will be mainly determined by the size of the population at risk
and the unit economic values used to value symptoms and statistical life.
Costs per capita in developing countries appear fairly consistent in the
range of $20–160, while the estimates for Bangkok suggest that overall
damages could be very much higher. If the dose-response function is
linear through the origin, as much of the epidemiology for PM_{10} suggests, per capita damage could be as high as $1,000 in Bangkok ($209 is
for a 20 percent reduction). Lead damage is similarly high in the
Bangkok study at $39–193 per capita. The Mexico and Jakarta studies
show much lower per capita damages at around $8 per person. Health
damage from lead shows up in the form of reduced IQ scores in children, hypertension in adults (mainly males), coronary heart disease,

Table 1. *Air Pollution Damage to Human Health in Cities*

Coverage	Mortality Cost	Morbidity Cost	Total Health Cost	Cost (In percent of GDP)	Cost per Capita (In U.S. dollars)
	(In millions of U.S. dollars)				
Particulate matter					
Costs of all exposure					
UK 1993[1]	11,800	9,400	21,150	2.7	848
China 1990[2]	41,670	19,300	60,970	11.1	52
Cairo 1990s[3]	186–992	157–472	343–1,464	n.a.	38–161
Jakarta 1990[4]	113	44	157	n.a.	19
Benefit of percentage reduction					
Mexico City 1990[5] 58 percent reduction	480	358	850	n.a.	50
Bangkok 1989[6] 20 percent reduction	138–1,315	302–309	440–1,624	n.a.	57–209
Santiago 1990s[7] 15 percent reduction	8	62	70	n.a.	15
Sulphur oxides					
Bangkok 1989 6 percent reduction	0	0.2	0.2	n.a.	<1
Santiago 1990s[7] 8 percent reduction	0	0.1	0.1	n.a.	<1
Nitrogen oxides					
Jakarta 1990[4]	0	1	1	n.a.	<1
Santiago 1990s[7] 49 percent reduction	0	1 or 17*	1 or 18	n.a.	<1 or 4
Ozone					
Cairo[3] 50 percent reduction	0	11**	11	n.a.	1
Mexico City 1990[5] 21 percent reduction	0	102	102	n.a.	6
Bangkok 1990s[6] 20 percent reduction	0	9–36	9–36	n.a.	1–5
Santiago 1990s[7] 69 percent reduction in VOCs and 49 percent reduction in NO$_x$	0	33	33	n.a.	7
Lead					
Jakarta 1990s[4] All exposure	26	36	62	n.a.	8
Mexico 1989[5] All exposure	n.a.	125–130	125–130	n.a.	7–8
Bangkok 1990s[6] 20 percent reduction	291–1,470	6–8	297–1,478	n.a.	39–193
Total health damage costs of air pollution					
Cairo[3] (50 all exposure, PM only)	186–992	157–472	343–1,464	n.a.	38–161
Jakarta[4] (All exposure, PM, lead, NO$_x$)	138	82	220	n.a.	27
Mexico[5] (All exposure, PM, lead, ozone)	480	590	1,070	n.a.	63

Table 1 *(concluded)*

	Mortality Cost	Morbidity Cost	Total Health Cost	Cost (In percent of GDP)	Cost per Capita (In U.S.
Coverage	(In millions of U.S. dollars)				dollars)
Bangkok[6] (Benefits of 20 percent reduction in PM, lead, SO$_x$, and ozone)	429–2,785	317–353	746–3,138	n.a.	97–402
Santiago[7] (Benefits of package of measures)	8	96 or 112	104 or 120	n.a.	22–25

[1]D.W. Pearce and T. Crowards, "Assessing the Health Costs of Particulate Air Pollution in the United Kingdom," Centre for Social and Economic Research on the Global Environment, University College London and University of East Anglia, 1995, unpublished. Assumes a value of statistical life of $2.25m and population at risk of 25.2 million. Damage done by PM$_{10}$ only.

[2]H.K. Florig, "The Benefits of Air Pollution Reduction in China," Resources for the Future, Washington, D.C., 1993, unpublished. Adjustments made to the original estimates to give a value of statistical life of $45,547 based on a US/UK VOSL of $2.25m multiplied by the ratio of GNP per capita in China to GNP per capita in the United States. For a justification for using this ratio see A. Alberini and others, *Valuing Health Effects of Air Pollution in Developing Countries: The Case of Taiwan*, Resources for the Future, Washington, D.C., Discussion Paper 95–01, 1995. Morbidity effects are restricted activity days (RADs), which are valued at a daily GNP per capita of $1.29.

[3]Estimates of mortality and RADs taken from Chemonics International and Associates, *Comparing Environmental Health Risks in Cairo, Egypt*, Vols. 1 and 2, Report to US AID, Egypt, September 1994. Value of statistical life taken to be $2.25m x GNP per capita Egypt/GNP per capita USA = $62,021. RADs valued at daily GNP per capita of $1.75 per day. Population taken to be 9.08 million. Estimates of hospital admissions from ozone pollution valued at $260; minor restricted activity days and days or respiratory symptoms valued at $0.4, asthma attacks valued at $2.5. Unit values taken from (Sources in footnote 4) as GNP per capita in Egypt and Indonesia is very similar.

[4]World Bank, "Indonesia Environment and Development: Challenges for the Future," Environment Unit, Country Department III, East Asia and Pacific Region, World Bank, Washington D.C., March, 1994. Value of statistical life of $75,000 and population at risk of 8.2 million. Morbidity effects include RADs, outpatient visits, hospital admissions, respiratory illness among children, asthma attacks, and respiratory symptoms. See also B. Ostro, "Estimating Health Effects of Air Pollution: A Methodology with an Application to Jakarta," PRDPE, World Bank, Washington, D.C., March 1994.

[5]World Bank, "Thailand: Mitigating Pollution and Congestion Impacts in a High Growth Economy," Country Operations Division, Country Department 1, East Asia and Pacific Region, World Bank, Washington D.C., February 1994. Bangkok population of 7.67 million assumed. Value of statistical life of $336,000 based on compensating wage differentials in Bangkok for risky occupations.

[6]S. Margulis, "Back of the Envelope Estimates of Environmental Damage Costs in Mexico," Working Paper WPS 824, Country Department 2, Latin America and the Caribbean Regional Office, World Bank, January 1992. Value of statistical life of $75,000 assumed based on human capital approach. Population of 17 million assumed.

[7]World Bank, "Chile: Managing Environmental Problems—Economic Analysis of Selected Issues," Environment and Urban Development Division, Country Department 1, Latin America and the Caribbean Region, World Bank, Washington D.C., December 1994. Estimates are based on dose-response functions for mortality and morbidity converted to work days lost, each work day being valued at US$9.55. Population of Santiago taken to be 4.8 million. Control costs for this package of measures were estimated at $60m, so that, even without considering other pollutants, the benefits of reduced PM$_{10}$ exceed the costs of control. Other benefits arise from the associated control of ozone, NO$_x$, and SO$_x$. Alternative estimate for NO$_x$ assumes NO$_x$ is credited with half the benefits of avoided ozone pollution damage.

and mortality. Table 1 suggests that tropospheric ozone may rank as a significant health-damaging pollutant, with consistent per capita cost estimates of perhaps $5 per person. Ozone is a secondary pollutant where main precursors are NO_x and volatile organic compounds (VOCs). In some studies, damage from VOCs is allocated to these two pollutants, although the allocation rule appears not to be generally agreed upon. Nitrogen oxides and sulphur oxides are generally revealed to be of limited relevance for health damage.

These observations bear on policy. They suggest that priority actions in countries where Western ambient standards are not met should focus on particulate matter and lead. The former can be addressed by energy conservation and vehicle-traffic control, especially the latter, since inhalable particulate matter tends to be associated with vehicle emissions rather than stationary sources, such as power stations. The practice of requiring new power stations in Eastern Europe and developing countries to be fitted with flue gas desulphurization equipment (FGD) becomes questionable since SO_x is not seen to be associated with significant health damage, although very high concentrations in black spots probably do have health consequences. Lead emissions can be addressed primarily through reductions in the lead content of gasoline. Overall, then, the air pollution studies suggest a focus on transport rather than on traditional power stations, although health damage from the latter can be significant.

The epidemiology of water pollution is well understood, but estimating dose-response functions for waterborne pollution and human health remains very difficult. Contamination of water supplies has known health effects, but these effects can vary substantially according to personal hygiene behavior and the amount of water available. It has been estimated that in 1979 some 360–400 billion working days were lost in Africa, South America, and Asia because of water-related diseases. At even a nominal 50 cents per day, this suggests that these continents lost $180–200 billion in forgone GNP each year. The combined GNP of the three continents in 1979 was about $370 billion, so that GNP was a staggering 35 percent below its potential value because of waterborne diseases alone. This figure would be offset only partially by the costs of treating water supplies and avoiding contamination.

A review of over 80 studies of water quality and quantity reveals that improved water and sanitation can be expected to reduce diarrhoeal mortality by 55–60 percent and morbidity by 25 percent (Esrey, 1990). Table 2 assembles some estimates of water pollution control benefits for two cities and one country. The Mexico study suggests that the benefits of control could be substantial and on a par with those from the control of particulate matter air pollution and lead exposure. A review of past poli-

Table 2. *Water Pollution Damage to Health, Selected Cities*

Coverage	Mortality Cost	Morbidity Cost	Total Health Cost	Cost (In percent of GDP)	Cost per Capita (In U.S. dollars)
	(In millions of U.S. dollars)				
Jakarta[1] Fecal contamination	300	3	303	n.a.	37
Mexico[2] Intestinal disease	3,600	small	3,600	n.a.	212
Santiago[3] Typhoid					
1985–90	0.5	0.9	1.4	n.a.	<1
1991	0.5	0.7	0.9	n.a.	<1

[1]World Bank, "Indonesia Environment and Development: Challenges for the Future," Environment Unit, Country Department III, East Asia and Pacific Region, World Bank, Washington D.C., March, 1994. Value of statistical life of $75,000 and population at risk of 8.2 million. Assumes 7,000 diarrhea related deaths per year. Improved water quality and sanitation can reduce such deaths by 55–60 percent a year, so that 3,800–4,200 deaths could be avoided. Some 360,000 fewer diarrhoeal episodes per year are estimated to be saved by improved water quality.

[2]S. Margulis, "Back of the Envelope Estimates of Environmental Damage Costs in Mexico," Working Paper WPS 824, Country Department 2, Latin America and the Caribbean Regional Office, World Bank, January 1992. Value of statistical life of $75,000 assumed based on human capital approach and applied to the whole of Mexico.

[3]World Bank, "Chile: Managing Environmental Problems—Economic Analysis of Selected Issues," Environment and Urban Development Division, Country Department 1, Latin America and the Caribbean Region, World Bank, Washington D.C., December 1994. Direct costs of typhoid only and based on forgone production, that is, the human capital approach. Indirect effects excluded from health effects include effects on farm profitability from loss of exports of farm produce.

cies in Chile on typhoid suggests that the modest actions taken in 1984 were justified on benefit-cost grounds, while more drastic action might well have had costs in excess of benefits. In 1991 a cholera outbreak prompted quick and effective action on educating the public concerning the consumption of unwashed vegetables and the banning of sewage irrigation for growing vegetables. Benefit-cost analysis suggests a benefit-cost ratio of 5:1 in favor of the emergency actions, with most of the benefits coming from the avoided costs of restrictions on food exports.

The limited analyses available on the control of water pollution in cities suggest that economic damages to human health can be very large and benefit-cost ratios typically favor intervention in water quality treatment. In terms of the human capital base, the air and water pollution studies suggest that both kinds of pollution are taking a heavy toll on human life and well-being. If so, pollution control is not a "luxury good" to be afforded after the development process has taken off, but a prior requirement for sustainable development. This suggests a wholly different picture to that implied by the neglect of environment in development economics generally.

Rate of Return on Environmental Investments

The social costs of health damage from pollution already hint at the high rate of return on environmental expenditures. These returns can, by and large, be expected to show up in conventional market terms as gains in GNP as traditionally measured. Other environmental investments, such as afforestation, may also generate high rates of return in conventional terms. The challenge for the analyst is to cast the net wide enough to ensure that all benefits and costs are measured. Anderson's study of afforestation in Northern Nigeria is a good example (Anderson, 1987, 1989). The benefits of afforestation included:

- halting the erosion of fertile soil (since trees typically reduce erosion)
- raising current levels of soil fertility
- producing tree products—fuelwood, poles, fruits
- producing fodder both from increased productivity of soils and from the use of forest fodder.

The economic rates of return (in percent) that resulted for shelterbelts (planting trees mainly for wind protection) and farm forestry (intermixing trees and crops) are indicated in the following table:

	Shelterbelts	Farm Forestry
Base case	14.9	19.1
Low yield, high cost	13.1	14.5
High yield	16.2	—
No erosion	13.5	16.6
More rapid erosion	13.6	15.5
Soil restored + yield jump	16.9	21.8
Wood and fruit benefits	4.7	7.4

Calculation of timber costs and benefits alone in the Kano area has tended to show rates of return of around 5 percent, which has to be compared with the cut-off rate, usually double this rate. In other words, afforestation for timber production does not pay. But once the other benefits are included, dramatic increases in rates of return can be secured. The analysis shows that counting wood benefits only produces negative net present value and correspondingly low economic rates of return. But if allowance is made for the effects of trees on crop yields and for expected rates of soil erosion in the absence of afforestation, the picture is transformed for both farm forestry and shelterbelts.

Other examples of high return environmental investments are given in Pearce, 1993.

Capturing Nonmarket Returns

Many environmental investments will yield mixes of market and non-market returns, where the distinction between market and nonmarket reflects the essentially arbitrary dividing line set by the way conventional accounting systems operate. While economists are right to insist that nonmarket gains and losses are intrinsically no different from market gains and losses (both translate into changes in the state of human well-being), nonmarket effects are by definition not traded and hence do not translate into empowerment over resources. Put simply, they do not by definition have associated cash (or in-kind) flows. This is why demonstrating the monetary value of environmental assets is not enough if change in the development planning ethos is to take place. It is as important to show how such nonmarket values can be captured by the developing countries. The issue of capture is now the subject of an emerging literature that aims to find ways in which developing countries can exploit their comparative advantage in environmental assets, from biological diversity to carbon storage in tropical forests. Table 3 shows estimates of the economic values residing in tropical forests. What stands out is the high value of tropical forests as stores of carbon, contingent on global warming being a proven phenomenon. Since the main proximate cause of deforestation is the burning of forests for conversion to agricultural or pasture land, one of the benefits of finding alternative land uses is the avoided global warming damage from released carbon dioxide through burning. These carbon values clearly exceed, sometimes by many multiples, the conversion value of the land. This suggests trades whereby the developed world seeks the attenuation of land-use options in tropical forests in return for encashable transfers. This is the essence of joint implementation, tradable development rights and franchise agreements (Panayotou, 1994). Early forms of such trades already exist in the form of joint implementation whereby carbon emissions in a developed economy are offset by carbon sequestration or carbon emission reduction in developing countries.

Asset Depletion and the Savings Rule

The final issue we address is the role that environmental assets and natural capital should play in development analysis. Given the central-

Table 3. *Local and Global Conservation Values in Tropical Forests*
(In U.S. dollars per hectare, present values at 8 percent)

	Mexico	Costa Rica (Carbon values adjusted)	Indonesia (Carbon values adjusted)	Malaysia	Peninsular
Timber	—	1,240	1,000–2,000	4,075	1,024
Non-timber products	775	—	38–125	325–1,238	96–487
Carbon storage	650–3,400	3,046	1,827–3,654	1,015–2,709	2,449
Pharmaceutical	1–90	2	—	—	1–103
Ecotourism/Recreation	8	209	—	—	13–35
Watershed protection	<1	—	—	—	
Option value	80	—	—	—	
Non-use value	15	—	—	—	

Note: Adapted from Kumari, 1994, but with additional material and some changed conversions. All values are present values at 8 percent discount rate, but carbon values are at 3 percent discount rate. Uniform damage estimates of $20.3 tC have been used (Fankhauser and Pearce, 1994), so that original carbon damage estimates in the World Bank studies have been reestimated.

ity of savings and investment in economic theory, it is perhaps surprising that the effects of depleting natural resources and degrading the environment have not, until recently, been considered in the measurement of national savings. This omission may be explained both by the models economists use and the fact that the UN System of National Accounts (SNA) ignores depletion and degradation of the natural environment. This is not intended to be excessively critical of the SNA, which measures market activity very well, as is its intent. It is nonetheless true that the glasses we look through as economists tend to color or restrict our view of the problems we face.

Valuing depletion and degradation within a national accounting framework is an increasingly viable proposition, as a result both of the progress in the techniques of valuation of environmental resources (Freeman, 1994) and of the expanding foundation that theoretical developments are placing under the methods of green national accounting (Mäler, 1991; Hamilton, 1994a). The first application of these accounting methods to the measurement of net savings appeared in Pearce and Atkinson, 1993. This study combined published estimates of depletion and degradation for 20 countries with standard national accounting data to examine the true savings behavior (what Hamilton, 1994a, calls "genuine saving"). By this measure many countries appear to be unsustainable.

Enlarging the concept of net saving to include the depletion of natural resources is in many ways the most natural alteration of traditional savings concepts, because the depletion of a natural resource is, in effect, the liquidation of an asset and so should not appear in any measure of net national product or, by extension, net savings. While minor technical issues remain, the methods of valuing the depletion, discovery and growth of commercial natural resources in the context of the SNA are by now well developed (Hamilton, 1994a; Hill and Harrison, 1994).

More problematic is the valuation of environmental degradation. While UN guidelines for environmental accounting (United Nations, 1993) favor valuing this degradation in terms of maintenance costs (the cost of restoring the environment to its state at the beginning of the accounting period), the latest theoretical approaches (Hamilton and Atkinson, 1995) suggest that the marginal social costs of pollution are the correct basis for valuing waste emissions to the environment. The model supporting this conclusion is included as an annex to this paper.

To give the flavor of what results from the formal approach to green national accounting, the following expression adapts the expression for economic welfare from Hamilton, 1994a:

$$MEW = C + I - n(R - g) - \sigma(e - d) + p_B B \tag{1}$$

Here C is consumption, I investment, n the unit resource rental rate net of emission taxes on production, R resource extraction, g resource growth, σ the marginal social costs of pollution emissions e, the natural dissipation of pollution d, and P_B the willingness of consumers to pay for environmental services B. For nonliving natural resources the term in g is zero, while d is zero for pollutants with cumulative effects. External trade is ignored in this expression for reasons of simplicity.

The measure of sustainable national income simply drops the last welfare term from this expression. The intuition behind this is clear: $I - n(R - g) - \sigma(e - d)$ is the value of *net* investment when changes in natural resource stocks and stocks of pollutants, appropriately shadow priced, are included in addition to increments to the stock of produced assets.

While it is important to know what constitutes the sustainable level of national income, this measure is not particularly relevant for policy purposes. A shift in the level of national income does not carry a policy signal with regard to sustainable development, while the relative growth rates of sustainable income and GNP, for instance, are liable to give equivocal signals. Given that concerns about sustainable development are fundamentally concerns about the future, this suggests that adjusted measures of savings and wealth are more fertile territory for policy purposes.

The expression for genuine saving follows directly from the preceding:

$$S_g = GNP - C - D - n(R - g) - \sigma(e - d). \tag{2}$$

Here *GNP – C* is gross saving as traditionally defined, with *C* being the sum of public and private consumption; gross saving includes the level of foreign saving as well. *D* is the value of depreciation of produced assets, while the last two terms represent the value of net depletion of natural resources and net accumulation of pollutants.

The importance of this measure of genuine saving is that it is a one-sided indicator of sustainability. While Asheim, 1994, and Pezzey, 1994, have shown that measuring positive genuine savings at a given point in time does not permit one to conclude that the economy is necessarily on a sustainable path, Hamilton and Atkinson, 1995, demonstrate that persistent negative genuine saving implies that the economy is not sustainable and that welfare will eventually decline. The foregoing references to "points in time" and "persistent negative savings" are important: sustainability is fundamentally a property of the path that the economy is on, rather than its instantaneous state.

It is possible to have apparently positive gross saving and negative genuine saving. So while it is easy to calculate gross savings rates from published national accounts data, this may give little indication of whether the economy is or is not on a sustainable path. This reinforces the point made earlier that economists may be biased in their conclusions with regard to economic performance.

Several policy issues are raised by negative genuine saving. All the policies concerning generating and mobilizing savings are relevant, including fiscal and monetary policy, levels of government current consumption, government investment policies (particularly with regard to the investment of resource rents), and the size and viability of the financial sector. Beyond these, there are questions of the performance of the resource sector, including tenurial arrangements and royalty regimes. Finally, there are questions regarding the policies for environmental protection and the optimality of pollution control levels.

Savings are not the only means to achieve economic sustainability. More efficient use of existing assets can lead to growth in many cases, although there is a limit, and the quality of investments arising from savings is also clearly important. Investment in primary education will give higher returns than many of the development projects seen historically in developing nations.

Evidence on Genuine Saving

Notions of genuine saving would have little impact if all countries were prudent managers of their portfolio of economic assets. There is abundant evidence, however, that many countries are not on a sustain-

Figure 1. *Genuine Savings Rate by Region*

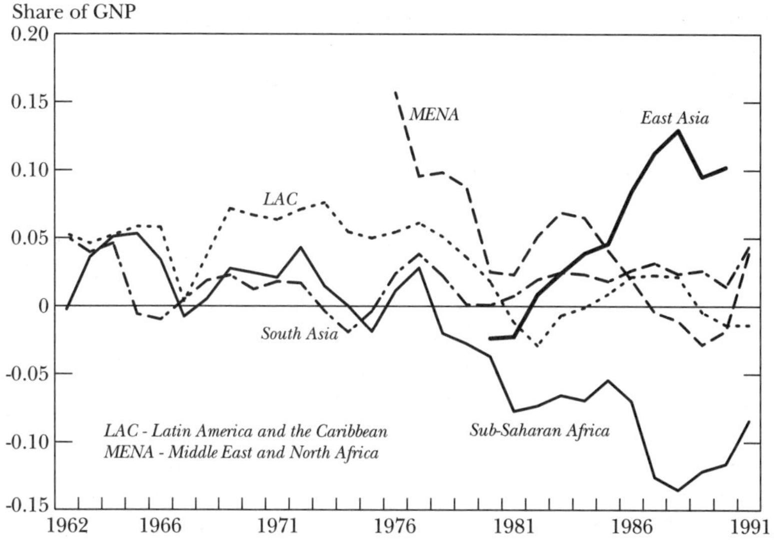

able path. Figure 1 plots genuine savings on a regional basis for a range of developing countries.

The saving rates in Figure 1 account for the depletion of oil, major minerals, and net deforestation. The calculations of resource rents are crude, assumed to be equal to 50 percent of the market value of re-source extraction and harvest, but sufficiently accurate (see Hamilton, 1994b) to serve as a useful indicator. Carbon emissions are the only pollutants considered in these calculations, with the global social costs of each ton of carbon valued at $20 in 1990 (Fankhauser, 1994). Depletion of fish stocks and degradation of soils, with the latter being particularly important in many developing countries, are not included in these figures.

The interregional comparison of savings behavior over this 30-year period turns up some interesting trends, although a number of caveats are required. Both South Asia and Latin America and the Caribbean had genuine saving rates that were moderately positive on average over this period, with savings briefly going negative at the time of the oil cri-sis in South Asia and at the time of the debt crisis (roughly speaking) in Latin America and the Caribbean. The short time series for the Middle East and North Africa shows a substantial decline in genuine saving, but the data coverage for these figures should encourage caution in their in-

Figure 2. *Malawi: Genuine Savings Rate, 1981–90*

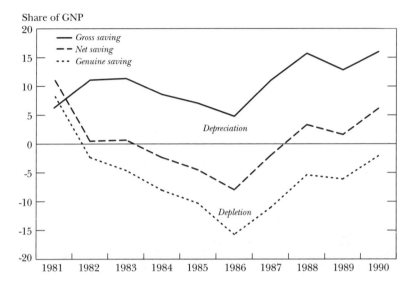

Source: data from Hamilton 1994b.

terpretation. In addition, the net price method of calculating rents may not be particularly appropriate for countries having many decades of reserves of oil (i.e., a discount factor should be factored into the depletion calculation, as in El Serafy, 1989).

The two trends that stand out in Figure 1 are for East Asia, where the rise of the "tigers" was associated with very strong saving performance and where primary resource activities are a declining proportion of GNP, and sub-Saharan Africa,[1] which started dissaving roughly at the time of the oil crisis and has continued on this unsustainable path into the 1990s.

Figure 2 shows the results of a more refined calculation of genuine savings (based on Hamilton, 1994b) for a sample country in sub-Saharan Africa, Malawi. One striking aspect of this figure is that traditional net saving in Malawi was negative in 1981 and 1984–87. By standard national accounting measures, therefore, Malawi was marginally sustainable during the 1980s. When the extra 5–7 percent of GNP for resource depletion and CO_2 emissions is included, Malawi was clearly

---

[1]The African figures are influenced by the performance of the oil states, especially Nigeria and Gabon. The earlier caveat about discount factors applies here as well.

unsustainable during this decade, and this excludes the value of soil erosion in this highly agricultural country.

There is ample evidence therefore that many countries have been on an unsustainable development path, at least since the mid-1970s. Sub-Saharan Africa is noteworthy in this regard, and it is to this region that we now turn our attention.

Genuine Savings and Sub-Saharan African Experience

In a paper reviewing the literature on long-term development and growth in sub-Saharan Africa, Ndulu and Elbadawi, 1994, cite a number of broad conclusions: (1) sub-Saharan Africa has grown more slowly than other developing countries since the mid-1970s; (2) lower saving rates and levels of human capital have prevented it from catching up with other developing countries; (3) the policy climate in sub-Saharan Africa has not been conducive to sustained growth, characterized as it has been by disincentives to save, overvalued and variable exchange rates, high public consumption, and underdeveloped financial systems; and (4) the economies of sub-Saharan Africa have been subject to many external shocks, both economic and physical (in the form of drought and other severe weather patterns), and political instability. Analysis of genuine savings provides further insights.

Table 4 presents the rates of genuine saving for selected countries in sub-Saharan Africa in the mid- to late 1980s. The rather eclectic selection of countries reflects limitations in data availability.

The pattern presented in Table 4 appears to be "the curse of the mineral-rich" (Gelb, 1988). Kenya, Rwanda, Burundi, and Niger, with relatively little exports of oil and minerals, have the most promising saving performance. On the other hand, mineral-rich South Africa and Zimbabwe both exhibited positive genuine savings. As noted earlier, the figures for Nigeria are probably skewed owing to the substantial size of the deposits of crude oil. Zaïre is the other anomalously large dissaver. While these effects may have been overstated for technical reasons, having to do with the valuation of resource depletion, it is also true that the economic policy climate has been particularly unfavorable in Zaïre for many years.

Conclusions

We have provided a brief overview of the ways in which environmental degradation affects the macroeconomy in developing countries and,

Table 4. *Genuine Saving Rates in Sub-Saharan Africa, 1986–90*

	1986	1987	1988	1989	1990
Burundi	1	-2	3	-1	5
Côte d'Ivoire	-6	-10	-14	-13	-17
Cameroon	-1	-3	0	-4	-9
Congo	-40	-69	-36	-51	-42
Ghana	-7	-4	-3	-2	-2
Kenya	7	7	4	6	3
Mali	-13	-5	1	1	2
Mauritania	-12	-18	-10	-3	-8
Malawi	-10	-16	-11	-5	-6
Niger	1	5	-5	6	-4
Nigeria	-15	-24	-31	-38	-41
Rwanda	9	8	5	5	4
Senegal	-14	-7	-3	0	-2
Sierra Leone	-2	-7	-11	-8	-9
Chad	-26	-22	-17	-10	-17
Uganda	-12	-7	-6	-15	-15
South Africa	5	7	11	10	9
Zaïre	-18	-21	-28	-30	-32
Zimbabwe	2	4	4	10	6

Source: Hamilton, 1994b.

for that matter, in the industrial world, since the principles do not change. Our basic conclusion is that environmental degradation gives rise to major economic costs in developing countries in terms of

- impairment of the human capital stock via premature mortality and morbidity
- loss of marketed GNP through health effects and degradation of assets such as soil and forests
- loss of nonmarketed GNP that could be the subject of capture via appropriately designed policies, domestic and international
- reductions in genuine savings, which amount to the mining of the capital base on which many developing countries depend.

The implications for policy are

- the need for revised accounting procedures, now well under way
- revised macroeconomic indicators that incorporate sustainability considerations—we advocate the genuine savings concept as the first step in such a revision
- the need for more and better economic valuation of nonmarketed resources—also now well under way
- a wholesale rethinking of mainstream development economics at the pedagogic level to reflect the rethinking that has already taken place at the research level.

Annex

Formal Green Accounting Model

We assume a simple closed economy with a single resource producing a composite good that may be consumed, invested, or used to abate pollution, so that $F(K,R) = C + \dot{K} + a$, where R is resource use and a is pollution abatement expenditures. Pollution emissions are a function of production and abatement, $e = e(F,a)$, and pollutants accumulate in a stock M such that $\dot{M} = e - d(M)$ where d is the quantity of natural dissipation of the pollution stock. The flow of environmental services B is negatively related to the size of the pollution stock, so that $\dot{B} = -\alpha\dot{M}$. Resource stocks S grow by an amount g and are depleted by extraction R, so that $\dot{S} = -R + g(S)$, and resources are assumed to be costless to produce. The utility of consumers is assumed to be a function of consumption and environmental services, $U = U(C,B)$.

If we assume that there is a social planner who wishes to maximize the present value of utility over an infinite time horizon, for some fixed pure rate of time preference r, then there is a close relationship between the Hamiltonian function for the optimal control problem and the measure of current welfare for the society. The Hamiltonian is given by

$$H = U + \gamma_K \dot{K} + \gamma_B \dot{B} + \gamma_S \dot{S} \tag{1}$$

where γ_K is the shadow price of capital, in utils, γ_B the shadow price of environmental services, and γ_S is the shadow price of the resource. The first order conditions for maximizing the Hamiltonian, setting the partial derivatives with respect to the control variables C, a, and R to 0, yield the following:

$$H = U + U_C K - U_C b(e - d) - U_C(1 - be_F)F_R(R - g). \tag{2}$$

Here b is the marginal cost of abating a unit of pollution, while F_R is the unit resource rental rate, and be_F is the effective emissions tax rate on production. The measure of economic welfare is derived by valuing each flow at its shadow price in utils, then converting to consumption units by dividing through by U_C, yielding

$$MEW = C + \dot{K} - b(e - d) - (1 - be_F)F_R(R - g) + \frac{U_B}{U_C} B. \tag{3}$$

It can be shown, for example, in Hamilton and Atkinson, 1995, that the marginal cost of abatement is equal to the marginal social cost of pollution emissions, which is in turn equal to the level of the optimal Pigouvian tax required to maximize welfare. Note that $p_B \equiv U_B/U_C$ is the price that a utility-maximizing consumer would be willing to pay for a unit of environmental service, and that resources are priced at their marginal product less the value of the emissions tax on production. Therefore this expression for welfare, although derived from optimal control, corresponds to what would be attained in a competitive equilibrium with a Pigouvian pollution tax.

This expression generalizes in obvious ways. Dropping the last welfare term yields sustainable income, since persistently consuming more than this implies negative genuine savings. A purely cumulative pollutant is handled by dropping the term in dissipation d. For a nonliving resource the term in growth g would be dropped.

References

Anderson, Denis, 1987, *The Economics of Afforestation: A Case Study in Africa* (Baltimore: Johns Hopkins University).

———, 1989, "Economic Aspects of Afforestation and Soil Conservation Projects," in *Environmental Management and Economic Development,* ed. by Gunter Schramm and Jeremy J. Warford (Baltimore: Johns Hopkins University).

Asheim, Geir B., 1994, "Net National Product as an Indicator of Sustainability," *Scandinavian Journal of Economics,* Vol. 96, No. 2, pp. 257–65.

Balasubramanian, V.N., and S. Lall, 1991, *Current Issues in Development Economics* (London: Macmillan).

Bartelmus, Peter, 1986, *Environment and Development* (London: Allen and Unwin).

El Serafy, Salah, 1989, "The Proper Calculation of Income from Depletable Natural Resources," in *Environmental Accounting for Sustainable Development,* ed. by Yusuf J. Ahmad, Salah El Serafy, and Ernst Lutz (Washington: World Bank).

Eröcal, Denizhan, ed., 1991, *Environmental Management in Developing Countries* (Paris: OECD).

Esrey, S. A., 1990, "Health Benefits from Improvements in Water Supply and Sanitation: Survey and Analysis of the Literature on Selected Diseases," Unpublished report to U.S. Agency for International Development, Washington, D.C.

Fankhauser, Samuel, 1994, "Evaluating the Social Costs of Greenhouse Gas Emissions," *The Energy Journal,* Vol. 15, No. 2, pp. 157–84.

———, and David W. Pearce, 1994, "The Social Costs of Greenhouse Gas Emissions," in *The Economics of Climate Change* (Paris: OECD).

Freeman, A. Myrick, 1994, *The Measurement of Environmental and Resource Values: Theory and Methods*, (Washington: Resources for the Future).

Gelb, Alan H., 1988, *Oil Windfalls: Blessing or Curse?* (New York: Oxford University).

Hamilton, Kirk, 1994a, "Green Adjustments to GDP," *Resources Policy*, Vol. 20, No. 3, pp. 155–68.

———, 1994b, "Estimated Rental Rates for Minerals and Crude Oil," Unpublished report, Environment Department (Washington: World Bank).

Hamilton, Kirk, and Giles Atkinson, 1995, "Valuing Air Pollution in the National Accounts," Unpublished paper presented to the London Group on National Accounts and the Environment, Washington, March 15–17, 1995.

Hartwick, John M., 1990, "Natural Resources, National Accounting and Economic Depreciation," *Journal of Public Economics*, Vol. 43, pp. 291–304.

Hill, P., and A. Harrison, 1994, "Accounting for Subsoil Assets in the 1993 SNA," Unpublished paper presented to the London Group on National Accounts and the Environment, London, March 15–18, 1994.

Hogendorn, Jan S., 1992, *Economic Development*, 2nd Edition (New York: Harper Collins).

Kumari, K., 1994, "An Environmental and Economic Assessment of Forestry Management Options: A Case Study in Peninsular Malaysia," in *Sustainable Forest Management in Malaysia*, Unpublished Ph.D. Thesis, K. Kumari, University of East Anglia.

Mäler, Karl-Goran, 1991, "National Accounts and Environmental Resources," *Environmental and Resource Economics*, Vol. 1, pp. 1–15.

Ndulu, B., and I. Elbadawi, I., 1994, "Long-Term Development and Sustainable Growth in Sub-Saharan Africa," Unpublished paper presented to the Colloquium on New Directions in Development Economics—Growth, Equity and Sustainable Development, SAREC, Stockholm, March 9–11, 1994.

Panayotou, T., 1994, "Financing Mechanisms for Environmental Investments and Sustainable Development," Unpublished paper, Harvard Institute for International Development (Cambridge, Massachusetts: Harvard University).

Pearce, David W., 1993, *Economic Values and the Natural World* (London: Earthscan).

——— (forthcoming), "North South Transfers and Global Environmental Change," in *Global Environmental Change*.

———, and Giles Atkinson, 1993, "Capital Theory and the Measurement of Sustainable Development: An Indicator of Weak Sustainability," *Ecological Economics*, Vol. 8, pp. 103–8.

Pearce, David W., and Jeremy J. Warford, 1993, *World Without End: Economics, Environment and Sustainable Development* (Oxford: Oxford University Press).

Pearce, David W., D. Whittington, and S. Georgiou, 1994, *Project and Policy Appraisal: Integrating Economics and Environment* (Paris: OECD).

Pezzey, John, 1994, "The Optimal Sustainable Depletion of Non-Renewable Resources," Unpublished paper, University College, London.

Ranis, Gustav, and T.P. Schultz, 1988, *The State of Development Economics: Progress and Perspectives*, (Oxford: Blackwell).

United Nations, 1993, *Integrated Environmental and Economic Accounting*. Series F No. 61 (New York: United Nations).

Walsh, J., and K. Warren, 1979, Selective Primary Health Care: An Interim Strategy for Disease Control in Developing Countries, *New England Journal of Medicine*, Vol. 301, No. 18, pp. 967–74.

Weitzman, Martin L., 1976, "On the Welfare Significance of National Product in a Dynamic Economy," *Quarterly Journal of Economics*, Vol. 90.

World Bank, 1995, *Monitoring Environmental Progress*, Environment Department (Washington: World Bank).

Discussion

Discussant's Comments

Kirit Parikh

Professor David Pearce has made very many valuable contributions in bringing environmental concerns into economics, and this paper is one of these contributions. I agree with the broad conclusion of the Pearce and Hamilton paper, that environmental degradation impairs human capital in developing countries, a conclusion that is usually recognized, but not adequately paid attention to. I have, however, some difficulty with the policy conclusions to be drawn, and particularly about the notion of genuine savings, on which I will elaborate.

Regarding the impact of air and water pollution, the authors have summarized estimates of mortality and morbidity costs owing to different air and water pollutants, and they rightly observe that comparison of absolute numbers may give rise to the view that one industrial country resident is worth less than one developed country resident. Unfortunately, they do not present relative numbers, but give absolute numbers, partly because for most cities estimates of gross products are not available. But I would have thought that one could have guestimated the gross products for different cities, with perhaps no more error than the error inherent in the costs of mortality and morbidity. That would have been less distorting and more clarifying of what the point is that they are trying to make.

I also have some difficulty with their policy conclusion that the focus should be on the transport sector rather than, say, on the traditional power sector. While the conclusion may be right, it does not necessarily follow from their argument. One should take into account the costs of abatement, and not just the benefits. For example, every dollar spent in the power sector may lead to a larger reduction in SO_2 or particulate matter or to the reduction in cost of mortality and morbidity than a dollar spent in effectively controlling pollutants from the transport sector. One does need to worry about the costs as well as the benefits on this side.

Regarding water pollution, the authors assert that cost-benefit analyses typically favor investment in water quality treatment. Water quality

---

Note: The discussion was chaired and moderated by Malcolm Knight.

and water treatment have been neglected in many developing countries and need much greater attention from governments and from international agencies (perhaps to finance it).

Turning to the nonmarket returns and joint implementation, the studies by Anderson on the value of forestation and Pearce's studies certainly point out the difficulty of capturing nonmarket returns from environmental investment. They suggest joint implementation, whereby carbon emissions in industrial economy are offset by carbon sequestration emission reduction in developing countries. Claiming offsets by carbon emissions in joint implementation projects raises a number of issues. Let me quote from a paper ("Joint Implementation and North-South Cooperation for Climate Change," *International Environmental Affairs*, Vol. 7, No. 1, 1995, p. 32) by Ms. J. Parikh:

> Let us take the example of agro-forestry projects in Guatemala to offset carbon releases in the United States. A U.S. power plant proposed a plan in which 40,000 farmers in Guatemala work for 10 years for a joint implementation project for the sum of 3.8 million dollars. The lifetime of a power plant is 40 years, and so the plantation will have to exist for 40 years. In addition, the Government of Guatemala is required to pay 1.2 million dollars. Apparently, this total of 5 million dollars is to pay for saplings, land, other inputs, and continued care for 52 million trees for 10 years. This works out to a mere 10 cents per tree. Is it possible to plant and nurture a tree for 10 cents? The project seems to expect that Guatemala will be perpetually living in poverty. Does it tie 40,000 farmers to this project for 40 years? What does Guatemala get for this? What happens to the trees after 40 years? And this is an important set of issues: If they are burned, would the carbon dioxide belong to the United States? If they are not burned, would the methane generated from the decay of leaves and roots after the trees are cut down belong to the United States? What if Guatemala needs this land for something else during these 40 years? Will it tie down generations for a paltry loan by the rich? What if the new generation wants a shopping complex or any other use for remunerative activity on this area? If the U.S. company receives tax breaks for this purpose, then it did not go through any pains for this project at all. Rather, it is the Guatemalans who have paid for this project. The purpose of presenting this case is not to discourage private enterprise from taking initiatives such as this, instead it highlights the need for institutional structures in joint implementation to channel such enthusiasm in the right direction.

One appreciates the opportunity to trade, but this opportunity needs the appropriate kind of institutional mechanism and setting to make it fair and just.

The global climate change problem is precipitated by the industrial countries, and poor developing countries cannot be justly expected to worry about carbon emissions unless a fair allocation of property rights in the global carbon sink is made. This may seem somewhat peripheral to the Pearce and Hamilton paper, but it is not, and I will show this later.

Let me turn to the notion of genuine savings and sustainability. The authors have made a heroic attempt to find one simple indicator of sustainability, so it is worth looking at in some detail. Pearce and Hamilton advanced the notion of savings, which they call genuine savings, as an indicator of sustainability, and referred to the weak sustainability rule advanced by Pearce and Atkinson in their 1993 paper. In that paper they advanced the indicator and suggested that the United States, among others, was a sustainable economy. Any test that classifies the United States as a sustainable society must be suspect. Their test for sustainability suggests that if GNP minus consumption, minus depreciation of produced assets, minus depreciation of resources, including quality of environment owing to pollutants, is positive, the economy is sustainable, but if it is negative, then it is not. I find a number of conceptual difficulties and empirical pitfalls in applying this test.

The most important difficulty is that the damage to environment done by a country is not limited to the country itself. For example, the damage done by the United States is not limited to U.S. territory. Thus, the United States has very high shares in the degradation to global commons. Their contributions to global warming, to the creation and enlargement of the hole in the ozone layer, degradation of the seas owing to oil spills, water pollution, nuclear testing and nuclear and other hazardous waste disposals in the seas, resulting from the U.S. lifestyle and policies, are substantial and very large in per capita terms. Should the United States be held accountable for these damages, I would be surprised if the U.S. savings would be sufficient to restore these damages to global commons.

A second difficulty is that the measure does not involve depreciation of natural capital embodied in trade. Some authors have estimated that U.S. imports are more pollution- or natural-resource-intensive than their exports. The loss to other countries' sustainability caused by their exports to the U.S. economy are not accounted for by the Pearce and Hamilton measure. If the United States were to satisfy its lifestyle entirely through domestic production, its savings may not be adequate to restore or substitute for degraded natural capital.

The third difficulty is that savings (or man-made capital) cannot substitute or make good natural capital. Thus, U.S. savings cannot make good the ozone layer, or Brazilian savings cannot restore virgin rain forests.

The fourth difficulty is with valuation of capital. We require the same capital stock to provide future generations with the ability to produce the same goods and services as are produced today. Even assuming that man-made capital can substitute for natural capital in the production of goods and services, such substitution need not be one dollar's worth of man-made capital for one dollar's worth of natural capital. This would be obvious if one looks at a production function with substitutability, such as a Cobb-Douglas function. It is possible to argue, however, that the valuation of capital and natural capital is done in a way that reflects appropriately the marginal productivity of each type of capital. Such an estimation would be complex, since it would have to account for the nonlinearities involved and would have to assume that prices are not distorted.

Finally, there is the fifth difficulty with the genuine savings estimates. Pearce and Hamilton have emphasized rightly the importance of human capital. Governments spend money on education and health services. These are in a real sense investments in human capital formation, but in an accounting sense are considered as current consumption. The same is true of private expenditure on education, which too is investment. I am afraid that the authors need to work harder to make their estimates more accurate.

One realizes that the strong sustainability rule, which is the appropriate measure, may be difficult to verify, but misleading calculations based on weak sustainability rule are worse than useless and would only lead to greater smugness in the industrial countries, whose lifestyles are thus wrongly shown to be sustainable. They would be even more reluctant to change their lifestyles.

The first four difficulties show that a positive genuine saving does not guarantee sustainability. The authors claim that their measure of genuine savings is a single indicator of sustainability. But because of the fourth and the fifth objections raised above and the way they have used it, I would argue that it is not even that. To wit, their calculations of negative genuine savings for sub-Saharan Africa cannot be taken to mean that countries with negative "genuine savings" that are depreciated by carbon emissions are on an unsustainable path. The value of carbon emissions should not be subtracted as long as there is no obligation on the part of a country to reduce its carbon emissions, or as long as its emissions are below its fair share in the global commons' absorptive capacity. To the extent that genuine savings have become negative because of subtraction of carbon emission values, sub-Saharan Africa cannot be classified as unsustainable.

In conclusion, let me emphasize that my comments are not just of academic interest. Unfortunately, joint implementation projects of dubious benefit and ambiguous offsets, together with erroneous interpretation of estimates of genuine savings, which lack conceptual clarity, seem to shift the burden of climate change adjustment on developing countries, which have not been responsible for precipitating it in the first place.

Response

David Pearce: Let me respond to Kirit Parikh. Kirit knows we have addressed the various issues that he has raised in papers that we have done over the years. I agree we should have presented the health impacts of urban pollution as a percentage of city-level incomes; however, we had no estimates of city incomes. But we have done this estimation nationally, and the proposition is valid that the health impacts as a percentage of incomes are high and are, in fact, larger in developing countries than they are in rich countries.

Second, we agree on the need to account for the cost of abatement of environmental damage owing to transport. In our opinion, many of these interventions are known to be extremely cheap, although the transport sector produces an incredible array of pollutants, many of which are extremely damaging to health. We are aware that joint implementation is controversial, but one has to recognize that the joint implementation deals are willingly entered into by two parties. We cannot be arguing that poor downtrodden peasants are being forced into these deals by some wicked multinational company or some wicked industrial-country government. Joint implementation is, in fact, one of a whole array of new financing mechanisms. If we do not exploit these mechanisms, you will not see the needed financing for environmental protection.

Kirit makes reference to our earlier paper, where the genuine savings concept was introduced and the United States came out to be sustainable, though barely. That was the whole point of the exercise. Two countries came out to be a big surprise in that paper. One was the United States, which was barely sustainable on the genuine savings rule, and the other was the United Kingdom, which was not sustainable. And if you ask why, the answer is quite simple. It fits very neatly with the popular view of the United States as a high-consumption economy. It also fits with the view in the United Kingdom that we have wasted and exploited our North Sea oil resources and have consumed them. This fact fits rather well with the nice consumption boom that the United Kingdom had in the 1980s.

Kirit says we should account for global damage. We do and that is what the CO_2 is doing in the paper. There is no great difficulty in putting the ozone depletion in this write-up.

We have written extensively about the issue of substitutability between natural resources. There are several problems. One is that ecologists and ecological economists have still not proven to the world in general that a large degree of nonsubstitutability actually exists.

I am ambivalent on the education issue. I know that some people build education back into the picture and use public expenditures on education as a surrogate for positive investment in human capital.

The issue is whether the mining of resources is adequately accounted for in economic policy formulation. If the IMF advises a country to adopt a macroeconomic adjustment policy that forces a country to mine its natural resources, in what sense has sustainable adjustment taken place? The answer has to be that it has not. That is all that we are stressing. The purpose of the genuine saving concept is to try to highlight those issues.

Some people are against single indicators. Just because we offer one measure does not mean that it is the only possible measure. I am quite happy to see a whole array of sustainability indicators. Ours is only one useful way of looking at those issues.

On the IMF again, at the end of the day, if we say that the IMF is not interested in how countries adjust, then something has gone seriously wrong, because if the adjustment takes place through the overmining of natural resources, it simply cannot be sustainable.

Other Discussion

Stein Hansen: If one is just looking at the fundamental question of whether economic growth is good or bad, then one has to look at the direct as well as indirect effects. I wonder if these are represented in the Pearce-Hamilton equation. Output enters with a positive sign in their genuine saving equation, but there are the indirect effects as well from an increase in output to the other variables, particularly the depletion of natural resources and the increase in pollution. So my question to David Pearce is what, in his view, is the net effect of economic growth on the genuine savings rate? Do the negative indirect effects of GNP growth, operating on depletion and on pollution (direct and indirect), outweigh the obvious positive direct effects of GNP growth that we macroeconomists have to deal with most of the time?

Malcolm Knight: For me, the real question is what should institutions like the IMF do and what criteria should we use in looking at the macroeconomic elements of stabilization programs? We have had two very interesting approaches today—the one of Pearce and Hamilton and the other of Stein Hansen—and both are actually quite different in their intellectual underpinnings.

Stein Hansen's approach is to have an environmental group establish the environmental priorities that he then took as given, to look at their economic impacts, and to experiment with the set of economic policies that would allow achievement of those goals along with their implications on the level and structure of consumption. That is a sort of war strategy—you have something you absolutely have to achieve and you run the macroeconomy subject to that constraint.

The Pearce and Hamilton approach appears to be more incremental, looking at the effect of macroeconomic policies on some index (and there has been a lot of discussion about whether the genuine savings measure is the proper index or not), but it is an index of incremental modifications that prompt changes in macroeconomic policies aimed at changing the level of economic growth or consumption. Now these seem to be very different approaches and perhaps the authors can comment on the relative merits of the two approaches.

Stein Hansen: As a response to this particular question, the dominant purpose of what we set out to do was to bring the NGOs and the Ministry of Finance (and the government) together and help establish mutual trust between these parties. As I said this morning, we did not just do computable general equilibrium work, we also did a lot of other analytic and fairly basic research work in parallel. Some of this work has addressed fundamental sustainability issues and, drawing on works that David Pearce, and others, and we ourselves had done, we come to the not-all-that-surprising conclusion that there were no simple sustainability rules. For that reason we decided to keep all possible indicators in mind and put them into practice within the operational framework already used routinely by the government, and also to help, along the way, bridge gaps of misunderstanding between the various camps.

Melting a number of things into one single indicator, whether it is green or brown or whatever color, helps alert people and create awareness about issues. But once you have done that, I think, you should move on to the more multidimensional picture and put it into operation, which, of course, requires data for the variables you have chosen.

David Pearce: I certainly would prefer to get an economic handle on resource-depreciation and on environmental damage. I know that these things are controversial, but they are now pretty standard fare in the World Bank, in national policies, and certainly in the European Community. So, my preference would be to begin that way and to try to establish environmental priorities. One of the exercises we are doing at the moment is in fact for the European Commission—trying to identify the environmental priorities of Europe itself. I am more than aware, after 30 years in this business, that you do not come up with a fully quantified risk-assessment ranking of all those goals. Those exercises have been done here in the United States by the EPA. They are fascinating, but also show the pitfalls of trying to come up with a ranking. But my argument is that this process is extremely important, even if at the end of the day you might not believe the actual numbers that emerge. We find in our European work that the process leads you to focus not so much on environmental issues but on selected economic sectors, such as transport, the policies of which can have a lot of environmental payoff.

I do not know how IMF adjustment policies are formulated. Perhaps the sectoral focus is not suited to the operational work of the IMF, but you must look at how adjustment takes place. One wants to know *how* economies adjust. If, for example, you are adjusting by running out of fuelwood and you have to import kerosene, then you are obviously affecting the balance of payments. As I understand it, this is of fundamental relevance to the IMF. If you react to economic difficulties, say, by mining your tourist sector, as some Caribbean Islands are doing, you may be creating a perfectly unsustainable situation as regards future growth and prosperity. The loss of the coral reefs and the disappearance of ground-water supplies are illustrations of that. So it seems to me that *how* people adjust is extremely important. And it is therefore important to quantify, as far as possible and as far as credible, the way in which countries adjust.

So, it does not matter whether it is genuine savings, green GNP, or physical indicators, so long as you start looking at the sustainability issue. The fact is that you have to do something and at the moment there is no evidence that the Fund is doing much by way of examining how those adjustments are taking place.

Mohan Munasinghe: We in the World bank have started asking the question: How do we engage those working on the environmental side and on the economic management side in the developing world to work together? A helpful tactic we have used is to get the environmental group to identify, say, the five most important environmental issues, not a hundred, but the five most important, and then ask them the question: Which of the current set of economic policies affect the selected environmental issues the most? At the same time you go to the Ministry of Finance or the Central Bank and you put the reverse question: Of the reform program you have in mind, which policies are likely to affect some aspect of the environment? And then in the next step you put these groups together and develop a composite, which we have called an Action Impact Matrix. This matrix has proven to be an extremely useful exercise for us in developing a consensus and also establishing priorities. So, in my view, you have to work from both sides and you have to ensure that the country gets the ownership of final decisions in order to make headway.

Salah El Serafy: Much more important than pursuing the impact of structural adjustment on the environment is actually to do the ground work of finding out what is harming the environment so as to rebut this with good microeconomic and macroeconomic policy.

Kirit Parikh: I completely agree with David Pearce that you use green accounting or natural resource accounting essentially to focus attention on the damage that we are doing to the environment. My only objection, however, is regarding the use of a single concept as an indicator of sustainability, especially when you use it in comparing countries, as the World Bank and the Fund often have to.

Benedicte Christensen: I want to come back to the issue that Malcolm Knight raised, namely the implications for the Fund. I do not want to leave the impression that the Fund is not concerned with environmental matters. I very much share the view that the key word is sustainability. What we are concerned with in the Fund are not environmental objectives per se, but the sustainability of economic growth and of external balance. And I think both of these involve important environmental concerns and issues. Even though we do not measure them by genuine savings rate or by other concepts, we do measure them indirectly.

When we have medium-term balance of payments projections for countries that rely on mining or natural resource exports, we are very much concerned with excessive depletion of such resources. Similarly, when we have countries relying on logging exports, we take them into account, both in our growth projections and export projections and discuss to some extent even the regulatory framework, especially, if it has an important bearing on the macroeconomic situation. I think the key to our work on the environment is to ask if the lack of an environmental policy has an important bearing on the macroeconomic outcome.

David Pearce: I think this is an extremely important comment. Now let us go a bit further and start looking at measures of soil erosion as well, because that is also extremely important for the longer-term viability of exports. There is a whole range of natural resources and their depletion and depreciation become relevant to macroeconomic exercise.

Vito Tanzi: As regards sustainability, it is unclear to me what we need to focus on—sustainability over what period? Over 2 years, 5 years, 100 years, 500 years, what period? It is easy to conceive of a situation in which something is not sustainable for 100 years, but might be acceptable for two or three years and helps you bring about other changes in the economy. So there might be a situation in which you might want to accelerate the exploitation of natural resources for a while, which can help you bring about other adjustments in the economy, after which you go back to a more sustainable path. Unless we define the time horizon, I am not sure what sustainability really means.

One more comment. As I was listening to the discussion, I was reminded of the discussion that took place in our Executive Board on the issue of the environment. One Executive Director noted that today you come with the environment, tomorrow you might come with the right of women, the next week with the aged, and still the next week with children. In other words, where do we draw the line? Why should the Fund get involved in the environment and not in the rights of women, or the rights of children, or something as important. If we say, because the environment has something to do with sustainability, that leads me to my first question: What does sustainability mean and over what length of time?

David Nellor: To follow up on what Benedicte Christensen said, in the cases where the Fund has dealt with resource-based economies, the staff have looked for advice from the World Bank and others on what sustainability means. However, we still require a quantitative target initially in order to be able to design the macroeconomic program.

The other issue is the time frame over which adjustment takes place. If you attempt to achieve sustainability over a very short time frame, the dislocation caused may in some cases just be as damaging as allowing the continuation of current practices. Maintaining a balance in the rate of adjustment and the rate of environmental protection is needed, which we have not really focused on in the discussion thus far.

Session 2

Integration of Economic and Environmental Accounts

Issues of Interest

Session 2 was intended to address the following questions.

- Are fully integrated accounts essential to integrating environmental objectives into macroeconomic policy formulation?
- How feasible is it to implement sound environmental accounting and fully integrate it into national accounts?
- Are there many countries that have fully integrated the environment into their national accounts and now regularly produce environmentally adjusted national accounts? If not, what prospects are there that most countries will soon have them?

The papers by Peter Bartelmus as well as by Adriaan Bloem and Ethan Weisman attempt to answer these questions. Michael Ward commented on both papers.

6

Environmental Accounting: A Framework for Assessment and Policy Integration

Peter Bartelmus

The compartmentalization of human activities and a corresponding neglect of ecological and socioeconomic interdependence have been blamed for policy failures in both environment and development (WCED, 1987). There can be hardly any doubt about the existence of interdependence between issues and policies of population, poverty, environment, and economic performance and growth. The Brundtland Commission (WCED, 1987) and the discussions and publications in the wake of the Earth Summit (UNEP, 1992; Bartelmus, 1994a; Brown and others, annual) give ample evidence of these interrelations as well as cross-boundary impacts of regional activities. The papers by Hansen and Gandhi and Mc-Morran in this volume elaborate on the effects of macroeconomic and mesoeconomic policies on the environment. The reverse, how the environment affects the economy through the erosion of natural capital and its impact on human capital, is described in the Pearce and Hamilton paper.

An Issue of Integration

The obvious answer is integration in assessing interdependence and in policy formulation and evaluation. Reorienting planning and policy toward integrated sustainable development has therefore been the *leitmotif*

Note: The author is a staff member of the United Nations Statistics Division (UNSD). The views expressed here are those of the author and do not necessarily reflect an expression of opinion on the part of the United Nations. Stimulating observations by S. Keuning, G.-M. Lange, F. Neto, and Jan van Tongeren are gratefully acknowledged.

of the Earth Summit, the 1992 United Nations Conference on Environment and Development (United Nations, 1993c), and follow-up sessions of the United Nations Commission on Sustainable Development.

Many countries continue to address environmental issues from the periphery of weak environmental protection agencies that are generally unable to incorporate environmental concerns into mainstream economic and fiscal policies. Proclamations on the need for sustainable development by governments and international organizations also can be deceptive—frequently they turn out to be mere rhetoric, a coverup for piecemeal and sporadic environmental action. Of course, such eclectic measures are a far cry from the full incorporation of environmental objectives into *all* stages and levels of decision-making.

What are the reasons? For one, recurrent exhortations by environmentalists fail to impress policymakers. Hard budgetary decisions for dealing with environmental effects of economic activities require hard evidence of the trade-offs between the two. This is a matter of compiling data and indicators not so much on the existence of interdependence, but on its comparative *strength*. In other words, indicators are needed that permit a comprehensive quantitative comparison of effects across disciplines and regional boundaries.

Another reason for inaction on or denial of interdependence is the inability of both decision-makers and data producers to translate the widely acclaimed paradigm of sustainable development into concrete policy advice, probably because of the absence of a generally accepted definition of such development. How can we expect to address perceived nonsustainability of human activity if we are not clear or disagree on what it is? In this sense, the murky notion of sustainability seems more of an impediment to policy integration than a framework for action. Operational (quantifiable) concepts of sustainable growth and development are needed.

The popular definition of sustainable development by the World Commission on Environment and Development as "development that meets the needs of the present without compromising the ability of future generations to meet their own needs" (WCED, 1987, p. 43) is vague. It does not specify the time horizon of future generations, gives no indication of the role of the environment, and refers to the opaque concept of human needs.[1]

---

[1]A development strategy focusing on the satisfaction of "basic human needs" was advanced in 1974 by a joint UNEP/UNCTAD symposium in Cocoyoc and widely publicized by the 1976 World Employment Conference. However, developing countries generally considered this strategy as a diversion from the negotiations for a New International Economic Order and as an intrusion into national sovereign development policies.

More operational concepts can be derived by examining the sustainability of providing economic goods and noneconomic amenities by the economy, nature, and the social system.[2] Accordingly, economic, environmental, and social sustainability of supply and production can be distinguished. Following the supply process through to the final uses and users permits a further distinction between the sustainability of supply and production and the sustainability of uses and users. This categorization links the concept of sustainability to well-defined economic production and consumption processes and to less well-defined qualities of life of human users of goods, services, and amenities.

Sustainable Supply

A significant part of the *economic sustainability* of production and income is already addressed in national accounts by making an allowance for the consumption of capital in production processes. Recently acknowledged scarcities of further inputs of natural resources and environmental services, notably of waste absorption, call for the extension of the sustainability criterion from produced capital maintenance to the maintenance of natural capital. In addition, the maintenance of human capital (skills and knowledge) and of institutional capital (the social, legal, and organizational infrastructure) for economic activities would also have to be considered in a comprehensive discussion of sustainable economic growth. Because of conceptual difficulties in measuring human and institutional capital, proposals for integrated environmental and economic accounting (United Nations, 1993b) have concentrated on produced and natural capital consumption.

The step from economic production to the supply of noneconomic, but welfare-relevant, amenities, and thus from economic growth to development, can be made by introducing two further sources of human welfare—nature and the social system.

Natural systems provide water, oxygen, nutrient flows, waste assimilation, and recreation. As long as these goods are not scarce, they do not affect the sustainability of economic consumption: they have, by definition, a zero economic value. Other value systems might give an "existence value" to ecological, aesthetic, or ethical attributes of natural systems. Changes in their stability or quality affect the noneconomic *ecological sustainability* of the supply of environmental services.

---

[2]Much of the following discussion of sustainability in growth and devc ,pment is based on Bartelmus, 1994a, which should be consulted for a more detailed treatment of the subject.

Social systems include public efforts to meet objectives of equity, freedom, health, security, and education. Some of the goods and services related to these objectives are supplied by market producers. Others, being collective goods and services, are typically provided by the government. They include law and order, public health, and environmental protection. For the supply of market-produced goods and services, the above-discussed criteria of economic sustainability apply. For collective goods and services, the *social sustainability* of their supply would have to be defined in terms of maintaining the government's institutional and fiscal capability for providing them.

Sustainable Use

A distinction can be made between final uses and the ultimate users of goods and amenities. Such analysis is more welfare- and people-oriented than the above description of cost- and technology-oriented production and supply.

Because national disposable income represents potential claims on final uses, it is a better measure of economic welfare than GDP. The incorporation into national income of the value of environmental services to consumers and of further welfare effects from the degradation of the environment thus facilitates a broader assessment of human welfare. The policy focus on market-based measures of economic growth has been criticized, however, by advocates of multidimensional development. Such development would have to address a variety of social concerns or human needs and aspirations. Much of the discussion of the human quality of life and corresponding social indicators has therefore focused on the inadequacy of development that concentrates on economic growth (OECD, 1973).

Indicators of final consumption and human needs focus already to some extent on the people who strive to meet those needs. Indeed, the ultimate objective of sustainability is not to sustain human activity but human beings themselves. Although the sustainability of income and consumption is easier to measure, it should be considered as a proxy only for the sustainability of human well-being. Attempts have been made, therefore, at concentrating more on the human factor in development by measuring the level of economic aggregates in per capita terms, defining an overall human development index (UNDP, 1991) and determining the carrying capacity of land for human populations (FAO, UNFPA, and IIASA, 1982; Vitousek and others, 1986).

The above discussion of sustainability concepts refers to various possibilities of merging environmental and socioeconomic concerns through operational indicators. Accounting for both economic activities and their environmental effects is probably the most significant step toward such integration. Accounting indicators have generally been used as the main operational variables to analyze economic performance and growth. Environmentally adjusted accounting aggregates can therefore be used in defining, measuring, and analyzing sustainable and environmentally sound economic performance and growth. Such analysis would have to consider substitution of capital in production, technological progress, and changes in consumption patterns (see below).

This paper explores the capabilities of integrated environmental-economic accounting for assessing the interaction between environment and economy. The limits of this accounting in measuring welfare effects and noneconomic development will also be discussed. Those goals are probably better assessed by other instruments of data collection and analysis.

Stress-Response Approach

The discussion of interdependence and sustainability above depicts widespread repercussions of human activity on the environment. To formulate and monitor integrated policies, social responses need to be related to the effects of human activities. The sequence of activity-impact/effect-response has therefore been used as the organizing principle for environmental and related social, demographic, and economic statistics in the United Nations (1984) Framework for the Development of Environment Statistics (FDES). The same principle has been taken up again in developing stress-response and other Frameworks for Indicators of Sustainable Development (FISD) (Bartelmus, 1994c).

All these frameworks present physical data in matrices that do not attempt to show functional relationships among statistical variables. Rather, they represent juxtapositions of such variables, leaving functional connections and the further integration of data to separate analysis. Unfortunately, models abound in the environmental and economic fields, and international consensus remains an elusive goal. However, one data *system*, the 1993 System of National Accounts (SNA), has been adopted worldwide to measure economic activity. The system presents accounting identities and uses a common numéraire, the market price, for integrating diverse activities through aggregation.

Given the interest in assessing the environmental sustainability of economic performance and growth, the UN Statistics Division (UNSD) explored possibilities of introducing environmental effects into the SNA. The idea was to incorporate environmental costs (and benefits where applicable), not into the SNA core system itself, but into a satellite System of integrated Environmental and Economic Accounts (SEEA) (United Nations, 1993b). Figure 1 illustrates how this incorporation is achieved by extending the asset boundary from conventional (produced) economic assets to include environmental assets and their depletion and degradation (shaded areas). In monetary terms, most of these changes represent environmental costs generated by economic agents.

The SEEA presents different modules for describing interrelations between the economy and environment according to alternative valuation principles. The different valuations can be categorized as the measurement of the environmental *costs caused* directly by economic activities, the (damage) *costs borne* ultimately by individuals, and the actual *costs incurred* in environmental protection. This distinction allows linking the above-mentioned stress-response sequence of integrated statistical frameworks to the different approaches proposed in SEEA. The following discussion of these cost categories will examine to what extent economy-environment-policy interrelationships can be measured in an integrated accounting framework.

Cost-Caused Accounting

Two categories of valuation are proposed in the SEEA for costing the direct impacts (stress) of economic (production and consumption) activities on the availability of natural resources and environmental services, such as the safe absorption of waste and residuals. The two categories refer to market values revealed in the sale of natural resources and the maintenance costs of the environment that would have avoided environmental impacts generated during the accounting period.

Market Valuation

Market values can be applied to the depletion of natural resource capital, caused mainly by extracting scarce raw materials from nature.[3] In the past, conventional accounts considered natural resources to be in unlimited supply, giving them a zero economic value. Their loss for fu-

---

[3]Various methods have been proposed for estimating the market value of natural "economic" assets and changes therein, including the calculation of the present value of future net returns from asset use, replacement cost derived from potential discoveries, and simplifications of the present-value method by using "net prices" or "user-cost allowances." See Bartelmus and van Tongeren, 1994, for a discussion of the advantages and drawbacks of these methods.

Table 1. *SEEA: Flow and Stock Accounts with Environmental Assets*

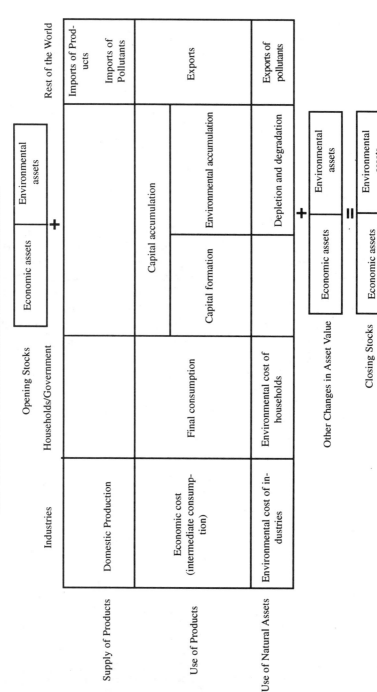

ture use in production was thus overlooked, undermining the long-term sustainability of production and economic growth.

Even from a purely economic point of view, some allowance for this type of natural capital consumption should be made at both the micro-economic (corporate) level and the macroeconomic and mesoeconomic levels; such an allowance would ensure that enough saving and investment would be generated for continuing production. Congo (Brazzaville) is an example of a country where oil riches have been si-phoned off by a foreign company without any effect on the living stan-dards of the population (*New York Times*, June 18, 1995, "Sleepy Congo, a Poor Land Once Very Rich"). It can be assumed that the company has kept good records of the depletion, while no such accounting seems to have been done for the nation.

The revised (1993) SNA records the depletion and degradation of economic natural resources in its asset accounts as economic disap-pearance.[4] However depletion and degradation (and discoveries) of natural resources are included under other volume changes, that is, outside the production accounts. As a consequence, they are not costed in the production accounts of the SNA and do not affect value added and national income and product. The SEEA, on the other hand, shifts the value of depletion and degradation of economic resources from other volume changes to production (as environmental costs) and to capital formation (as a decrease in natural capital).

Maintenance Costing

A major drawback of market valuation is its restriction to the scope and coverage of economic assets. The impact of economic activities on environmental assets, such as forests, and on the quality of air, water, and land is not accounted for. It can be argued that the use of scarce en-vironmental services represents a factor input of the environment into production. Such an input represents economic cost, beyond what is implied by the narrow SNA definition of "economic" assets. Mainte-nance costing is therefore proposed to capture the impact on all natural assets irrespective of their economic or environmental functions. Main-tenance costs are defined in the SEEA as the costs that would have been incurred if the environment had been used during the accounting pe-riod in such a way that its future use had not been affected. These costs

---

[4]Economic assets are defined in the 1993 SNA as those assets (including natural assets) over which ownership rights are enforced and which provide economic benefits to their owners.

are, of course, hypothetical because actual depletion and degradation do affect future uses of the environment.

The maintenance cost concept reflects a conservationist view of the environment. Uncertainties about long-term hazards from disturbing the natural environment and possible irreversibility of environmental impact from economic activities call for a high degree of risk aversion and the maintenance of at least the present level of environmental quality. Also, the use of maintenance costs for valuing environmental functions is similar to valuing the services of man-made capital: allowances made for capital consumption in national accounts can be taken as the amount necessary to keep capital intact.

In the case of nonrenewable subsoil resources, the application of a strong sustainability (full conservation of the resource) concept would lead to the non-use of certain resources and indeed squandering of other resources whose extraction involves limited environmental impact. A weaker sustainability concept would allow for substituting subsoil assets by other natural or man-made assets with a view to maintaining income levels rather than particular categories of natural capital. The market or user-cost valuation, noted above, caters to this approach.

Cost Internalization and Integration

Accounting in this manner for the environmental costs caused by natural resource depletion and pollution reflects the widely accepted philosophy of the user/polluter-pays-principle (OECD, 1989). Cost-caused accounting thus helps to assess the sources of environmental depletion and degradation with a view to prompting economic agents— through appropriate (dis)incentives—to internalize these costs into their accounts and budgets. It has been argued, however, that hypothetical costing of environmental impacts cannot be compared with observed, that is, realized, benefits in the market (de Haan and Keuning, 1995). A counter-argument is that maintenance costs reflect a pragmatic first-step assessment of externalities that *should* be internalized by causing agents. In this sense it provides necessary information for setting the level of "economic instruments" for cost internalization.[5]

From a macroeconomic point of view, maintenance costs serve as weights needed to aggregate different environmental impacts occur-

---

[5]The reservations of some national accountants about such "normative costing" are not quite comprehensible, since it is in line with the equally normative costing of capital consumption in conventional accounts—as the cost of maintaining intact the stock of fixed assets used up in production and that "should be sufficient to enable the assets to be replaced, if desired" (1993 SNA).

ring during the accounting period. Any aggregate comparison of environmental and economic effects has to resort to some type of weighing, reflecting their relative importance. Alternatively, one would have to content oneself with either juxtaposing partially aggregated physical indicators and monetary indicators, or to resort to shadow pricing in models that usually represent only a shadow of reality. Monetary weighing by means of prices or unit costs permits full integration of environmental impacts and effects with economic costs and benefits. The SEEA therefore proposes to deduct environmental costs from the economic benefits generated in production, obtaining environmentally adjusted value added and, as its sum total, an Environmentally adjusted net Domestic Product (EDP).

Cost-Borne Accounting

Optimal levels of environmental externalities are reached when marginal costs of abatement equal marginal damage reduced. As a consequence, cost internalization instruments should be set at this level where environmental cost reflects the environmental damage borne by economic agents (households and enterprises). One issue is how to determine individual marginal cost and damage curves and aggregate them at the sectoral or national levels. Another issue, discussed below, is to what extent optimality criteria apply in the absence of perfect competition and transparency in real-world markets.

The measurement of environmental damage is addressed in a separate version of the SEEA by means of cost-borne valuation. This valuation combines the market valuation of natural resource depletion, mainly borne by enterprises, with contingent or similar valuations of the welfare effects from environmental deterioration borne by households. Well-known problems of applying contingent and related valuations in cost-benefit analyses at the project level[6] accumulate at the national level. At least for the time being, such valuation does not seem to be applicable in routine national accounting, but could be further explored in more experimental studies for selected environmental subjects or (subnational) regions.

It is also doubtful whether contingent valuations are at all suitable for incorporation into national accounts. National accounts are based on market prices that are not capable of assessing welfare owing to their ex-

---

[6]Such as free-rider attitudes, short-sightedness of consumers about long-term environmental impacts, and effects of income levels and distribution when questioning individuals in opinion surveys and other attempts at revealing and aggregating preferences for environmental quality and related social values.

clusion of consumer surpluses. Contingent valuations on the other hand include these surpluses when assessing the willingness to pay for environmental services. Mixing these valuations would create aggregates that being neither performance nor welfare measures are difficult to interpret.

It appears that national accounts can contribute little to the assessment of environmental damage generated and borne by the different economic units. Closest to assessing environmental and social costs within the national accounts framework is probably the above-described maintenance costing. Such costing represents a least-cost approach, based on available technologies and desirable standards. To the extent that these standards, typically set by enlightened governmental institutions, approximate the optimal damage reduction level, minimum compliance cost would be consistent with optimal cost internalization into a perfectly competitive market price system. In reality, of course, compliance and maintenance cost do not equal optimal damage values. Under these circumstances, maintenance costing can be considered as a pragmatic combination of technological solutions to environmental problems and social preferences for environmental conservation.

Cost-Incurred Accounting

Responses to environmental impacts can be proactive, reactive, regulatory, or incentive. A classification of those responses that incur actual expenses is incorporated in a separate module of the SEEA dealing with the segregation of environmental protection expenditures. Since these expenditures are already part of conventional accounts they are fully consistent with the market valuation of the SNA, but they may pose difficult measurement and classification problems, notably in the case of inputs and outputs that can serve both environmental and other (economic) purposes.

The analysis of current (intermediate and final consumption, labor cost) and capital expenditures in national accounts could be usefully extended to the sources of expenditures, as measured in financial accounts. Financial accounts are an integral part of national accounts and can thus be directly linked to nonfinancial transactions in the economy. This link facilitates the integrated analysis of environment-economy interaction in debt, savings, inflation, fiscal policy, and income distribution. However, little work has been done on the financial aspects of environmental accounting, owing to its focus on the physical environment and its role in sustaining growth and development.

In line with the focus of the SEEA on environmental stress caused by economic activities, its Classification of Environmental Protection Activities (CEPA) reflects responses to environmental degradation only. In principle, classifications of expenditures made to mitigate or avoid environmental welfare effects borne by human beings, in particular health-related expenses, could also be introduced into the SEEA. Several scholars propose the deduction of both types of expenditures from national income. In their view, they represent "defensive" expenditures, which compensate only for negative environmental effects of economic growth and urbanization (Leipert, 1989; Daly, 1989; Pearce, Markandya, and Barbier, 1989). However, this deduction is questionable since it would draw the transaction-based accounting approach into the murky waters of welfare measurement. Necessarily, the exclusion of defensive or any other undesirable activity from the economy would change the production boundary quite arbitrarily, since it is hardly possible to obtain a consensus on what is desirable or regrettable in society.

The separate identification of total (current and capital) expenses for environmental protection seems to provide a comprehensive picture of the efforts undertaken by different sectors and institutions to protect the environment. However, this aggregate is not directly comparable to the net productive effort of the economy, reflected in GDP. The value of total expenditure includes double counting of the cost of intermediate uses contained in the value of final ones (capital and consumption).

Two alternative approaches suggest themselves. One is to create a new (broader) environmental service sector, combining internal (ancillary) and external environmental activities. In this sector, internal environmental services that are not transacted between establishments (production units) of enterprises would be externalized, increasing gross output, but leaving value added and GDP unchanged. Alternatively, input-output analysis could be used to assess the direct and indirect value-added contributions to net domestic product (NDP) in connection with environmental protection expenses (Schäfer and Stahmer, 1989). This approach would assess the total involvement of the economy in environmental protection as far as production and income generation are concerned.

Environmentally Adjusted Indicators

The above stress-response analysis of monetary valuation showed how environment-economy interactions can be assessed within an integrated accounting framework. The following takes the next step by describing how environmental values can be incorporated into the aggregation process provided by integrated accounts. This process can be seen as the highest form of integration, merging environmental and economic issues in a few macroeconomic indicators. While it is impossible to describe here all the potential applications of environmentally modified aggregates, some immediate uses in policy formulation and modeling are suggested in the following paragraphs.

The scope of indicators derived from integrated accounts depends on how far conventional accounts are expanded to incorporate environmental and related socioeconomic concerns. A relatively narrow approach expands only the asset boundary. Noneconomic (in the SNA sense) environmental assets, such as air, water, tropical forests, and wildlife, for which no ownership and managerial control has been established, are added to economic tangible assets. Further extensions of the production boundary introduce households as producers of economic goods and services and related environmental effects and the environment as a producer of waste disposal, space, and other physiological and recreational services. These expansions are more controversial but have been elaborated in principle in additional modules of the SEEA.

Figure 1 describes the narrow approach of incorporating environmental assets only. Even in this simplified presentation, the figure reveals the main aggregates that can be derived from this version of the SEEA. They are

- measures of wealth, including the endowment with environmental assets, in opening and closing stocks of asset accounts
- changes in those assets as economic and environmental capital accumulation and capital consumption
- the mirror effect of capital consumption, that is, economic and environmental cost generated by industries and households
- transnational environmental effects of pollution as imports and exports of waste and pollutants
- the sum total of net production, environmentally adjusted net domestic product (EDP), obtained by deducting total (environmental and economic) cost from gross output of industries, or by adding environmentally adjusted final demand categories of consumption, net capital accumulation, and (net) exports
- total expenditure for environmental protection as part of intermediate consumption and final uses (consumption, accumulation, and foreign trade) in conventional accounts.

Wealth: Value of Nature

Accounting for wealth and its distribution measures the availability of productive and financial capacities, as well as the concentration of economic power within and among nations and between current and future generations. Wealth accounts thus address issues of economic efficiency and equity. Of course, these issues are also relevant in the generation and distribution of income flows.

The focus of economic concern seems to have vacillated in the past between stock (wealth) and flow (income) analysis. The declining sway of socialist doctrines, preoccupied with the concentration of wealth in the hands of few, is probably the reason why national accounts, until recently, gave little attention to asset accounting. On the other hand, the explicit inclusion of stock/asset accounts in the 1993 revision of the SNA seems to have been prompted by increased attention to noneconomic aspects of human wealth, notably natural and human capital.[7]

The above discussion of environmental asset valuation distinguishes between natural assets "transferred" to the economy because of their use in production and consumption and environmental assets that remain outside the economic system, but may be affected (destroyed, degraded, or restored) by economic activities. The former can be valued and measured in monetary terms (market values) and their changes incorporated in the flow accounts. It is much more difficult to assign a monetary value to the latter, and usually only their *change* is measured through maintenance or contingent valuation.

The part in national wealth of transferred economic assets, such as mineral resources, timber from forests, or fish in the oceans, can thus be measured in national asset accounts. Just as for conventional tangible and financial economic assets and liabilities, several avenues of analytical and policy uses of broadened (produced and natural) wealth indicators can be identified.

- *Ownership and distribution of assets.* Generation of individual property rights for "common-property" natural assets has been proposed to facilitate greater care and more efficient use by owners. Equity aspects of the ownership allocation need to be considered in this context. Such equity concerns include not only intra-national but also international aspects (e.g., for global commons or internationally shared resources), as well as intergenerational ones, that is, wealth to be shared with future generations.
- *Wealth and production.* The analysis of the role of natural capital in economic production and growth would have to consider short-, medium-, and long-term productivity effects of capital availability and substitution of natural capital by produced and human capital.

---

[7]As already discussed natural economic assets are included in the 1993 SNA asset accounts and balance sheets. Less attention is paid to human capital, except for suggestions of reclassifying education and health expenditures from final consumption to capital formation. Further work on "human resource accounting" is currently being done by UNSD (van Tongeren and Becker, 1994).

- *Wealth and consumption*. Running down (through sale and non-replacement) of economic wealth, required in production, for purposes of consumption is usually not an option for prudent behavior, as reflected in the widely accepted income definition of Hicks, 1946. To the extent that natural assets are complementary (nonsubstitutable) factors in production, their depletion poses indeed a threat to the sustainability of production and income generation.
- *Financial aspects of wealth accounting*. Owing to a general preoccupation with physical impacts on and from the environment, integrated accounting has focused on tangible asset accounts. Financial implications of the accumulation and reimbursement of "environmental debt," that is, the total value of depletion and degradation generated in the past, have therefore been largely neglected.

Noneconomic environmental assets can be seen as providing directly to final users services, including recreation and health, but those assets may also reflect inherent values of cherished natural biota or ecosystems. These values also need to be assessed in comprehensive wealth measurements. There are, however, major valuation problems in measuring existence or option values (Munasinghe, 1993), which would have to be established through the above-described contingent or similar valuations. As already discussed, such valuations of environmental wealth are generally beyond the capability of integrated accounting. Other physical indicators would have to be used for measuring the presence and distribution of noneconomic environmental assets.

Changes in Wealth: Sustainability of Economic Growth

Economic behavior has typically been reactive, responding to observed *changes* in wealth. A benign neglect (World Bank, 1995) of the stock aspects of wealth in measurement, theory, and policymaking has been the result. For practical policy advice it may thus be more useful to focus on activities that create changes in wealth rather than on the results of the changes in the availability and distribution of asset stocks at a particular point of time.

As far as the capital function of wealth is concerned, activities of capital formation, capital consumption, and saving and borrowing—the sources of funding capital formation—are defined and measured in national accounts. Those indicators describe a major part of demand for the result of economic activity, NDP generated; they are also the key macroeconomic variables monitored and used to steer the economy through short- and medium-term fluctuations into long-term sustainable economic growth.

Measuring Sustainable Growth

The sustainability of economic growth was discussed above as a question of capital maintenance. Environmental depletion and degradation were blamed for the lack of sustainability that went unrecorded in accounting and thus in the minds of most decision-makers. Denial and neglect of the environmental impact of economic activity at the macroeconomic and microeconomic levels are the result. The SEEA was designed therefore to capture environmental impacts and communicate them to the decision-makers in their own—economic (money)—language. This is achieved by defining environmentally adjusted accounting indicators that can be introduced as "eco-variables" into conventional economic analysis (Bartelmus, 1994a).

The trend of national income and product is generally used to measure economic growth. Allowing not only for produced but also for natural capital maintenance in these indicators permits the definition of more sustainable economic growth as upward trend of eco-domestic product (EDP). Of course, a number of factors other than capital maintenance may affect the sustainability of future (potential) trends of the EDP. They include technological progress, discovery of natural resources, changes in production and consumption patterns, natural and man-made disasters, inflation, indebtedness, and the productivity of human and institutional capital.

Most of these factors are interrelated, affecting the potential use and substitution of capital and consumption goods and services. To the extent that substitutes avoid depletion or degradation, a weak sustainability concept would require changes in production and consumption patterns only; no (or little for adjusting production and consumption processes) cost allowances would have to be made in accounting, and no further action of resource conservation would be needed. On the other hand, a strong sustainability approach of full environmental cost accounting and conservation would be the answer to complementarities of natural asset use in production and consumption. Sensible sustainability has been advocated as a criterion that takes both complementarity and substitution in the different types of capital into account (Serageldin and Steer, 1994).

Concepts of Capital Accumulation

A key policy variable of sustainable economic growth is obtained by turning capital formation into the eco-variable of capital accumulation. Capital accumulation is defined in integrated environmental and economic accounts by introducing a broader concept of capital consumption incorporating the depletion and degradation of nature. Of course, the same alteration can also be applied to the accounting mirror of capital formation, savings, obtaining a net concept that reflects dissavings or liquidation of natural capital (World Bank, 1995).

In principle, three concepts of capital accumulation can be distinguished in integrated accounts, depending on the coverage of activities and events that affect the availability of economic and environmental wealth.

- Capital accumulation, net of depletion and degradation costs. This indicator reflects an expanded depreciation concept, covering the loss of future uses of the environment for natural resource supply and waste disposal. The indicator is incorporated in the production accounts of the SEEA.
- Capital accumulation, including other accumulation, that is, discoveries of subsoil assets and transfers of land and natural resources into the economic system. This indicator is based on economic decisions but accounted for outside the production and income accounts in the SEEA. The purpose is to avoid major fluctuations of income and production and to reflect the fact that natural wealth is not the result of economic production.
- Total capital accumulation, including additionally other volume changes in natural assets. Other volume changes are largely noneconomic, such as effects of natural disasters, accidents, warfare, or natural growth.

For the first concept, the national accounts identity between investment (capital formation) and savings is maintained. For the other concepts, this identity does not hold, unless transfers and noneconomic changes of environmental assets are introduced as capital formation into the production and income accounts. It is difficult to see, however, how discoveries or natural disasters can be interpreted as economic production or capital consumption.[8] In these cases, saving cannot any longer be interpreted as a source of capital formation from forgone consumption. The interpretation of these concepts would thus have to be outside national income and production analysis and possibly in terms of wealth accounting and modeling, which, as indicated above, appear to be of less use and appeal to policymakers.

The treatment of depletion of mineral resources in accounts, prepared by the Bureau of Economic Analysis (1994) in the United States,

---

[8]It has been argued, on the other hand, that such "windfalls" of capital gains and losses would make national income "a useful measure of real social income" (Hicks, 1946, p. 180).

is an example of how different concepts and definitions may affect the interpretation and analysis of environmentally adjusted indicators. Discoveries of mineral resources were accounted for as capital formation, which more or less compensates for the depletion of these resources. If the exploitation of this nonrenewable resource had been entered as intermediate consumption of a raw material or as depreciation of the natural capital stock, income (value added) generated in mineral production would have been reduced by an average of 50 percent over the 1977–91 period.

Funding Capital Accumulation

As already mentioned, the current interim version of the SEEA stops short of following the process of accumulation through to its financial sources, that is, saving, capital transfers, and net lending and borrowing. International organizations, notably the International Monetary Fund and the World Bank, have been particularly concerned with this aspect of (non)sustainability or (in)stability of economies, prescribing measures of structural adjustment to indebted nations. They have been criticized for focusing on the "unsustainable raise in national liabilities" of indebted nations, neglecting at the same time unsustainability on the asset side, that is, natural-capital depletion (Repetto, 1994).

Clearly, the connections between an environmentally modified concept of capital accumulation and the financial sources available for capital maintenance deserve further scrutiny. The SNA already provides the framework for linking production and income accounts to capital and financial accounts, facilitating a corresponding extension of the SNA-based SEEA. Such extension could indicate to what extent current consumption is indeed financed by dissaving through selling off natural assets, as suggested by the World Bank, 1995.

Moreover, the relationship between long-term sustainability and short-term financial stability could also be usefully explored in this framework. For instance, it has been argued that macroeconomic stability is a precondition for preserving the environment (Gandhi and McMorran in this volume). Does this argument justify the separation of macroeconomic from environmental policy? Extended green accounting could help to assess the relevance of well-known relationships among wealth, accumulation, saving, and dissaving for environmental asset conservation and use. At the international level, pertinent questions refer to the connections between international liabilities and environmental exploitation. On one hand, natural resource exploitation might have intensified for purposes of debt servicing; on the other hand, debt-for-nature swaps could be considered as a direct response to this situation.

Of course, capital formation and liquidation are only two of the many determinants of economic performance and growth. The greening of the elements in the basic accounting identities between supply and use and between production and income points to possibilities of modifying consumption, production, and export/import functions in economic models. Such analysis might provide quite different policy advice regarding foreign trade, public and private consumption, and, by analytical extension, employment and inflation. It is beyond the scope of this paper to discuss the implications of such modified analysis for short-term and long-term macroeconomic policymaking.[9]

Comparing Conventional and Environmentally Adjusted Indicators

A few immediate conclusions can already be drawn from the direct comparison of conventional and environmentally adjusted indicators. Table 1 illustrates this for two experimental case studies carried out in Papua New Guinea (PNG) and Mexico.

Overall, the table indicates a reduction of NDP by 13 percentage points in Mexico and between 3 and 10 percentage points in PNG (for the 1986–90 period)[10] when environmental costs are accounted for in EDP. The table also illustrates the effects of greening the national accounts on capital formation, capital productivity, and final consumption. In Mexico, net capital accumulation (CAP net) turned into a disinvestment while PNG's capital formation was halved under the green accounting calculations. Changes in capital productivity (NDP/CAP) resulting from the inclusion of natural capital paint a different picture of capital efficiencies for the economy and its sectors (with wide fluctuations in sectoral ratios). Increases in the share of final consumption in

---

[9]For a discussion of some of the possible implications of environmental costing in planning and policies for sustainable growth and development, see Bartelmus, 1994a, Chapters 4 and 5. It should be noted in this context that, while environmental questions are usually viewed as long-term accumulation of depletion and degradation, some of those impacts may result also in the short-term and may be intensified or lessened by short- and medium-term fluctuations in economic activity. Short- and medium-term effects and repercussions of business cycles between the economy and environment might thus deserve greater attention in planning and policymaking (Munasinghe, 1995).

[10]Of course, such a period is too short to demonstrate any differences in trend between NDP and EDP; for a more detailed discussion of the use of these and other macroindicators in national (PNG) strategies for sustainable development, see Bartelmus, 1994b.

Table 1. *Conventional and Environmentally Adjusted Indicators:*
Mexico and Papua New Guinea

	Mexico (1985)		Papua New Guinea (1986–1990)[1]	
	Conventional Accounts (NDP)	Integrated ("Green") Accounts (EDP)	Conventional Accounts (NDP)	Integrated ("Green") Accounts (EDP)
NDP or EDP	P 42.1 billion	P 36.4 billion	K 2.8 billion[2]	K 2.6 billion[2]
EDP/NDP	—	87%	—	90–97%
C/NDP	83%	96%	89–100%	95–109%
Δ CAP (net)	P 4.6 billion	P –0.7 billion	K 0.5 billion[2]	K 0.2 billion[2]
Δ CAP/NDP	11%	–2%	12–20%	3–16%
NDP/CAP	37%	10%[3]	59%	—

Sources: Van Tongeren and others, 1991; Bartelmus, Lutz, and Schweinfest, 1992.
[1]Lowest and highest percentage.
[2]For 1990.
[3]Natural resource depletion only.

NDP (C/NDP), to close to and over 100 percent, indicate a nonsustainable consumption pattern of living off the natural capital base.

Cost Internalization for Structural Change

Decisions about environmentally adjusted economic variables would not only be made at the macroeconomic level. Households and enterprises use the very same variables of investment, saving, and consumption in their own decision-making. Given the inefficiencies of command-and-control measures in central planning and policies, the use of different policy instruments (of cost internalization) to influence microeconomic behavior has therefore been advocated. The following shows that these microeconomic aspects of environmental policy can also be incorporated in an integrated accounting framework. As a result, linkage and consistency between micro- and macroeconomic analysis might be improved.

Accounting for Accountability

Structural distortion of the economy may result either directly from environmental impact or from responses to this impact. In the case of an environmental impact, scarce resources are misallocated to economic activities because market prices do not reflect environmental cost and thus send wrong signals of exaggerated social benefits to economic agents. On the other hand, the increasing allocation of human and financial resources to "defensive" activities has also been blamed for creating a distorted economy that allocates fewer and fewer of its resources to the generation of human well-being (Leipert, 1989).

The first step toward redirecting an increasingly defensive and destructive economy is the measurement of environmental impact and responses to this impact. Actual environmental expenditures and imputed environmental costs are therefore shown in the SEEA in connection with the economic activities that incur or cause them. Such accounting for accountability facilitates budgetary decisions about environmental expenses and the setting of measures of cost internalization for full-cost pricing. These measures include effluent charges, user fees for natural resources, deposit-refund systems, and tradable pollution permits.

The monetary valuation of environmental costs also permits their aggregation for the different sectors of the economy. Sectoral cost measurement facilitates the move from microeconomic to mesoeconomic analysis and thus the assessment of structural effects of defensive expenditures and underpricing. Of course, further aggregation for the whole economy permits the modification of conventional macroeconomic aggregates, such as NDP, national income, and capital formation.

The above-mentioned case studies in Mexico (van Tongeren and others, 1991) and Papua New Guinea (Bartelmus, Lutz, and Schweinfest, 1992) provide examples for significant distortions in the economy owing to the environmental costs generated by different industries. In Mexico, for instance, value added dropped to –13 percent of its original value in the forestry sector and to about 18 percent in the mining (largely oil) sector, if environmental depletion and degradation were accounted for. Less dramatic, but still significant, is the reduction to 73 percent (1989) for Papua New Guinea's main industry of (gold and silver) mining.

Accounting versus Modeling

These figures show the significance of environmental costs, in particular resource-intensive or highly polluting or degrading industries. They do not provide an answer to the question of whether cost internalization is justified in real-world situations where other—mainly monopolistic—market imperfections cast doubt on the assumptions of perfect competition and market transparency. Those assumptions usually underlie the claim of optimality in resource allocation, resulting from full-cost pricing.

The semi-fiction (Solow, 1992) of these assumptions and the murky issue of justifying second-best solutions in this situation could explain why economic policy has focused mostly on the direct use of macroeconomic variables rather than on optimizing models that may be quite removed from reality. Perhaps the time has come now to reassess cherished optimality criteria at the microeconomic level, with a view to replacing them, at least in part, by more strategic approaches. The recent Nobel Prize award in economics to pioneers in game theory might be an indication that economic behavior needs explanation in strategic terms rather than by the invisible hand.

Still, those models provide the theoretical justification and definitions for most economic variables and indicators. From this point of view it can be questioned if the accounting system can, at least on theoretical grounds, provide the correct information for setting up fiscal (dis)incentives, that is, market instruments, in integrated environmental-economic policymaking. To the extent that imputed environmental costs are already accounted for in microeconomic budgets, integrated accounting represents just a correction of inaccurate national accounts. There is indeed some indication that such accounting is carried out at the corporate level in the case of depletion of natural resources and in anticipation of liabilities for hazard-prone activities.[11] On the other hand, when such accounting does not take place, the ultimate incidence of hypothetical costs caused can be traced only through modeling microeconomic behavior. The above-described first-step allocation of imputed costs would provide the starting-point information for such modeling.

These issues are sometimes raised when questioning the need for incorporating environmental costs into the national accounts, even as satellite accounts. The argument is that the accounting for hypothetical environmental costs is an analytical approach that should be dealt with by modeling rather than solid (in the sense of actual observation) accounting.[12] There is, however, a difference in modeling and accounting that should be borne in mind before relegating environmental (monetary) accounting to modeling. While environmental accounts make use of real costs, either observed as actual expenditures or derived from engineering studies, analytical models, for example, of cost incidence, have to make assumptions about the optimizing *behavior* of economic agents.

---

[11]For example, balance sheet provisions for potential toxic waste cleanup seem to have been made by U.S. chemical concerns (Monsanto, Du Pont, Cyanamid Corporations) (*Wall Street Journal*, March 23, 1992).

[12]See, for instance the discussions and contributions to the second meeting of the so-called "London Group" of national accountants in Washington, D.C. (March 15–17, 1995), in particular papers presented by Hill and Harrison, 1995, and de Haan and Keuning, 1995.

Ideally, close links between accounting and modeling should be maintained, making the question of cutoff between accounting and analysis somewhat esoteric. In practice, however, official statisticians seem to shy away from analysis, supposedly to guard their reputation of providing validated observations of the real world. On the other hand, the capabilities of statistical frameworks, such as the SEEA, to provide standard concepts of links among indicators that can be used as policy variables get lost if they are left to myriads of modelers and analysts. Rather than walking away from any particular accounting result, national accountants should make a greater effort at shaping their data to be relevant for policy analysis. This applies particularly to the field of environment, which has become a mainstream issue of sustainable growth and development.

Limits of Monetary Accounting

From Valuation to Evaluation

Monetary valuation and much of economic analysis reach their limits where such valuation becomes arbitrary with increasing remoteness of the effects of economic and noneconomic activities and natural processes from economic production. Social goals and values of equity, political freedom, culture, or the health of humans and ecosystems are difficult to measure in physical terms and quite impossible in money terms. The above-described cost-borne (contingent) valuations attempt to capture some of these welfare effects—with limited success.

A comprehensive concept of development—as opposed to economic growth—would have to consider all these noneconomic amenities as part of the overall goal of improving the quality of human life. As indicated above, concepts of maintaining the capital base of the provision of these amenities do not apply when focusing directly on the sustainability of (the welfare of) human beings.

In the absence of consensus on human needs and aspirations, targets or standards will have to be set by governmental fiat or expertocratic decision. At the same time, limits and constraints in meeting needs and aspirations, posed by nature and by overriding social values (e.g., equity, tradition, or culture), would also have to be considered in formulating development programs.[13] Such standard and limit setting would turn

---

[13]Minimum standards and maximum limits or thresholds relevant in such analysis can be categorized as (a) standards of living, (b) natural resource capacities and pollution standards, (c) limits of ecological carrying capacity, (d) equity standards of the distribution of income and wealth and environmental costs and benefits, and (e) other cultural, political, and sociodemographic standards or targets (Bartelmus, 1994a, p. 72).

the analysis of the sustainability of development into one of the *feasibility* of development programs, complying (or not) with an exogenously set normative framework (Bartelmus, 1994a). Monetary valuation is replaced by social evaluation.

Indicators of Sustainable Development

Measures of standard compliance or violation are difficult to integrate or compare, since the pertinent indicators are measured in different units and may be intercorrelated. Overall indices such as the Human Development Index (HDI), proposed by the United Nations Development Program (UNDP, 1991), can therefore be criticized for applying arbitrary weights in adding or averaging the underlying indicators.

A compromise is to select key indicators that either reflect a broad area of analysis (such as the average life expectancy of a population) or can be aggregated through equivalence factors reflecting their relative contribution to particular themes (de Haan and Keuning, 1995). Of course these indicators or indices can still not be fully integrated with economic indicators in the absence of a common numéraire. Attempts have been made at least to juxtapose environmental indicators next to economic ones within an accounting system; there is a risk, however, of overloading the system with physical data or, alternatively, under-representing noneconomic phenomena through arbitrary selection of indicators.[14]

Probably, a more transparent way of organizing and displaying indicators is to develop and present them in a Framework for Indicators of Sustainable Development (FISD) (Bartelmus, 1994c). Such a framework would facilitate the rapid identification of indicators and their linkage with interactive processes.[15] It remains to be seen to what extent these indicators and indicator systems can supplement or replace integrated accounting aggregates and systems. The above stress-response analysis of integrated accounting is a starting point for linking physical

---

[14]This seems to be the case in several proposals from national accountants who attempt to meet the demand for green accounts by listing environmental and related social indicators together with conventional accounting information. The Dutch NAMEA (de Haan and Keuning, 1995) is a protagonist of these approaches.

[15]The proposed FISD attempts to link aspects of indicator use, reflected in Agenda 21 (United Nations, 1993c), with issues of data availability and production, reflected in the United Nations (1984) Framework for the Development of Environment Statistics (FDES). Other, similar frameworks have been proposed mostly by the user community (United Nations, 1995; SCOPE, 1994; World Bank, 1995). One drawback of these proposals is that they seem to be more of wish lists (of desirable information) than realistic proposals for recurrent data collection at national and international levels.

indicators and monetary accounting aggregates since it applies the same organizational criteria commonly used in indicator frameworks.

Outlook for Implementation of Integrated Accounting

National Programs of Environmental Accounting

UNSD has assisted developing countries in carrying out projects of SEEA implementation. To date, projects have been or are being conducted, with the support of UNEP, UNDP, or the World Bank, in Colombia, Ghana, Indonesia, Republic of Korea, Mexico, Papua New Guinea, and the Philippines. Given the novelty of the proposed concepts and methods, these projects are experimental. Their purpose has been to demonstrate the feasibility of integrated accounting and possible uses of their results in integrated planning and policymaking.

A phased implementation has therefore been favored by most developing countries. In the first phase, a pilot project is typically carried out by a research institute in collaboration with key data users and producers. After assessing the results, the second phase is to institutionalize integrated accounting through incorporation into official statistical work. The Korean and Philippine projects are examples of where such institutionalization is contemplated (by the Bank of Korea) or actually pursued (by the National Statistical Coordination Board of the Philippines).

Most pilot projects were initiated by a national seminar that brought together policymakers, nongovernmental organizations, researchers, and data producers. In several cases, these seminars were an innovation in cross-disciplinary collaboration of national organizations in environment and development. This collaboration was then anchored in a supervisory committee that had the task of following closely the progress in the implementation of integrated accounts and supporting data compilation. In line with the pilot character of the projects, no new data collection efforts were carried out; rather, existing data were compiled within the SEEA framework. Missing data were identified for possible estimations or inclusion in future surveys.

If nothing else, this process identified significant data gaps and called attention to major interactions and repercussions among diverse areas of natural resource management and economic policy. It appears, from the above-mentioned case studies, that integrated accounts can be compiled in both physical and monetary terms even in countries with limited statistical capabilities. The argument that basic environment statistics programs have to be established first before an integrated counting project can be initiated is thus not confirmed by experience to date. Another argument for delayed action in this area has been the need to gain experience first with selected natural resource accounts, such as forest or water accounts. While such accounting might indeed provide useful information for the *management* of a particular resource, it is hardly useful for comprehensive, integrative *policies* of sustaining growth and development. Moreover, accounting for selected natural resources has typically been conducted outside the national accounts framework, impairing consistency with national accounts identities and aggregates, and making it a one-time research effort.

Of course, these tentative conclusions from a few case studies require confirmation through further experience with integrated accounting in developing and industrialized countries. Considering the above-mentioned stimulation of cross-disciplinary cooperation and experience gained in data collection and analysis, the benefits of embarking on an integrated accounting project seem to outweigh the relatively modest costs of a pilot project (of about US$120,000).

International Cooperation

International seminars on environmental and natural resource accounting, conducted jointly by UNSD with UNDP or UNEP, generated numerous requests for advisory services, training, and financial support of country projects. This was anticipated by UNCED, which requested UNSD to support, in collaboration with relevant UN agencies, countries in establishing integrated environmental and economic accounts (United Nations, 1993c).

However, UNSD's technical cooperation program, which covers a wide range of applied statistics, could not cope with all these demands. At the same time, a large variety of national, international, governmental, and nongovernmental institutions used this surge in interest about green accounting for experimenting with their own particular approaches in different developing countries. Duplication of work, confusion about methodologies, and turf fighting were the result.

There is an urgent need for better use of existing mechanisms of coordinating international statistical work in environmental accounting. In environment statistics, several mechanisms are in place. An Inter-Governmental Working Group on the Advancement of Environment Statistics has met regularly to discuss the development and coordination of environmental and sustainable development indicators and their links with environmental accounting. Also, a Task Force on Environment Statistics was created by the Statistical Commission of the United Nations to develop an "integrated work program" in environmental statistics, indicators, and accounting. However, the Task Force, at its first meeting, cautioned that differing mandates of international organizations do not yet permit the full integration of programs.

Perhaps more promising are recent plans advanced by UNDP and the World Bank to address specifically the area of environmental accounting by creating a "global project" of such accounting (UNDP), or by organizing a working group of developing countries that already compile integrated accounts (World Bank). The latter would be similar in nature to the "London Group" of national environmental accountants, which decided to restrict its membership to industrialized countries only. The aim of both efforts should be to reach some consensus on concepts and methods and to coordinate international support of national programs.

The second special conference of the International Association for Research in Income and Wealth in Tokyo (March 5–8, 1996) will examine to what extent such consensus has already been reached or where further standardization needs to be developed. Eventually this process could lead to a revision of the interim United Nations, 1993a, proposals on *Integrated Environmental and Economic Accounting* and the adoption of international guidelines or recommendations in this area. UNSD, in collaboration with other international organizations, is prepared to play its part in this revision.

References

Bartelmus, Peter, 1994a, *Environment, Growth and Development—The Concepts and Strategies of Sustainability* (London and New York: Routledge).

———, 1994b, "Green Accounting for a National Strategy of Sustainable Development—the Case of Papua New Guinea," *Ambio*, Vol. 23, No. 8, pp. 509–14.

———, 1994c, *Towards a Framework for Indicators of Sustainable Development.* Department for Economic and Social Information and Policy Analysis, Working Paper Series No. 7 (New York: United Nations).

———, Ernst Lutz, and Stefan Schweinfest, 1992, *Integrated Environmental and Economic Accounting: A Case Study for Papua New Guinea*, Environment Working Paper No. 54 (Washington: World Bank).

Bartelmus, Peter, and Jan van Tongeren, 1994, *Environmental Accounting: An Operational Perspective*, Department for Economic and Social Information and Policy Analysis, Working Paper Series No. 1 (New York: United Nations).

Brown, Lester R., and others, *State of the World 19__*, annual (London and New York: Norton).

Bureau of Economic Analysis (U.S.), 1994, "Accounting for Mineral Resources: Issues and BEA's Initial Estimates," *Survey of Current Business*, April 1994.

Daly, Herman E., 1989, "Toward a Measure of Sustainable Social Net National Product," *Environmental Accounting for Sustainable Development*, ed. by Yusuf J. Ahmad, Salah El Serafy, and Ernst Lutz (Washington: World Bank).

de Haan, M., and Steven J. Keuning, 1995, "Taking the Environment Into Account," Paper submitted to the London Group meeting on "Natural Resource and Environmental Accounting" (Washington, D.C., March 15–17, 1995).

Food and Agriculture Organization of the United Nations (FAO), United Nations Fund for Population Activities (UNFPA), and International Institute for Applied Systems Analysis (IIASA), 1982, *Potential Population Supporting Capacities of Lands in the Developing World* (Rome: FAO).

Hicks, John R., 1946, *Value and Capital*, 2nd edition (Oxford: Oxford University Press).

Hill, P., and A. Harrison, 1995, "Accounting for Depletion in the 1993 SNA," unpublished paper submitted to the London Group meeting on "Natural Resource and Environmental Accounting" (Washington, D.C., March 15–17, 1995).

Leipert, Christian, 1989, "National Income and Economic Growth: the Conceptual Side of Defensive Expenditures," *Journal of Economic Issues*, Vol. 23, No. 3, pp. 843–56.

Munasinghe, Mohan, 1993, *Environmental Economics and Sustainable Development*, World Bank Environment Paper No. 3 (Washington: World Bank).

———, 1995, Oral statement to the London Group meeting on "Natural Resources and Environmental Accounting" (Washington, D.C., March 15–17, 1995).

Organization for Economic Cooperation and Development (OECD), 1973, *List of Social Concerns Common to Most OECD Countries* (Paris: OECD).

———, 1989, *Economic Instruments for Environmental Protection* (Paris: OECD).

Pearce, David W., Anil Markandya, and Edward B. Barbier, 1989, *Blueprint for a Green Economy* (London: Earthscan Publications).

Repetto, Robert C., 1994, "Discussant Remarks," in *Valuing the Environment*, Proceedings of the First Annual International Conference on Environmentally Sustainable Development, ed. by Ismael Serageldin and Andrew Steer (Washington: World Bank).

Schäfer, D., and C. Stahmer, 1989, "Input-Output Model for the Analysis of Environmental Protection Activities." *Economic Systems Research*, Vol. 1, No. 2, pp. 203–28.

Scientific Committee on Problems of the Environment (SCOPE), 1994, "Environmental indicators—A Draft Report by the Project on Indicators of Sustainable Development," unpublished.

Serageldin, Ismael, and Andrew Steer, 1994, "Epilogue: expanding the Capital Stock," in *Making Development Sustainable—From Concepts to Action*, ed. by Ismael Serageldin and Andrew Steer, Environmentally Sustainable Development Occasional Paper Series No. 2 (Washington: World Bank).

Solow, Robert, 1992, *An Almost Practical Step Toward Sustainability* (Washington: Resources for the Future).

United Nations, 1984, *A Framework for the Development of Environment Statistics* (E.84.XVII.12) (New York: United Nations).

———, 1993a, *System of National Accounts* (E.94.XVII.4) (New York: United Nations).

———, 1993b, *Integrated Environmental and Economic Accounting* (E.93.XVII.12) (New York: United Nations).

———, 1993c, *Report of the United Nations Conference on Environment and Development, Rio de Janeiro, 3–14 June 1992—Vol. I. Resolutions Adopted by the Conference* (E.93.I.8) (New York: United Nations).

———, 1995, "Information for Decision-Making and Earthwatch—Report of the Secretary-General" (doc. E/CN.17/1995/18, submitted to the third session of the UN Commission on Sustainable Development).

United Nations Development Program (UNDP), 1991, *Human Development Report* (New York and Oxford: Oxford University).

United Nations Environment Program (UNEP), 1992, *Saving our Planet—Challenges and Hopes* (Nairobi: UNDP).

van Tongeren, Jan, and others, 1991, *Integrated Environmental and Economic Accounting: A Case Study for Mexico,* Environment Working Paper No. 50 (Washington: World Bank).

van Tongeren, Jan, and B. Becker, 1994, "Integrated Satellite Accounting, Socio-economic Concerns and Modeling" (paper prepared for the Twenty-third General Conference of the International Association for Research in Income and Wealth, St. Andrews, Canada, August 21–27, 1994).

Vitousek, P.M., and others, 1986, "Human appropriation of the Products of Photosynthesis," *Bioscience,* Vol. 36, No. 6, pp. 368–73.

World Bank, 1995, *Monitoring Environmental Progress—A Report on Work in Progress* (March 1995 draft) (Washington: World Bank).

World Commission on Environment and Development (WCED), 1987, *Our Common Future* (Oxford: Oxford University).

7

National Accounts and the Environment

Adriaan M. Bloem and Ethan Weisman

The environment is generally accepted as an area of government and popular concern, and it is of great importance to have information on the environment properly reflected in statistics. While environmental statistics cover a broad range of topics and issues, this paper concentrates on economic aspects of environmental statistics. As economic activities, such as production and consumption, impact on the environment and the environment impacts on economic activities, it is important to link information on the environment with information on the economy.

The system of national accounts, one of the most powerful tools for economic analysis, is an eminent framework for reporting links between the environment and the economy. The *System of National Accounts 1993* (1993 SNA) argues that this should be developed from the central framework (through a system of satellite accounts) rather than changing or replacing the basic system. This paper studies alternative approaches and outlines some thoughts for the implementation of environmental accounting, given the status of the basic data and currently available methodologies.

Economic and environment-accounting issues concern the depletion of natural resources as well as the degradation of the environment. The

Note: Adriaan Bloem (Division Chief) and Ethan Weisman (Economist) are in the Real Sector Division of the IMF Statistics Department. The opinions expressed in this paper are those of the authors and not necessarily those of the IMF. The authors express their gratitude to Paul Cotterell, Michael Ward, and the other participants at the seminar for their useful comments. Of course, the authors are responsible for any errors that remain in the paper. Paul Cotterell presented this paper at the seminar.

two approaches to the development of a system of environmental satellite accounts are a physical and a monetary approach. Both approaches are based on physical data on the environment; but in the physical approach these data are linked to the national accounts, while in the monetary approach they are internalized in an accounting system through monetization. The basic thrust of the monetary approach is to monetize the depletion of natural resources and environmental degradation and to record these as costs. This does not seem viable in the short term, since valuation and other problems still need to be resolved before this approach can be successfully implemented. Nevertheless, a case could be made for improving the accounting of natural resource depletion within the core system. In the short term it would be more promising to link national accounts data with physical data on the environment through the accounts or in the framework of supply and use tables. Studies in the Netherlands, for example, demonstrate that environmental supply and use tables could be used to estimate levels of pollution associated with various levels of production.

The paper begins by outlining the main approaches to environmental accounting, assessing the relative merits and problems of each approach. The paper then discusses whether green national accounting should replace the traditional national accounts, or whether green accounts should be developed as a supplement to the system. Subsequently, the paper describes the practical experiences of two countries that have attempted to incorporate information on the environment in their national accounts. Based on these assessments, the paper concludes with suggestions for possible future actions and research regarding environmental accounting, including possibilities for practical statistical implementation.

Methods and Problems

Environmental Indicators and Statistics

Traditionally, environmental statistics have concentrated on the collection of physical data about a wide variety of environmental aspects of the quality of life, such as information on pollution levels and environmental degradation. Physical data on the quality of life also may concern the variety and viability of species, often indicated by the number of survivors of a threatened species. Welfare issues also have been raised regarding health, life expectancy, and poverty.

On the basis of these data, environmental indicators have been constructed ". . . to reduce a large quantity of data down to its simplest form, retaining essential meaning for the questions that are being asked of the data" (Ott, 1978). According to Tunstall (1979), environmental indicators can (1) assess environmental conditions and trends on a national, regional, and global scale; (2) compare countries and regions; (3) forecast and project trends; (4) provide early warning information; and (5) assess conditions in relation to goals and targets.

Although statistics on the environment have been collected for a long time (some countries began collecting these statistics in the 1970s) and have provided valuable insights into environmental problems, in the view of many people concerned with the progressive deterioration of the environment, they did not have a sufficient impact on public awareness and government policies because these statistics did not sufficiently demonstrate economic impacts. Answers to this problem have been sought through the development of sustainable growth indicators and green (or environmental) national accounts. This paper focuses on the latter.

Resource Depletion and Environmental Degradation

Analysis of environmental issues is often divided into natural resource depletion (using up oil, gas, minerals, fish, or forests) and environmental degradation (air, soil, and water pollution). Although all economies must confront both sets of issues, depletion of natural resources is often seen as a problem primarily for developing countries, while industrial countries tend to focus more attention on the impacts of pollution. Adjustments to national accounts for natural resource depletion are sometimes referred to as "green" national accounts, while national accounts adjusted for environmental degradation are sometimes referred to as "brown" national accounts. This paper will not pursue this distinction further, but will refer to both as "green" national accounts. The development of a system of integrated environmental and economic accounting will need to take both sets of issues into account. The approaches described below attempt to begin that process.

Two Approaches to Environmental Accounting: Physical and Monetary

A system of green accounts can be developed through a physical approach or a monetary approach. In the physical approach to green national accounting, physical data are linked to the national accounts, while the basic thrust of the monetary approach is to monetize environmental degradation and depletion of natural resources and record these as costs. Although this may seem obvious, it should be pointed out that both approaches need physical data on the environment.[1]

The importance that national accountants attach to environmental issues is illustrated by the fact that the most recent version of the globally accepted handbook on national accounts, the 1993 SNA,[2] includes a chapter, "Satellite Analysis and Accounts," describing a system of environmental economic accounts (SEEA) based to a large extent on *Integrated Environmental and Economic Accounting* (UN Handbook). The 1993 SNA describes both natural resource accounting, which focuses on physical aspects of the accounts, and monetary accounting, which identifies expenditures on environmental protection and the treatment of environmental costs. As noted in the 1993 SNA, this description is to be considered a work in progress.

Physical Approach

The 1993 SNA notes that substantial progress has been achieved in developing the physical approach to environmental accounts. The central framework of the national accounts already depicts aspects of environmental accounting. Nonproduced natural assets, which are under the effective control of institutional units and may be expected to yield benefits to their owners, are deemed economic assets and therefore are included within the boundary of the system of national accounts. However, the central framework does not include externalities concerned with the use of the environment. The core innovations of the approach taken in the 1993 SNA chapter that describes environmental accounting are additions of the "use of non-produced natural assets" and "other accumulation of non-produced natural assets." These extensions are needed to account fully for natural resource degradation, depletion, and transfer of natural assets to economic activities. Although natural assets that do not fulfill the criteria of ownership and economic benefits are excluded from the central framework, they can be included in environmental satellite accounts. Environmental degradation and depletion can be measured in physical and monetary terms, but the 1993 SNA admonishes readers to use extreme caution with the monetary ap-

---

[1]". . . physical data and accounts need to be established first. Monetary data could then be established as a second step" (United Nations, 1993, paragraph 390).

[2]The 1993 SNA has recently been published under the auspices of the IMF, the OECD, the United Nations, EUROSTAT (the statistical bureau of the European Union), and the World Bank.

proach, owing to the controversial nature of the valuation of environment costs and capital.

The inclusion of data on the environment, proposed in the 1993 SNA
chapter on environmental accounting, is developed mainly through matrices that show the traditional national accounts data on production
and consumption in combination with data on the use of natural resources. It has been argued that green national accounting should be
extended to include the full sequence of the national accounts in order
to demonstrate all effects of the use of the environment. The UN Handbook recognizes that "the use of environmental functions not only has
impacts on the production and use of goods and services but also affects
the income and accumulation accounts" (United Nations, 1993, paragraph 96), but it does not pursue this idea further.

The 1993 SNA and the UN Handbook mention the possibility of linking physical data on the environment to the national accounts through
input-output tables. The UN Handbook refers to the classic article by
Leontief (1970), but this possibility is not developed further in these
manuals. A type of input-output table particularly suited to linking production and consumption with environmental effects concerns supply
and use tables combining detail on products with detail on producers
(input-output tables usually focus either on products or on producers).
The rows of supply and use tables provide information on the supply of
goods and services through domestic production and imports, and the
use of those products through domestic consumption and exports; this
information can be supplemented with information on the pollution
that the production and use of those goods and services entails.
Likewise, through the columns of these tables that provide, inter alia,
information on the producing industries, pollution can be linked to
industries.

Supply and use tables are limited in the sense that they focus on production and consumption, but this approach can be further extended
through the use of social accounting matrices that provide a link to
other economic processes, such as the sectoral distribution of income,
saving, and capital formation. Further, through social accounting matrices the national accounts can be related to data relevant to welfare,
including data on employment, education, poverty, and health.

This approach could yield estimates concerning levels of pollution
corresponding with expected or projected levels of activity or use, or
vice versa, levels of activity corresponding with predetermined levels of
pollution. Through the use of scaling techniques, such as linear programming, this approach would also allow the estimation of sustainable
levels of economic activity and concomitant growth rates. Critics of
these methods have mentioned that this type of economic analysis goes

beyond pure statistics and involves economic modeling.[3] However, the use of these methods to depict the relationships between economic activities and the environment seems extremely relevant.

Monetary Approach

Historically, efforts to monetize the use of natural resources have been triggered primarily by the concern that national accounts aggregates, such as GDP, which are generally accepted indicators of economic growth, do not adequately reflect the effects of the environment on the economy. Even though, arguably, certain elements concerning the environment are already included in the national accounts (for example, costs to abate pollution are included that reflect taxes imposed on production or consumption causing pollution), it should be recognized that the national accounts currently do not include externalities associated with the use of the environment that in the view of many are far more significant than the environmental elements presently included. An important aspect of the monetary approach is that it could generate alternative measures of economic activity, such as "eco GDP" or "green GDP," that take into account environmental externalities and that could serve as indicators of sustainable growth.

The basic idea behind the monetary approach is that (presumably negative) externalities connected with the uses of natural resources may involve costs (just like the use of any other scarce resources), and that these costs should be internalized to facilitate a more balanced view of the economy and of economic development. From this perspective, market prices are misleading because they do not reflect these externalities. Therefore, the fundamental issue facing those attempting to implement this approach is the search for prices that accurately reflect these externalities.

The methods used to value these environmental externalities have included (1) the willingness-to-pay and other shadow prices, and (2) abatement, avoidance, defensive, maintenance, and other cost measures. Estimating shadow prices requires large amounts of data for the construction of marginal costs and marginal benefit curves. In addition, willingness-to-pay and other shadow prices have been controversial for conceptual reasons[4]

---

[3]In the UN Handbook the use of input-output techniques is contrasted to the SEEA, which "should avoid data that are the result of modeling" (United Nations, 1993, paragraph 302). However, this does not seem consistent with SEEA's commitment to monetization that, as will be discussed in the next subsection, also implies modeling.

[4]For instance, it can be debated whether the willingness-to-pay prices that individuals claim in surveys would be affected if these individuals actually faced these expenditure decisions in reality.

and also have turned out to be difficult to estimate. Shadow price estimates require behavioral assumptions and are sensitive to the selection of modeling techniques.

At present, the use of abatement or maintenance costs is advocated widely, especially in the context of the assessment of externalities through levels of pollution or other physical deterioration and environmental degradation. The underlying philosophy of the valuation approach through abatement costs parallels the Hicksian income concept, that is, a sustainable use of the environment implies that the quality of the environment should be the same at the end of the accounting period as it was at the beginning. Under this approach, deterioration of the environment should be valued at the cost of preventing or redeeming the deterioration. Although this method is concrete and practicable, as estimations of these costs can be derived from engineering projects, the required estimates are sensitive to the underlying assumptions. Further, these costs do not intrinsically relate to the quality of the environment and they may not correspond to the amount of damage incurred (substantial damage may be abated at little expense, while insignificant damage may require extensive outlays). Another objection concerns the validity of the growth rates derived from this method as indicators for sustainable growth. Because engineering costs can be expected to dwindle over time as a result of technological developments, corresponding abatement costs also will diminish. Thus, a deterioration in the environment can be masked by diminishing abatement costs.

The inclusion of externalities in the national accounts would change the emphasis of the national accounts from observed statistics to economic modeling. The 1993 SNA uses two kinds of output prices: basic prices and producer prices. Both are actual transaction prices, which can be directly observed and recorded (1993 SNA, paragraph 6.205). The prices used in the national accounts are mainly observed market prices irrespective of market structures; however, prices do not appear in the market for many of the items needed to determine values in a set of green (or brown) national accounts. It is at this point that producers of environmental accounts would need to make assumptions about market structures and competitive behavior. Because externalities, such as costs inflicted on other parties without compensation, are not reflected in economic transactions, their inclusion requires assumptions about economic behavior that are not based on observed facts.

The monetary approach to green national accounts is increasingly recognized as involving the distinction between observed statistical data and economic modeling. For instance, estimating green GDP through the deduction of abatement costs from traditional GDP introduces a departure from observed reality and is in fact a model exercise on the basis of assumed relations between variables. This recognition is important because observed statistics and model estimates differ with respect to their reliability.

Although the assumptions of green GDP models have not been spelled out, one apparent implicit assumption is that the inclusion of environmental costs would not invoke a reaction from the economic actors. Critics have pointed out that this is not a realistic assumption, since both producers and consumers are likely to change their behavior if either bears abatement costs. This would probably affect production, consumption, and other economic processes, such as income distribution and saving.

A much less contested aspect of the inclusion of abatement costs in the national accounts is the inclusion of the depletion of natural assets (Levin, 1993). It has been argued for countries with production processes that are largely dependent on the depletion of subsoil assets, such as oil, gas, or coal, that the use of these assets has not been well described previously by the traditional national accounts, which did not recognize this nonproduced wealth as an economic good. The 1993 SNA recognizes that these nonproduced goods are economic assets because they can be subject to ownership and provide benefits to their owners, but does not include the use of these assets in the description of the production process in the core accounts. At present national accountants tend to recognize this as a deficiency, and it is argued that the 1993 SNA should be revised accordingly. However, a consensus has yet to be reached on whether the depletion of natural resources should be recorded as a depletion of capital (which would leave GDP unaffected) or as a use of stocks (which would affect both gross and net aggregates).[5] Furthermore, it should be decided how the depletion should be valued; alternatives include (1) valuation on the basis of actual market prices of the assets, (2) valuation of the present discounted value of expected net proceeds, and (3) valuation on the basis of net prices that reflect actual market prices of the raw products, exploitation costs, and a rate of return on invested produced capital.

---

[5]Adherents of recording the depletion of natural resources as depreciation of capital point to the vast resources that are used over an extensive time period, while proponents of recording depletion as a use of stocks point out that the natural resources are actually used up while a capital good should, through maintenance, stay intact during its lifetime apart from normal wear (see El Serafy, 1991a).

Environmental National Accounting: Supplement or Substitute?

Whether environmental accounting should be seen as a supplement to the central framework of the national accounts or should replace the traditional national accounts altogether is hotly debated. Since the physical approach to national accounting does not provide monetary values, this debate primarily concerns the monetary approach to environmental accounting. For instance, a brochure circulated ahead of a conference on environmental accounting, hosted by the European Union Parliament in Brussels during May 31–June 1, 1995, strongly indicated a preference by the organizers to replace the traditional national accounts through a "global adoption of Green Accounting." Although many national accountants, to a greater or lesser degree, recognize the validity of the environment-based critiques and embrace the development of green national accounts, they prefer to see this development as a supplement to the core national accounts through the satellite accounts rather than as a substitute.

This preference for green accounting as a supplement rather than a substitute is reflected in the 1993 SNA and the UN Handbook. The 1993 SNA proposes the development of environmental accounts as a satellite system linked to the core national accounts; and the UN Handbook mentions as its immediate objective "to provide a framework for implementing an SNA (satellite) system for integrated environmental and economic accounting (SEEA). . . ." Neither the 1993 SNA chapter on environmental accounting nor the UN Handbook would provide a sufficiently comprehensive framework to allow replacement of the traditional national accounts. As has been mentioned above, both the 1993 SNA chapter on environmental accounting and the UN Handbook relate to aspects of production and consumption and do not comprise a full system of accounts, which would include financial accounts, transactions with the rest of the world, and balance sheets.

This preference for a satellite SEEA linked to the traditional national accounts is caused by problems with green accounting (as noted above) and also by the nature and use of traditional national accounts. Although the national accounts constitute a multipurpose system, it would be impossible to create a system to respond to all demands concerning national accounting; answering demands from specific users would frustrate other users. For instance, the national accounts' focus on observed data, mainly based on market values or costs, impedes their use for analyses of welfare issues, such as distribution of wealth, income, and labor. Similarly, this focus impedes the inclusion of nonmonetary market activities, such as unpaid household activities, voluntary services, and externalities. On the contrary, inclusion of these aspects would hamper many traditional uses of the national accounts, such as economic forecasting, and the development and monitoring of economic policies. For example, the inclusion in the national accounts of unpaid household activities would hamper the use of GDP as a denominator for important financial and fiscal indicators, such as measures of liquidity and the government budget deficit. Since these indicators are of a purely monetary nature, they could not be related sensibly to a denominator including substantive nonmonetary elements.[6]

For these reasons, it has been argued that although the traditional national accounts may be deficient in some respects, they are too important to be abolished or replaced. Metaphorically, physicians use body temperature as an indicator of a patient's health. Even though they know that this does not provide the whole picture, they do not want to throw away the thermometer.

This preference for a satellite account approach is recognized on a political level, as indicated by a 1994 communication from the Commission of the European Communities to the Council of the European Parliament stating that further integration of economic and environmental information systems aimed at "greening" national accounts following the satellite approach should be intensified.

Practical Experience

The United States and the Netherlands have made significant efforts to incorporate environmental links to their national accounts.[7] Both countries have taken the recommendations of the 1993 SNA as a point of departure. They have not altered the central framework of the national accounts, but have developed satellite accounts to show the connections between the national economy and the environment.

---

[6]Another problem with inclusion of nonmonetary elements is that they elude measurement (in part because they are not reflected in actual prices). Currently, the national accounts include some nonmonetary elements, such as owner-occupied housing and food production for own consumption; however, in most countries these elements are not large enough to disturb the use of national accounts data for economic policymaking. On the other hand, inclusion of elements such as unpaid household labor would change the national accounts aggregates substantially. For instance, a 1992 study by Kazemier and Exel for the Netherlands indicated that, if unpaid household labor would be valued at a minimum wage level, equivalent GDP would be 25 percent higher than standard GDP.

[7]Norway also provides some interesting lessons. Interested readers may wish to consult the papers and references contained in this volume.

United States

In 1992 the U.S. Bureau of Economic Analysis (BEA), Department of Commerce, began its work on natural resource satellite accounts and accelerated this project following President Clinton's 1993 Earth Day address making work on developing a "green GDP" a priority. In May 1994 the BEA released results of their efforts to develop integrated economic and environmental satellite accounts, in which mineral resources were treated as productive assets. This work builds on and complements the BEA's national accounts and is designed to highlight the interaction of the economy and the environment. The BEA also has formulated plans to extend this work to fish stocks and forests; however, budgetary constraints have prevented further work in this area.

The BEA study covering 1958–91 included oil, gas, coal, metals, and other minerals. The study applied four alternative valuation methods, and two of these applied different present discount values of 3 percent and 10 percent, respectively. To illustrate the economic importance of mineral resources, the BEA's analysis revealed the following. First, that "proved" mineral reserves added up to 3–7 percent of private capital stock in the national economy. Second, the 1991 value of the stock of proved subsoil mineral resources was approximately equal to two to four times the mining industry's stock of structures, equipment, and inventories. Third, average rates of return in the mining industry were lower when resource depletion and additions to income and production were taken into account. For the study period, 1958–91, the industry rate of return was only 4–5 percent, in contrast to the roughly 23 percent before the impacts on mineral resources were included in the national accounts. Fourth and perhaps most important, in constant 1987 dollars, additions to mineral resources as productive capital roughly offset depletions, leading to a negligible impact on net domestic product.

The Netherlands

Statistics Netherlands has produced and published a National Accounts Matrix extended with Environmental Accounts in physical units (NAMEA) for each year covering 1989–91. The NAMEAs identify, for each economic activity, an overview of related pollutants, such as carbon dioxide, CFCs, nitrogen oxide, ammonia, and phosphorus. Subsequently, these pollutants were grouped according to the environmental problems with which they were associated. Based on the contributions of the pollutants to each problem, five summary environmental indicators were estimated. Both the environmental indicators and traditional economic indicators were included in one information system. One of the advantages of this satellite system and the available time series is that (ex-ante and ex-post) forecasting and policy-based models can be developed using this information to estimate green GDP (through scaling techniques such as linear programming), as well as to estimate social indicators. Communication by the Commission of the European Communities to the Council of the European Parliament in December 1994 proposed to establish a European System of Economic Environmental Indices based on work similar to the NAMEAs.

Conclusions

The statistical coverage of environmental concerns in a national accounts framework commands widespread support, primarily because this would further public awareness and benefit the development and the monitoring of environmental policies. Several approaches, each having its merits and limitations, have been applied to achieve improved coverage. Among statisticians, and certainly among national accountants, it is generally recognized that whatever approach is taken, coverage of the environment in a national accounts context should be provided through the development of satellite systems linked to the national accounts, and not through a replacement of the national accounts.

Concerning the relative merits of the physical and monetary approach to national accounting, the debate should continue, and it seems useful to develop both approaches further. Although statistical considerations have to play a prominent role in this debate, it is of great importance also to take a user-oriented perspective. An important element in this respect is to determine how to further public awareness and environmental policies in an optimal manner. A single macroeconomic indicator such as green GDP may well serve to promote general awareness concerning the environment, but is less useful for the development and the monitoring of specific environmental policies. To serve the latter objective, environmental statistics need to be linked to the national accounts on a detailed level. It might be useful also to develop a range of relevant national indicators.

Both the physical and the monetary approach require further development. Concerning statistical implementation, whatever approach is used to link environmental statistics to the national accounts, there is a primary need for physical data on the environment. All applications of the physical and monetary approaches need these data. The development of environmental statistics clearly should precede coverage of the environment in the national accounts. Developing standards in this area also is an issue for international coordination, but decisions on the relevance of various environmental concerns will have to be made at the national level.

The physical approach is much less fraught with theoretical problems than the monetary approach. Techniques such as input-output analyses and linear programming are well developed. This is not to argue that these techniques are not amenable to further development, but there is a well-established framework for data presentation and manipulation, and no valuation of externalities is needed. The main problem facing the physical approach seems the availability of the basic data to develop supply and use tables. Many countries find it difficult to implement these tables in view of resource constraints and the lack of sufficiently detailed source data.

To further develop applications of the monetary approach, clearly more theoretical work has to be done on improving valuation techniques; eventually a global consensus should be sought on this issue to ensure the international comparability of the national statistics. However, this is not only a matter of developing theoretical concepts, but also of collecting data and building up experience with the use of these data in a national accounts framework. Although it is encouraging that practical experience has already been gained in a number of countries, these experiences also demonstrate that there still is more work to be done to achieve reliable results.

References

Aaheim, Asbjørn, and Karine Nyborg, March 1995, "On the Interpretation and Applicability of a 'Green National Product'," *Review of Income and Wealth*, Series 41, Number 1, pp. 57–71.

Ahmad, Yusuf J., Salah El Serafy, and Ernst Lutz (eds.), 1989, *Environmental Accounting for Sustainable Development: A UNEP-World Bank Symposium* (Washington: World Bank).

Bureau of Economic Analysis, "Integrated Economic and Environmental Satellite Accounts," *United States Department of Commerce News*, May 10, 1994.

El Serafy, Salah, 1991a, "Depletable Resources: Fixed Capital or Inventories?" unpublished, Special Conference of the International Association of Research in Income and Wealth on Environmental Accounting, Baden, Austria, May 27–31.

―――――, 1991b, "Natural Resource Accounting: An Overview," *The Environmental Challenge* (London: Overseas Development Institute), pp. 205–19.

Institut Français de l'Environnement, 1995, "Physical Environmental Accounting: Land Use/Land Cover, Nutrients, and the Environment" (Orleans, France: IFEN).

IMF, OECD, UN, EEC, and IBRD, 1993, *System of National Accounts 1993* (1993 SNA) (New York: United Nations).

Kazemier, Brugt, and Janet Exel, 1992, "The Allocation of Time in the Netherlands in the Context of the SNA: A Module," *National Accounts Occasional Papers*, NA–052 (Amsterdam: Netherlands Central Bureau of Statistics).

Keuning, Steven J., 1995, "Environmental Accounting in the Netherlands," *SNA News and Notes*, Issue 1 (New York: United Nations).

Landefeld, J. Steven, 1995, "Implementation of the 1993 SNA in the United States," *SNA News and Notes*, Issue 1 (New York: United Nations).

Leontief, Wassily W., 1970, "Environmental Repercussions and Economic Structure: An Input-Output Approach," *Review of Economics and Statistics*, Vol. 52, pp. 262–71.

Levin, Jonathan, 1993, "An Analytical Framework of Environmental Issues," IMF Working Paper 93/53 (Washington: International Monetary Fund).

———, 1991, "Valuation and Treatment of Depletable Resources in the National Accounts," IMF Working Paper 91/73 (Washington: International Monetary Fund).

Lutz, Ernst (ed.), 1993, *Toward Improved Accounting for the Environment: A UNSTAT-World Bank Symposium* (Washington: World Bank).

Ott, Wayne, 1978, *Environmental Indices: Theory and Practice* (Ann Arbor, Michigan: Ann Arbor Science).

Rutledge, Gary L., and Christine R. Vogan, May 1994, "Pollution Abatement and Control Expenditures, 1972–92," *Survey of Current Business*, pp. 36–49.

Tunstall, Daniel B., 1979, "Developing Indicators of Economic Quality: The Experience of the Council on Environmental Quality," *Social Indicators Research*, Vol. 6, pp. 301–47.

United Nations (UN Handbook), 1993, *Integrated Environmental and Economic Accounting: A United Nations Handbook of National Accounting*, interim version, Series F, No. 61 (New York: United Nations).

van den Born, G.J., and others, December 1993, "An Overview of Environmental Indicators: State of the Art and Perspectives," unpublished, National Institute of Public Health and Environmental Protection, Bilthoven, the Netherlands, in cooperation with Cambridge University.

Discussion

Discussant's Comments

Michael Ward

As befits someone who has served longer in the trenches of environmental accounting than almost anyone else, Peter Bartelmus, with his customary eloquence and erudition, discusses in his paper the issues and problems the approach to integrated environmental and economic accounting raises from a conceptual and generic perspective. But for reasons that become apparent in the detailed thread of his argument—to which I will refer later—his finely tempered enthusiasm does not quite border on an unrestrained exuberance for a fully integrated and comprehensive environmental accounting system. As nobody's trencherman, Peter also raises a number of pertinent practical questions concerning the relevance of the primary direction of this approach.

The paper by Bloem and Weisman, as might be expected from such a strong policy-oriented institution as the Fund, is more pragmatic. It focuses on some of the more intractable and systemic measurement concerns. The authors question implicitly the relevance of environmental accounting to fiscal and monetary management and overall macroeconomics strategy. Understandably, they see the need to preserve the integrity of GNP within existing SNA concepts, assigning environmental questions to the realms of a statistical hyperspace inhabited by freely orbiting satellite accounts. The essential difference between "integrated," on the one hand, and "national accounts and (separately) the environment," on the other, emerges very clearly.

I approach this subject from both a conceptual and practical point of view, recognizing in the process that the protagonists for different positions must tread delicately over a path strewn with institutional eggshells. Were it possible by common agreement to marshall all the resources of statistical alchemy and illusionism on this fascinating topic, it would still be doubtful whether the numerologists could convincingly demonstrate the superior power of statistics over environmental phenomena, at least in improving official understanding of how every development strategy gives rise to a different environmental issue.

Note: The discussion was chaired and moderated by Mohamed El-Erian.

With comparatively little fanfare, economists have been able to establish themselves as the new, self-appointed global guardians of green living. As well-trained bloodhounds, with good noses for sniffing out anything that smacks of a resource utilization or allocation issue, they have been able to highjack the environment and redefine popular basic concern within the acclaimed paradigm of sustainability. Now, while this may seem eminently sensible from the standpoint of macroeconomic policy and the Bretton Woods Institutions, it does tend to narrow down the scope of the issue from its original broader public perspective. It may be recalled that public awareness of the environment came first to general attention through a justifiable genuine concern with a perceived decline in the overall quality of life. Worries about global warming, pollution, and environmental degradation, especially as these have impacted on the survival of natural species and affected human well-being, have been far more to the forefront than sustainability per se.

Bringing environmental concerns into an economic context, nevertheless, does recognize that many present problems encountered by policymakers find their roots in a past "hands off" attitude that implicitly condoned the unbridled pursuit of economic gain. This approach prevailed despite the fact it could lead visibly to the deterioration of resources through excessive exploitation and thus result in the eventual depletion of limited exhaustible and nonrenewable natural resources previously thought of as being abundantly available and hence free. Peter Bartelmus understandably remains uncomfortable with this paradigmatic shift to sustainability, referring to the notion as opaque and murky. He underlines the fact that sustainable development stresses the importance of economic activities over human beings and the natural environment. Consequently, he seriously questions whether the sustainability of production is an acceptable proxy for sustainable human well-being. In noting that the capabilities of integrated environmental-economic accounting are currently limited, one has a clearer sense of his preference for pursuing a stress-response approach to an analysis of these complex issues that refer to concerns beyond economic performance and growth. He shows, however, that integrated accounting is capable of capturing direct environment-economy interactions in stress-response terms, facilitating a link-up with broader indicators of sustainable development.

Once the principle is accepted and the issue is established as an essentially economic lacuna, however, the task of the statistician is to determine the appropriate analytical structure (and related empirical framework) to be mapped onto the conceptual or theoretical model. From the outset it is also necessary to identify the value set for which that data structure is valid. The compilation of a relevant value set involves the careful selection of the pertinent quantities to be incorpo-rated into the analytical structure and the assignment of applicable prices by which to weigh their relative significance. While there has been considerable convergence in recent years as to what quantities are relevant to an assessment of environmental change, there has been much less agreement on the choice of prices to apply. The basic problem, of course, is that the fundamental price structure underlying the conceptual coherence of the system of national accounts—which deals predominantly with current value flows—is not the same as that which is relevant to an evaluation of environmental conditions because the latter attaches overriding significance to the importance of stocks and future reserves of natural capital. A variety of approaches have been suggested, such as shadow prices, willingness to pay (effectively shadow prices), avoidance costs, defensive costs, abatement costs, and maintenance costs, each of which stresses a somewhat different princi-ple. All valuations, however, are answers to different questions and each of the above contingent valuations suffers from some sort of drawback as a measure of environmental cost in *maintaining human wel-fare intact.*

Traditionally, environmental statistics have focused on the compila-tion of physical data. Investigators have tended to concentrate on the primacy of resource depletion concerns and have carried out assess-ments of the direct and indirect physical impacts of environmental degradation, perhaps to the exclusion of gaining a fuller understanding of the underlying factors that influenced such activities in the first place. The greatest attention therefore has been paid to the use, pre-dominantly in the economic production of material goods and services, of nonproduced natural assets, most of which can be classified as scarce because they are nonrenewable and hence exhaustible. Using up these resources has had very clear *direct,* but sometimes less obvious *indirect,* effects on the environment and on the economy. More recently, re-searchers have been examining some of these issues through evalua-tions of the impact of production activity itself on the environment in respect of residual output, polluting effluents, waste generation, and energy losses. Approximate emissions coefficients and elasticities have been calculated in relation to different industrial sector outputs. David Wheeler's work in the World Bank on constructing matrices of pollu-tants, effluents, and emissions associated with different forms of indus-trial output has been a pioneering effort in this regard. But perhaps the real question is how to link such emissions and unwelcome subsidiary output to the nature of the technology in use. Even dirty industrial ac-tivities like coal burning, as the Swedes have shown, can be turned into relatively clean activities.

There are in addition other "nonbenign" physical environmental impacts arising from development and production activity such as the construction of dams, roads, street lighting, and office blocks, which give rise not so much to pollution and ongoing waste disposal problems, but to other ecological and environmental changes that may impose costs on society. In this area, as elsewhere, the devil lies in the details, lending added emphasis to the need to pay close attention to sectoral data and keep track of the microeconomic policy decisions.

The question of how to identify the appropriate physical components of environmental change, however, is overshadowed by the valuation problem. Since the pricing issue is widely debated and well known (although the solution remains elusive), I will simply and briefly refer to some of the *major concerns.*

Overall Price Structure and SNA

The monetary value of the various components of the SNA is predicated on the assumption that the aggregates and their magnitude are the outcome of the operation of market forces and that individual component prices reflect relative scarcities in both the product and factor markets. But, even in the details of the SNA, most of the flows measured represent a consolidation of activities transacted under different price regimes and market interventions. In the national accounts, the self-selecting common numéraire to integrate quantities is (internal) market prices. In theory, prices (or average revenues) are related to a level of output where marginal revenues are equated with marginal costs. This represents the point at which, if marginal costs are rising, prices properly reflect relative scarcities in a fully informed, open, unregulated economic system. Prices therefore provide reliable and effective signals for efficient current resource allocation decisions and transactions. Unfortunately, when people rely on the efficient operation of the invisible hand in economics they rarely question whether it reflects a strong right hand wielded by zealots of a new American conservatism or the more malleable left hand of a revisionist British socialism. Nor indeed do they notice whether any fingers are missing on account of ill-considered interventions by well-meaning public officials intent on donating subsidies or other forms of support to their political constituents. Only rarely do policymakers search deeper and look at the underlying distribution of wealth, income, and power that helps determine the price structure, or acknowledge intergenerational factors shaping economic and social policy. Certainly, neo-Ricardians—with a Sraffian perspective of production in an environmental context—would have some difficulty in agreeing on the formation of appropriate prices in a nonmechanistic system.

Environmental versus Economic-Policy Boundaries

While in principle national economic policies are bounded within each respective country's political territory, the impact of those policies and more general environmental effects are frequently felt outside. In transcending national boundaries, such factors cause shifts in relative values (and costs) as well as changes in prices. The example of extensive logging and consequent deforestation by one country, with its widespread ecological implications for neighboring countries, is especially relevant in this context. ·

Price Levels and Relative Prices

Recent research on international comparisons of output and expenditure, involving the calculation of overall and sectoral level purchasing power parities, demonstrates that clear and significant differences exist between countries not only in absolute price levels but also in their respective structures of relative prices. This makes it difficult to view various environmental trade-offs in a more scientific, institutionally independent, and structurally detached conceptual manner. What is perhaps more important, the variability in prices across countries at different stages of economic development underlines critical differences in the relative importance attached to the environment by the rich and the poor. The lower price levels in low-income countries demonstrate clearly why the poor are prepared to ignore environmental costs and to take the benefits of economic activity upfront. They would clearly prefer to draw on their private gains now rather than hold on for the prospect of some better collective world in the future, even when firms are forced to internalize their costs according to an existing price structure.

Sector-Specific Issues

In most countries, and particularly the resource-rich developing countries, the all-important production activity of resource extraction is not conducted by industries readily characterized by a large number of well-informed small firms openly competing with each other. In this market, the organizing hand is not only invisible, it is also far from transparent. Attaching values to the use of resources (or reserves) in this context, where the dominant firm may also be a key corporate player in an international market already subject to oligopolistic forces, may make little sense and not lead to optimal resource allocations, whatever time dimension is under consideration.

Internalized Cost

Price structures are a reflection of power systems as well as power systems in their own right. If current price structures, which do not take into account future losses and changes in the relative scarcities of available resources, are not somehow adjusted to reflect the true full costs of present economic activity, the use of those resources will remain suboptimal. A more realistic price structure that can reflect better the time dimension of productive activity would encompass prices more closely representing the present discounted flow of future income earnings from resource use, that is, if available resources are used up very rapidly now, their prices would be much higher in the future, making present prices appear far too cheap.

For these and other reasons, as well as in the physical environmental context, it is important not to view the market simply as an excuse for allowing governments to abdicate the responsibility accorded to them by popular mandate. Governments need to be concerned with ensuring a safe and comfortable future for all citizens, particularly the poor and weak, who have little economic voice. The government needs to intervene in the market because it has a clear responsibility to take into account the wider social and collective costs (which the government itself must usually meet out of taxpayers' funds) to try and ensure, for public benefit, that existing prices reflect all costs of economic production.

These problems of quantification and the basic values attached to the numbers have led some to argue that the transient quality of human life and the impermanence of the world dominion cannot be properly captured within all-embracing statistical artifacts that do not intrinsically possess a common underlying value system. But a tentative path from craft and magical sleights of hand to more generally accepted and authentic environmental economic framework has been carved out by a few statistical Merlins assisted by pragmatic empiricists and other more adventurous numerologists (sometimes in admittedly rather free-form carnivalesque constructions). These models now need to be endorsed not only by the scientific virtuosi, but also by the policy gurus and cognoscenti in applied operational use.

For the present, however, the policy practitioners in the international agencies and at the country level have been unable to reach a firm decision on the need for environmental accounting and its analytical use.

There is consequently a need to break the present logjam of methodological debate. The question of whether governments should go for an environmentally adjusted set of national accounts (as Bartelmus recommends) or live with a satellite system in juxtaposition with the conventional national accounts (as Bloem and Weisman suggest) is more of a "horses for courses" problem than a "one-zero" acceptance/rejection issue. There is even room to settle astride a suitable saddle. Clearly, many key environmental issues with a large social payoff in low-income countries can be taken upfront without any strict accounting framework or huge outlays in cost. These issues include the provision of, and access to, safe water, efficient solid waste disposal, and clean sanitation. In 19th century Europe, irrespective of whether policymakers were humanitarians or utilitarians, such environmental requirements were considered basic rights, fundamental to human needs. Their provisions was part of the social overhead cost of building a more cohesive and civilized society.

In terms of action by the international financial institutions, the present position would argue forcibly for the adoption of an essential practical initiative on the part of the World Bank to select perhaps as many as a dozen developing countries where prima facie environmental issues seem important, and seize on the "big ticket" items of resource depletion and ecological deterioration to assess their significance for future development. This would be in preference to trying to take a more comprehensive (but still incomplete) view of the environment as has been attempted in the United States and Norway. But the key is to strengthen individual countries' own capacity to carry out such adjustments to their standard accounts on a regular basis.

For the Fund, ongoing concerns with the impact of structural adjustment programs with their emphasis on output growth (and hence more extensive input use) and the need for sound and sustainable macroeconomic policies will remain of overriding interest. But a more holistic view of development, guided by environmental accounts, could open up the possibility of a review of where so-called green taxes could be applied in certain sectors to achieve a more balanced and rational pattern of progress.

Other Discussion

Mohamed El-Erian: It is clear from just listening to the two papers that we should go quickly to the world of second best and try to come up with some views as how best to approximate, to use Michael Ward's words, an appropriate methodology, an appropriate implementation strategy, and derivation of appropriate policy implications.

Salah El Serafy: I have worked for a long time trying to get economists to appreciate the fact that the economic aggregates being measured may not be the right ones. Environmental changes that are actually marketable and that have prices should be integrated in the national economic accounting system. One can draw a comparison between integrating the environment in the national accounts and Pigou's approach to economic welfare. Pigou realized that economic welfare is only part of human welfare and that economists can deal with only those aspects that can be measured by money. Hence, the economist's function differs from the environmentalist's function, and I would like to particularly see an improvement in the way we look at economies that depend fundamentally on natural resources.

The new SNA and its extension to satellite accounts are perhaps the proper way to proceed, and as Michael Ward has rightly said, putting a value on the stock and adding it to national income may not be the best way of approaching the environmental change. I continue to believe that it is idiotic to think that when you discover some oil, you add it to national income, and then when you have extracted the oil, no change should take place in the economy. It is well known that the U.S. administration was very sympathetic to having green accounts, but has given up the initiative because of the controversies they caused.

I do not blame the revised UN national accounting system, which is essentially a compromise, under which, when new mineral finds are discovered, they can be allocated to some mysterious reconciliation account (which is devoid of significance). I believe that we need six months to a year to discuss the various methodologies, and I am delighted that the IMF has brought experts together to start a constructive discussion.

Knut Alfsen: There are many ways of valuing environmental resources and natural resources. No system can give all the answers. So, one should keep in mind the sort of questions one wants to address. The development of national accounts or of integrated national accounts should all be demand driven: one must focus on the questions the politicians and the decision-makers really want to address. From that, one should be able to fashion the sort of tools one needs, the sort of models or other analytical techniques one needs, and it is from these that one should be able to derive the sort of data one needs. So, the determination of statistics and the data is really the very last step in this process, and one should not start a discussion by focusing on the data.

Ian Johnson: As to the shadow prices of exhaustible resources, the methodological hurdles are not so great, and we really could do a much better job of coming up with economic costs and associating them with a depletion premium. The problem, I suspect, lies in the political consequences of looking at exhaustible resources and asking the authorities to charge shadow prices reflecting the true economic costs of, say, water. That is going to be a bigger hurdle than the methodological one.

Mohamed El-Erian: It seems to me that our speakers need to address four general questions. The first question relates to the value of the selective approach that says, "Let's be selective, especially where it matters." Second, should we rely on demand-driven effort for data generation? Third, is the binding constraint methodological or does it have political implications? Fourth, are the SNA satellite accounts the right way to approach the issue?

Responses

Peter Bartelmus: Let me start with the first question. The selective approach is selective in the sense that we focus on the most important issues in, say, green accounting. I believe it is not a correct approach. When we at the United Nations did our country projects, we had many surprises. Things that looked irrelevant in physical terms became very relevant in monetary terms. And even things we suspected were irrelevant in physical terms became, after some research, relevant. We should not simply do things because in the first meeting a few experts said this was important and that was not important. Of course, we have to be selective in terms of countries, and Michael Ward was correct on this.

The demand-driven effort would be the ideal approach, but the problem is that the demanders are usually inarticulate. They cannot say what they really want, especially in relation to a complex subject such as integrated accounting. Furthermore, if we permit people to ask questions, they will surely come up with very many questions that can become a clear impediment to standardization. I believe we must aim at standardization.

As to the satellite approach, except for the extreme green and the extreme brown people, I believe there is a consensus that parallel systems should be developed. Conventional economic accounts serve the medium- and short-term purposes of measurement of economic performance and they do it rather well, so one need not overburden them with controversial valuation and estimation methods. So, for the time being, the consensus is to let the two systems, environmentally adjusted national accounts and conventional national accounts, answer somewhat different questions—one long term and the other short term, one focused on environment-economy integration, and the other on the whole range of macroeconomic policies.

To provide Salah El Serafy the rationale for the reconciliation accounts, a number of impacts on the environment and on natural resources are not based on economic rationales and economic decisions, such as effects of natural disasters, natural growth of resources, and replenishments in the wilderness. Their discovery is something quite different from the creation of these resources. They are not produced. This is why noneconomic activities that affect natural resources have been separated from other activities that are part of the economic decision-making process. And they are put along with other volume changes, not reconciliation accounts (that's a new terminology).

Paul Cotterell: We would agree that there is a strong case for selective approach in terms of the countries as well as the timetable of all the issues that one needs to address. We cannot address everything at once—issues such as resource depletion should be dealt with first—and on a priority basis. The Fund position on a satellite approach is quite clear from the paper.

As regards the question of being demand driven. While we all agree with it, the problem with national accounts is that a variety of users have a variety of needs, which we cannot meet all at once. This is part of the reason, and Peter Bartelmus has already said so, that a satellite approach is needed as an adjunct. There are obviously a number of methodological and practical issues that we do need to work on, but that should not stop us from progressing as well as we can with the available data and available understandings.

On reconciliation accounts, I find the comment by Salah El Serafy a little amusing, because if you do not put the new discoveries into reconciliation accounts, and you do not put them in income and production accounts, where do you put them? Not all reconciliation comes from the transactions and flows in the core of the accounts. Some comes from other sources. One of the reasons for not wanting to put the addition to natural resources into income, it seems to me, is that it is in reconciliation. There may be a better way of doing this in terms of the satellite accounting for the environment, but I do not quite know yet what it is, and this issue, I think, needs some further work.

David Reed: It is only appropriate as we move to the closing sessions of the seminar that we give our attention to how to push ahead in this area. In the Bloem-Weisman paper there is a reference to a conference that is being organized by the European Parliament. In fact, it is being organized by World Wildlife Federation, and is cosponsored by the European Parliament, European Commission, and the Club of Rome. I would like to point out that a similar conference will be held in Washington at the beginning of October 1995, and its focus will not be on EUROSTAT/European community per se, but rather on international financial institutions, the Bank, the Fund, and United Nations agencies.

The conference will cover a period of reflection, as Salah El Serafy has suggested, there will be a selection of 10 to 12 countries in a pilot phase, as Michael Ward has suggested, and there will be application of various methods included in the SEEA to those pilot countries; an assessment, derivation, and conclusions from those experiences; and a proposal of a more ambitious implementation plan. I am glad to say that the response from the Bank has been positive and negotiations are moving forward. I hope that the response from the Fund will also be positive.

Further Discussion

Naheed Kirmani: I am interested in knowing how Fund economists going out in the field, having to do their balance of payments analysis, and trying to churn out medium-term scenarios, can use the discussion on green accounting. Forgetting about all the controversies on methods and statistics, supposing the statisticians gave us a perfectly agreed set of national accounts, where environment was fully taken into account, would it really make a fundamental difference in the aggregate advice that the Fund would give or the components of that advice? For example, would we, having the new set of data, be in a position to advise a country to appreciate or depreciate its currency? Similarly, would the advice on the components be any different? Would we be advising the country to expand its budget or follow a contractionary policy? This is the sort of practical question that would help the economists in the Fund to realize exactly what the implications of green national accounts are.

Salah El Serafy: Perhaps I can attempt to answer this question. Given our state of knowledge, the satellite accounts are the proper place where we should attempt to make the adjustments, because it hurts to use the economic accounts, since the economic accounts are wrong! When Peter Bartelmus tells us, that we should be happy with the conventional calculations of GDP, I think it is wrong. The GDP is based on the fundamental concept of value added, and selling assets, as some countries do, does not create value. The method is thus wrong, totally, conceptually, and practically. And then, not only is GDP wrong, the saving is wrong (as David Pearce said earlier), the investment is wrong, the current account of the balance of payments is wrong, and all these clever calculations about the incremental capital-output ratio are wrong. We cannot get a good measure of whether a country is growing or is simply selling its assets. When a country is selling its timber, or selling its petroleum and mineral resources and overfishing its stock, to say that it is growing is wrong.

Kirit Parikh: I might be echoing what others have said. I am still not clear in my own mind the direction in which we should proceed to develop our estimates. I do recall, following the Pigouvian tradition, that Samuelson, in one of his articles, mentioned that an indicator useful in a production sense would not be useful in a value sense. So, in terms of future development (i.e., where we should be going in terms of our estimates?), I would like to know what direction we should follow. Are we going to attempt to develop value indicators or are we going to develop production indicators?

Michael Ward: I really have only two comments to make. First, on reconciliation accounts, the rationale, of course, is that we simply need a catch-all, jumbled-up residual, which it is. The degrees of freedom in the reconciliation accounts in the SNA, of both the quantities and the prices, are so wide that I do not think you can really make head or tail of them. In theory, you can, but my suspicions are that nobody is going to calculate them.

On valuation of assets, the separation between asset change and the price change, I think, is going to be very difficult. In relation to this, and coming back to the point about shadow prices, what concerns me most is that you have a structure of market prices (internal domestic prices), which in some sense are not the valid prices. If you think of prices as the present value of some future discounted income stream, you have to think of them in a broader sense than the purely domestic economy, because environmental issues are much broader than the context of the specific economy, or at least some of them are.

On the specific point made about Fund policies, I detect a conscious and commendable attempt during the last few years to rethink Fund strategy on fiscal policy and its impact on poverty and its fiscal policy advice and its impact on environmental concerns. The two are closely interlinked.

We heard arguments from Gandhi, McMorran, and Hansen this morning that economic growth and economic stability are key to improving the environment. These arguments were persuasive because they also addressed policy failures and the issues of the generation of material well-being. But my problem is that if your structure of prices reflects a given pattern of purchasing powers in an economy, and growth is a reflection of rates of return on capital and rates of return on labor, then it does matter very much (in terms of its impact on environmental issues) where you are getting your economic growth from.

Final Responses

Peter Bartelmus: The point made by Salah El Serafy that natural-capital consumption needs to be incorporated is incontestable; this is why we do integrated accounting. On the other hand, we should not overlook that the conventional national accounting system has been and continues to be a valuable information system measuring what is actually going on at the microeconomic and macroeconomic levels. Individual corporations, in most cases, do not yet account for resource depletion and for environmental degradation. There are exceptions, of course, and some corporations do account for natural resources if they own them, and some corporations have also started accounting for liabilities from pollution. (To the extent that these result in actual accounting at the microeconomic level, I suppose macroeconomic accounts would indeed incorporate these values.) In the meantime, the system still measures economic transactions and the financial flows behind them, while avoiding any imputations. I say this as an environmentalist at heart, that for the short-term measurement of economic performance, conventional economic accounts still have a very valuable role to play.

I share concern with everyone who believes that the attempt to introduce physical indicators into monetary accounts would overload the system. Can you imagine the impact of environmental statistical systems on national accounts, if, for instance, pollution from emissions and in concentration, contamination, and health indicators were all to be allocated to the different sectors? I do not think we yet have a feasible information system for doing this. The solution of the Netherlands was to create indices, and in producing indices that contributed to many political themes they avoided the overload. But they introduced another arbitrariness, by weighting a number of things together as contributors to a particular problem, such as global warming.

Paul Cotterell: I want to reemphasize that we should not be trying to make the national accounts the catch-all for everything to meet all sorts of needs and policy requirements, but rather that we should be developing particular systems that answer the particular questions being asked.

Session 3

Experience

Issues of Interest

Session 3 was intended to draw on the experience of industrial and developing countries to see what lessons can be learned about the interrelationships between macroeconomics and the environment.

In relation to industrial countries, the following questions seem pertinent.
- Is there any evidence that pursuing environmental goals has hurt macroeconomic stability and growth seriously?
- What approaches have industrial countries adopted to integrate their environmental and macroeconomic policy objectives and how far are these approaches replicable in other industrial countries?

Knut Alfsen attempts to answer these questions in his paper on the experience of Norway and Peter Clark comments on the paper.

In relation to developing countries, the following questions need answers.
- Is there much evidence, based on methodologically sound and empirically based studies, showing that reforms of macroeconomic policies have either damaged or not damaged the environment?
- How far are environmental damages the result of economic policy failures and of environmental policy failures in developing countries?
- What steps can be taken to facilitate economic and environmental policy reforms in developing countries?

Mohan Munasinghe and Wilfrido Cruz attempt to answer these questions in their paper. Cielito Habito brings to bear his experience in the Philippines in commenting on the paper.

8

Macroeconomics and the Environment: Norwegian Experience

Knut H. Alfsen

The links between macroeconomic policymaking and the environment are numerous. Some are obvious although sometimes difficult to quantify, others are more elusive. For instance, energy taxes and subsidies have direct impacts on the amount and type of fuel used, and hence on air pollution. Agricultural policy has well-known impacts on soil degradation and water pollution, to mention just a few obvious examples of interrelationships. Less obvious links are perhaps those working through the input-output structure of the economy. Thus, the economic cost of environmental regulations may sometimes be found to depend crucially on, for instance, the way wages are formed in the society. Also, environmental regulation of one set of sectors, for instance, the manufacturing industry, may shift economic activity to another set, for example, the service sectors, giving rise to a new set of environmental problems stemming from other sources than those originally controlled. Finally, there are sometimes important links among different environmental problems, for example, the greenhouse problem and local air pollution, which make a partial approach to one of the problems extremely cost inefficient compared with an integrated solution comprising both types of problems. Thus, important relationships exist not only between the macroeconomy and the environment, but also among economic sectors and their associated environmental issues. All of these will have to be taken into account to some degree in pursuing an integrated policy approach.

Note: The author thanks Adne Cappelen for comments and ideas.

165

In discussing the relationship between macroeconomic and environmental policymaking in industrial countries, I have chosen to concentrate on Norway's experience in integrating macroeconomic policy and the environment. Norway is a small and, in a global context, insignificant country. Nevertheless, Norway has, together with a few other industrial countries (Canada, France, and the Netherlands), played a pioneering role in Natural Resource Accounting (NRA). Over the years, this has led to the development of integrated macroeconomic and environmental models in Norway, now routinely employed not only by the Ministry of Finance but also other ministries, such as the Ministry of Environment and even some major nongovernmental organizations (NGOs). The early start has allowed us to make a fair number of errors and to gather some useful experience. The outcome to date has been a rather tight integration of at least a part of the environmental policymaking and macroeconomic policymaking in Norway. The integrating activity takes place both with regard to environmental issues, allowing a discussion of several interdependent environmental problems simultaneously, with regard to the links between economic and environmental issues and to the actors participating in the economic and environmental policy debate. I will try to explain how this has come about and some of its effects on both environmental and economic policymaking. These experiences are, we feel, relevant to other industrial countries and international organizations.

Underlying the description of the history and current position in Norway with regard to the integration of macroeconomic and environmental policymaking is the belief that in the majority of industrial countries there is no lack of data or expertise on environmental and economic issues. Rather what is often lacking is an awareness of the relationships between the policies. The challenge is therefore to establish an operational framework facilitating communication between the prime actors, that is, the Ministry of Finance, the Ministry of Environment, and various NGOs. It is the process leading up to this and its consequences for policymaking that I want to comment upon in this paper.

Natural Resource Accounting

In the early 1970s, concern for the management of natural resources in Norway was accompanied by political conflict. Decades of intensive expansion of the hydroelectric power system gradually led to increased opposition from conservationists seeking to preserve at least some of the more spectacular waterfalls. Oil and gas were discovered off the

Norwegian coast and, with rising petroleum prices, this augmented concern for proper management of these valuable resources. Some of the fish stocks were overexploited, threatening the resource base of the coastal population.[1] Agricultural questions, among them the question of the optimal degree of agricultural self-sufficiency, were raised, and plans for the use of scarce arable land were requested.

These concerns resulted in the initiation of work on natural resource accounting in Norway some 20 years ago. The aim was to ensure a better long-term resource management by

- providing new and better-suited data for monitoring resource use and long-term management
- avoiding duplication of effort in data collection and analysis
- providing data in a form compatible with traditional economic statistics to facilitate integrated analyses of natural resource and economic issues
- developing a standard procedure for presentation of data and analyses on natural resources and the environment.

History of Natural Resource Accounting

The work on the Norwegian natural resource accounting system, initiated by the Ministry of Environment in the early 1970s, has since 1978 been operated and further developed by Statistics Norway (SN). Statistics Norway is also responsible for national accounting and development and operation of some of the economic policy models employed by the Ministry of Finance. Coordinating the work on the natural resource accounting with ongoing work on national accounting and economic models has been useful for a number of reasons.

- Locating the work on natural resource accounting in Statistics Norway has assured access to statistical expertise and closeness to primary statistics used in the development of the natural resource accounts.
- In Statistics Norway, the resource accounting framework was naturally based on existing economic standards and sector classification schemes, thus ensuring general consistency in the sectoral classification of economic and resource related data and statistics. In particular, links to the UN System of National Accounts (SNA) has

---

[1]Interestingly, the overfishing was largely a consequence of subsidies to shipyards and the building of larger and more efficient fishing boats, a subsidy that was meant to support the coastal population.

Figure 1. *Organizational Set-up in Norway*

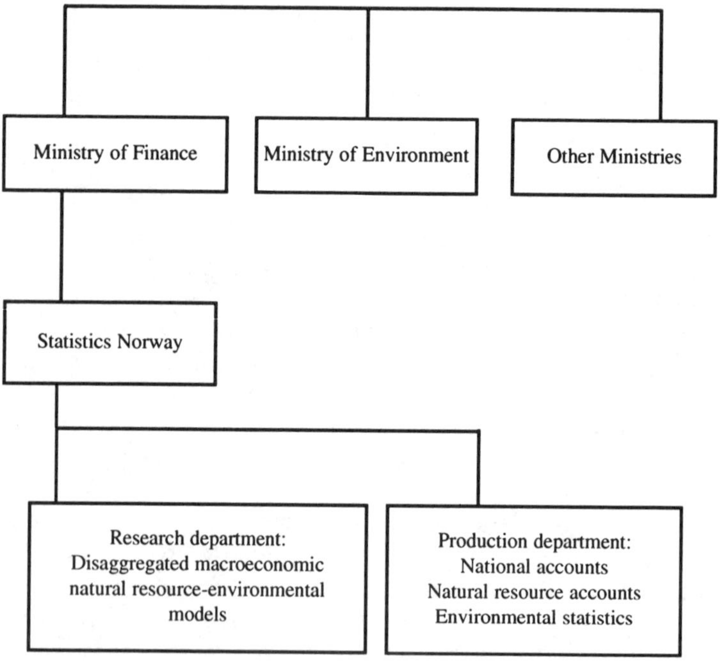

made it possible to integrate natural resource variables and relations within existing macroeconomic models developed by the Research Department of Statistics Norway and extensively used by, for instance, the Ministry of Finance.

• Use of a common set of economic standards and models in the analysis of resource issues have facilitated the communication between the ministries responsible for the management of the economy and the ministries responsible for the management of the natural resources, in particular, between the Ministry of Finance and the Ministry of Environment (see Figure 1).

In the initial phase of resource accounting, considerable effort was made to establish resource accounts for a large number of resources. Among the most important were energy, fish, and land use. In addition, less detailed accounts were made for minerals, forests, and sand and

Figure 2. *Structure of National Resource Accounts (NRA)*

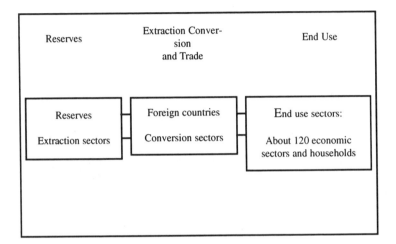

gravel.[2] The accounts consisted of three subaccounts covering (1) reserves, (2) extraction, transformation, and trade, and (3) domestic end use, and were kept in physical units (see Figure 2). In all parts of the accounts emphasis was put on consistency with the classifications and definitions of the national accounts. Later, based mainly on the energy accounts, inventories of emissions to air were established.

Thus, many resources were covered in the initial phase. The main reasons for this were a growing general concern over the scarcity and mismanagement of these resources, so typical of the early 1970s, and a belief that one of the greatest stumbling blocks for a rational management was the lack of adequate and systematically organized data. These concerns have, however, changed over time.

The two oil price shocks of the 1970s and the reactions to these shocks seemed to indicate that there was no immediate danger of depletion of nonrenewable resources. It became clear that doomsday prophecies brought forward by, for instance, the Club of Rome had ignored important behavioral changes brought about by increases in resource prices. Thus, problems with the management of natural re-

---

[2]See Alfsen and others, 1987; Statistics Norway, 1981; Lone, 1987, 1988; and Sæbø, 1994, for more detailed descriptions of the accounts and their development over time.

sources turned out to be different from those that originally motivated the establishment of the resource accounts. It also emerged that the problems of rational management of natural resources were not primarily due to lack of data. Rather, political and governmental bodies appeared to resist the introduction of new and additional constraints and considerations in the existing planning and decision-making procedures. Finally, the effort necessary to develop and maintain a comprehensive accounting system was clearly underestimated in the first period.

Basically, of all the accounts developed, only the energy account was used actively by the government. The reason for this can be sought in the tight integration of energy issues achieved in the macroeconomic modeling tools employed by the government. Already at an early stage the economic models were extended to include energy as a separate input factor in production as well as to include at a disaggregated level the energy-producing sectors. Later, the energy accounts were supplemented by emission inventories of a number of polluting compounds and the models modified accordingly. The harmonization of the classification scheme used in the energy accounts, the emission inventories and the national accounts were crucial in this respect. Thus, of all the accounts established, only the one applicable for answering questions about the future was in real demand.

Presently there is a continuing effort to integrate resource and environmental issues into the *existing* economic policy procedures in Norway. This is seen as a more useful approach than striving to establish parallel and more or less separate resource and environmental planning procedures. In addition to covering energy demand and emissions into the atmosphere, the integrated models now also cover generation of various types of waste. Furthermore, functions linking the state of the environment with the economic productivity of capital and labor are implemented on an experimental basis in the macroeconomic models.

Summarizing, the development of natural resource accounting in Norway has been from a broad coverage of many resource categories to a more selective approach with greater emphasis on analysis and integration of resource issues in economic policymaking.

Tradition of Modeling

Basic to this process is the special Norwegian tradition of relying to a great extent on model-based studies in formulation of economic policy (Figure 3). The Ministry of Finance has a long tradition, going back to the 1960s, of using large and disaggregated models for policy pur-

Figure 3. *Extended Macroeconomic Modeling*

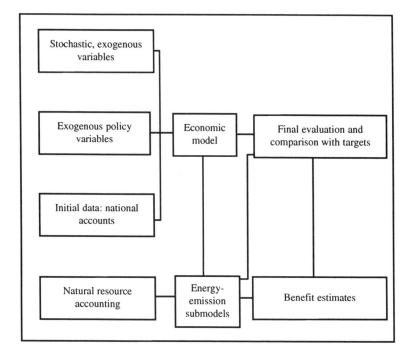

poses.[3] These models were developed, updated, and partially operated by the Research Department in Statistics Norway as an extension of the work on national accounting. Today the models form the backbone of the effort of integrating natural resource and environmental issues in macroeconomic policymaking. As well as the standard economic variables, the models project energy use (electricity based on hydroelectric or gas power, transport oil, and fossil fuels for heating purposes) and the associated emissions into the atmosphere of some nine polluting compounds. In addition, generations of various types of waste are calculated on the basis of the economic growth paths generated by the models. Also, an effort is made to incorporate some physical effects,

---

[3]For elaborations and details of the economic core models, see Johansen, 1974; Bjerkholt and others, 1983; Offerdal and others, 1987; and Holmøy and others, 1994.

like corrosion of materials and lower labor productivity owing to air pollution and waste generation, in the economic model. This opens up for an economic valuation of the environmental deterioration within the model framework (using shadow prices for capital and labor from the model).

By integrating the resource and environmental data with economic models, several aims are achieved. First, consistency between economic planning, expected growth in energy use, and the resulting emission to air is secured in the model-based forecasts. Second, by providing output tables covering economics, energy, and environmental variables, the links between these policy areas are brought to the attention of the policymakers. Finally, by making a single modeling tool available to both the Ministry of Finance and the Ministry of the Environment (among others), communication among the different branches of the government is enhanced.

Typically, three types of questions are addressed by the integrated model.

- What are the likely future developments with regard to economic growth, demand for energy, and emissions to the atmosphere? Are environmental targets compatible with the economic goals?
- How will a change of policy (e.g., introduction of environmentally motivated taxes or regulations) affect the projected development with respect to the economy and the environment?
- How will future developments in the state of the environment and availability of energy resource affect economic development?

Presently the model apparatus is utilized on a routine basis not only by the Ministry of Finance, but also by other ministries, such as the Ministry of Environment and the Ministry of Industry and Energy.[4] Lately some of the larger Norwegian NGOs have used the model in order to illustrate the feasibility of alternative and, in their view, more sustainable policies. Thus the models function like a mediator among several politically important agents, forcing the environmental aspects of economic policy to be taken into account by the Ministry of Finance, while at the same time showing the Ministry of the Environment and the NGOs some of the economic consequences of pursuing a "greener" pol-

---

[4]Some recent examples of their use are reported by the Green Tax Commission (Norges Offentlige Utredninger (NOU), 1992) and the government's Long-Term Program 1994–97 (Ministry of Finance, 1993). Earlier studies include SIMEN (Studies of Industry, Environment and Energy Toward 2000), (Bye and others, 1989), an analysis of climate policy problems on a national scale (Moum, 1992), and a white paper on structural adjustments of the Norwegian economy (NOU, 1988).

icy. As such, the development of integrated models can be said to be a success in Norway, and it has certainly brought the policy debate forward.

This multiple use of the models allows all participants in the debate to learn about the shortcomings of the models, the impact of alternative assumptions regarding exogenous variables, the conclusions of the models, and the inherent uncertainties always present in forecasting exercises. This has diminished the traditional "owner" of the model (the Ministry of Finance) of some of the magic often associated with large numerical models and therefore to some extent leveled the playing field for the participants in the economic and environmental policy debate.

Modeling the Costs and Benefits of Environmental Control

Around 1985 Norway signed a number of international treaties and protocols obliging her to stabilize or reduce the emission of several polluting compounds. At that time the initial use of the models was to produce emission projections based on official economic scenarios. It turned out, and this will be illustrated later, that the projection showed that Norway would have difficulty in reaching all the emission targets (Figure 4). Publication of the projections therefore provided environmental groups and the Ministry of Environment with ammunition in their fight with the Ministry of Finance over resources.

The logical next step was to include environmental control policies of various kinds in the model simulations. Of course, it then emerged that a—sometimes substantial—economic cost was associated with the environmental targets. In some cases, for instance, in setting a national target for future carbon emission, this lead to a downward revision of initially very ambitious targets. In other cases, for instance, when the NO_x target for Norway was decided, the ambition level was retained despite clear evidence that it would prove prohibitively expensive to reach.

The question of the economic costs of not improving the state of the environment was also raised and this has been addressed in a recent, perhaps more controversial, development of the models. The focus has been on quantifying benefits associated with reductions in local pollution levels of SO_2, NO_x, CO_2, and particulate matter. The benefits covered are reduction in local environmental damage to forests and lakes, damage to health, and damage to certain types of materials. In addition, benefits accruing from reduced traffic congestion, road damage, traffic accidents, and traffic noise levels are quantified. This is not the place to

Figure 4. *Emission to Atmosphere Compared With National Target*
(Deviation in percent)

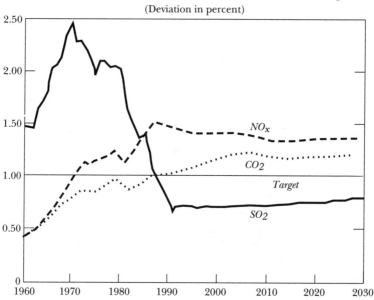

discuss the many methodological issues arising in these types of studies.[5] Here, we only briefly mention the issues relating to the benefit estimates of environmental-control policies.

Environmental Benefits

The economic cost of damage to freshwater lakes in Norway from deposition of sulphur and nitrogen is estimated on the basis of willingness-to-pay surveys carried out in the 1970s. Damage to Norwegian forests from sulphur deposition has been assessed by an official commission. Given an estimate of physical damage, the economic loss owing to reduced timber production is relatively easy to assess. The estimation of loss in recreational value from damage to forests is roughly assessed in proportion to recreational loss from damage of freshwater lakes.

Damage owing to corrosion of building materials and machinery has been estimated on the basis of data of capital exposure to atmospheric sulphur, the cost of maintenance and replacement, and detailed physi-

[5]For a more detailed discussion of data and assumptions, refer to Alfsen and others, 1992, and Brendemoen and others, 1992.

cal damage functions (e.g., amount of material corroded under different atmospheric conditions).

Estimates of health damage owing to air pollution are based on two official Norwegian reports on health damages induced by air pollution and their costs in some Norwegian cities. These, in turn, build on international dose-response studies adjusted to correspond to Norwegian conditions.

Traffic-Related Benefits

In the same reports marginal external costs of road traffic owing to congestion, traffic accidents, damage to roads, and noise are estimated. The submodel assumed future road traffic to be proportional to the demand for transport fuels. Multiplying the marginal cost of the various damage components by changes in emission into the atmosphere of the relevant compounds and by the change in demand for transport fuels yields a rough estimate of some of the direct benefits of environmental control policy compared with a baseline scenario. It is difficult to measure correctly the economic cost of introducing a control policy, but a rough indicator is the calculated reduction in GDP.

Examples of Empirical Analyses

In this section we provide several examples of the use of integrated environment-energy-economy models. The first example is an analysis of the economic and environmental effects of the introduction of carbon taxes. The secondary benefit (i.e., secondary with respect to potential climate effects) of a specific carbon tax is presented in some detail, before an overview of secondary benefits and GDP losses in several studies is offered. The next example shows emission elasticities with respect to changes in the price of electricity and fuel oil. The final example illustrates that the indirect costs of an environmental control policy directed at a specific economic sector may be substantial.

Emission Forecasts and Carbon Tax

Figures 5–7 show historical development and projected values for the emission of SO_2, NO_x, and CO_2 in Norway. The projections cover one reference or baseline alternative and two carbon tax alternatives. In the Tax-1 alternative the tax in year 2030 is of the order of $800/tons of carbon (tC) (in 1989 dollars, corresponding to $93/barrel of oil), while the Tax-2 alternative assumes a much lower tax of $160/tC ($19/barrel

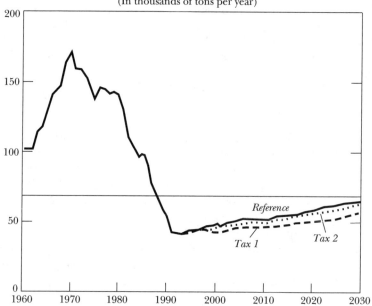

Figure 5. *Emission Levels of SO2*
(In thousands of tons per year)

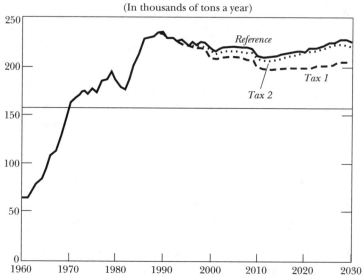

Figure 6. *Emission Levels of NO2*
(In thousands of tons a year)

Figure 7. *Emission Levels of CO₂*
(In millions of tons per year)

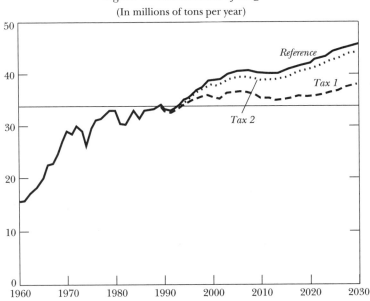

of oil). In both cases the taxes are presumed to be part of an international agreement imposing similar taxes on all other industrial countries and therefore affecting both economic growth in world markets and the price of important commodities, such as crude oil and natural gas. An important assumption in the calculation is that the trade balance of Norway should be unchanged from the reference alternative. Norway has national emission targets for all three compounds shown here. Although specified for different years, the targets are shown as horizontal lines in the figures.

From the figure we note that the SO_2 emissions have declined substantially since the early 1970s, mainly because of vigorous use of administrative control measures and the shutting down of polluting industries. The decision to implement these control measures was to some extent influenced by an early analysis of expected future growth in SO_2 emissions carried out by use of an extended macroeconomic model (Ministry of Finance, 1972). Future emission growth is expected to be small, and few problems are envisaged with respect to the fulfillment of the national target even in the long run. NO_x emissions have grown substantially over the years from 1960 to 1990. New control measures, such as catalytic cleaning of automobile exhausts, are expected to curb this growth in the future, but this is not enough to ensure a fulfill-

Figure 8. *Secondary Benefits of Carbon Tax in 2030, Composition*
(In millions of Norwegian kroner)

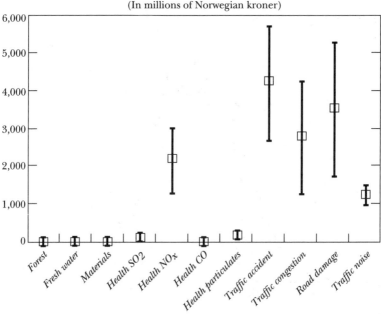

ment of the national target even with a high carbon tax. However, a carbon tax is not likely to be the most efficient mean of reducing NO_x emissions. CO_2 emissions have also grown over 1960–90, although at a declining rate over the last ten years or so. However, further expected growth makes it hard to achieve the national target, even with a high carbon tax.

It is obvious from the figures that the main problem for Norway in achieving its air pollution targets is related to the emission of NO_x unless new affordable technology offers, for instance, low-NO_x combustion engines for use in ships and heavy vehicles.

Cost and Benefits of Carbon Taxes

Estimates of (secondary) economic benefits of introducing a carbon tax have been calculated according to the procedure briefly outlined previously. They are of course highly uncertain, and for this reason Monte Carlo simulations are carried out to map the effect of the uncertainty in the marginal cost figures on the final benefit estimate. Figures 8 and 9 illustrate the composition and probability distribution

Figure 9. *Secondary Benefits of Carbon Tax in 2030, Probability Distribution*
(In billions of 1990 Norwegian kroner)

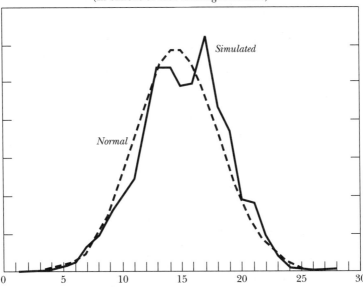

of the secondary benefit in year 2030 of introducing a carbon tax of approximately \$800/tC on all CO_2 emissions in Norway, assuming that similar measures are introduced by our most important trading partners.

While the benefit is estimated to be between 10 and 20 billion 1990 Nkr in 2030, the calculated reduction in GDP is 34 billion Nkr in the specific example considered here. Thus, a sizable fraction of the economic cost of introducing a carbon tax is recouped by the fact that emissions of local pollutants, such as SO_2, NO_x, CO_2, and particulate matter, are also reduced. These benefits are in addition to benefits that may accrue from a reduction in the greenhouse effect.

Costs and Benefits in Other Studies

The results cited above are from just one of many similar studies carried out in Statistics Norway over the years. Table 1 summarizes some of the results.

The studies referred to in Table 1 are based on different models employing different assumptions regarding how the tax is implemented (e.g., unilaterally or through an international agreement). Also the time horizon of the studies varies from 2000 to 2030. The results are therefore not strictly comparable.

Table 1. *Environmental Taxes: Benefits versus GDP Losses*

	Secondary Benefits			Loss in	Benefit/		
Study	Environmental (US$/tC)	Traffic (US$/tC)	Total (US$/tC)	GDP (US$/tC)	GDP Ratio	Year	Model
1	179	309	489	2	300	2000	MODAG
2	52	74	126	177	0.71	2010	MSG-TAX
3	306	392	698	795	0.88	2000	MSG-TAX
4	151	228	379	897	0.42	2000	MODAG
5	169	255	424	1,974	0.21	2025	MSG-5
6	184	828	1,012	2,757	0.37	2030	MSG-5
7	138	228	366	3,634	0.10	2030	MSG-5
8	213	365	578	5,974	0.10	2030	MSG-4
9	222	256	478	8,219	0.06	2000	MODAG
10	1,426	1,630	3,056	37,672	0.08	2000	MODAG

Note: tC = ton of carbon.

The estimates of GDP reductions (measured per ton of carbon removed) vary widely. This is of course due to varying assumptions made in the course of the studies related, for instance, to reactions in the world oil market to an international climate treaty or consequences for energy-intensive industry based mainly on hydroelectric power in Norway. The variability clearly points out the difficulties associated with assigning a *single* cost figure to an environmental target.

The assessment of the local benefits associated with reduction in local pollutants only (neglecting the benefit from reduced road traffic) is in the range of $50 to $300, with most of the studies showing benefits between $150 and $200 when measured per ton of carbon removed. This is of the same order of magnitude as found by Pearce, 1992, in a separate study of secondary benefits from climate policies for the United Kingdom. Also it is of the same order of magnitude as the carbon tax calculated to be necessary in order to stabilize global CO_2 emissions (see, for instance, Cline, 1992, for a summary of such studies; Burniaux and others, 1992, provide evidence of the global effects of a CO_2 tax, based on OECD's GREEN model).

The variations both in benefit estimates and in the loss of GDP illustrate that many factors besides the strength of the policy measure (the tax rate) are involved in determining the final impact of the environmental policy. Thus, it is in general impossible to assign a single number to the cost of an environmental control policy without specifying in detail what other assumptions the projections are based on (for example, impacts on world trade and world market prices of energy, other tax reforms). Finally, the benefits of mitigated climate change (the primary benefit) owing to the introduction of a carbon tax of this size is com-

Figure 10. *Emission Elasticities of Various Compounds*
(With respect to oil price)

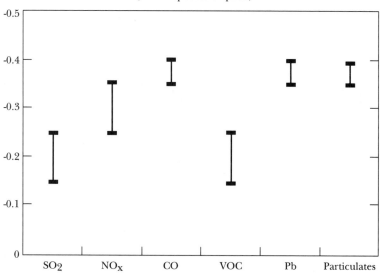

monly estimated to be an order of magnitude less than the above range
(see Nordhaus, 1991a,b; and Cline, 1992). Thus, the inclusion of the
secondary local benefit estimates in the evaluation of climate policies
might be crucial to an evaluation of such policies.

Emission Sensitivity to Energy Prices

Any forecast is contingent on uncertain assumptions. The future
world-market price of crude oil is crucial in this respect, owing to its
close link to emissions into the atmosphere.[6] Figure 10 shows calculated
emission elasticities for several compounds with respect to the oil price.
In the model-based calculation, effects on foreign trade from changes
in the oil price are also taken into account. Generally, emissions of compounds stemming mainly from transportation activities show the greatest sensitivity to changes in the oil price. For further discussion and references, see Alfsen, 1991, 1992.

---

[6]The situation in Norway is somewhat special since its power supply is 100 percent based
on hydroelectric power.

Emission Tax on Sulphur

In a study based on the MSG-4 model, the effects on economic activity and emissions into the atmosphere of introducing a tax on sulphur emissions from the manufacturing industries were calculated (Alfsen, Hanson, and Lorentsen, 1987). According to the model, which has empirically estimated relations with predominantly energy-capital complementarity, taxation of sulphur emissions reduces long-term economic growth. Furthermore, the reduction in GDP inferred from the model calculation was considerably greater than the tax payment from the sectors directly affected by the tax. Although substitution possibilities can be expected to reduce the total impact of the tax on the economic results of a sector, the energy-capital complementarity leads to less investment when the price of energy increases, thus reducing the long-term growth of that particular sector. Taxation is obviously a cost-effective means of lowering emissions from polluting sectors. Nevertheless, the indirect allocation costs of the control policy should be recognized from the outset, as these costs may dominate the more easily calculated direct costs of the taxed sectors.

Relevance for Other Countries

In summarizing a tentative answer to the question of applicability of Norwegian experience to other countries, it is useful to separate the discussion into economic, institutional, and political factors that may have made the integration of macroeconomic and environmental policies possible. Beginning with the economic preconditions, we would like to emphasize the importance of natural resources for the Norwegian economy. While most OECD countries have gradually reduced their dependence on "nature" as basis for their production, Norway has retained an economic structure closely linked to natural resources, such as fish, timber, hydroelectric power, and more recently crude oil and gas. Norway's wealth is to a larger extent than any other OECD country (except Iceland) based on how we manage our natural resources.

In terms of political factors, Norway was the first country in the world to have a separate ministry for environment (1972). The reasons for this are partly the economic factors just indicated and partly the political interest in environmental issues in the late 1960s. In particular, national conflicts over the use of the countryside for economic purposes rather than leisure activities were important from the late 1960s onwards. Political groups, as well as lobbyists, organized themselves and became important in the policy debate. This feature is not of course a specifically Norwegian phenomenon, but took place in many countries. What seems to be a particularly Norwegian factor is the way the politicians responded and that the setup of a separate ministry gave the NGOs a better target for their activities. It is also worth mentioning the corporatist tradition in Norwegian society through which political organizations of nearly all kinds are supported by government funds. This tradition reflects a political attitude where organized labor, farmers, fishermen, industry, and organizations focusing on particular environmental issues are seen as a positive part of the parliamentary system.

Turning finally to the institutional factors, we would like to emphasize the modeling tradition within government and the centralized collection of statistics as factors that helped the integration of macroeconomic and environmental policy discussion. The responsibility for most of the relevant data collection as well as modeling work is centralized within Statistics Norway. The need for better and more relevant statistics in national resource accounting and the like, both for purely statistical purposes and for modeling, could perhaps be met easier within this institutional framework. It is perhaps also easier to accumulate knowledge in data collection and modeling when this takes place in institutions that are supposed to have a long life. In many countries (e.g., Sweden) model building is a largely academic exercise and models live only for short periods. In other countries such as the Netherlands (The Central Planning Bureau) and Canada (Statistics Canada), the development and operation of models has been a permanent activity for decades. Establishing operational integrated models is obviously easier within such stable frameworks.

Although we have managed to establish a useful and operational model framework for integrated policy discussions in Norway, this does not imply that it was an easy task or that the framework has worked perfectly. Initially, the Ministry of Finance was rather skeptical and hesitant in taking additional constraints into account in their policy deliberations, but public exposure through newspapers and other media of the inconsistencies between economic and environmental policy targets, together with pressure from the Ministry of Environment, convinced the Ministry of Finance of the usefulness of employing the integrated model in their own policy studies. It may also have played a role that the Ministry of Finance, through environmental taxes, saw the possibility of extending the taxation base in the society.

As mentioned previously, output from studies based on the integrated models has sometimes been heeded and sometimes been ignored in formulating environmental policy targets. Model results have also sometimes been used for more than they are worth in selling specific political positions. A particularly difficult topic here has been the relation between employment and environmental policy. We sometimes find that the policy debate focuses more on how the economy works rather than on explicit targets for economic or environmental development or on ways to achieve these targets. This tends to draw the model builders into the political arena and may undermine their role as providers of impartial information.

Overall, however, we feel that the availability of the models to several political actors has by and large improved communication and understanding among the parties. This has come about not least because the models are useful for delimiting the potential space for political actions. By highlighting links between economic activities and the environment, the models ensure that real trade-offs are faced by all parties taking part in the policy process. The models can, of course, never provide the right political answer to political question, but by using the same modeling framework for analyses of both economic and environmental policies, consistency in behavioral and other key assumptions are secured. Furthermore, linking physical resource accounts and environmental statistics to economy-wide models provides for better and more comprehensive information on the value of natural resources and environmental services than is available through more partial studies. For these reasons, we strongly recommend a strategy in which resource and environmental issues through their physical characteristics are integrated into already operational economic planning tools. This is in opposition to a strategy where new and separate models for resource and environmental analysis are developed in addition to existing models.

Finally, let me end by mentioning a rather neglected, but potentially important, dimension of the many interrelationships between macroeconomic development and the environment. Many industrial countries were rebuilt and reformed after World War II. In this process a number of strong lobbying groups were created, representing various sectoral interests, such as the agricultural community and industrial groups. These groups have often retained great political influence on economic policymaking. While the influence in a sense was necessary and perhaps useful in the reconstruction of the economies in the wake of the war, a time eventually comes when the structure of the economy has changed to such an extent that these lobbying activities become counterproductive in economic terms. A typical example is the agricultural policies in place in many industrial countries today. The emergence of strong environmental interest groups in the last couple of decades is interesting in this light, since they have the potential of breaking up the outmoded power structure established over the last 40 years and hence of dismantling at least some of the inefficient power structures prevailing in today's industrial countries. To some extent the environmental groups in industrial countries also reduce some of the imbalance found between producers on one side and consumers on the other side.

References

Alfsen, Knut H., 1991, "Environmental Economics Based on General Equilibrium Models: The Norwegian Experience," *Swiss Journal of Statistics and Economics*, Vol. 127(2), pp. 225–43.

————, 1992, "Use of Macroeconomic Models in Analysis of Environmental Problems in Norway and Consequences for Environmental Statistics," *Statistical Journal of United Nations Economic Commission for Europe*, Vol. 9(1), pp. 51–72.

————, 1994, "Natural Resource Accounting and Analysis in Norway," *Documents 94/2* (Oslo: Statistics Norway).

————, A. Brendemoen, and S. Glomsrød, 1992, "Benefits of Climate Policies: Some Tentative Calculations," *Discussion Paper No. 69* (Oslo: Statistics Norway).

Alfsen, Knut H., T. Bye, and L. Lorentsen, 1987, "Natural Resource Accounting and Analysis: The Norwegian Experience 1978–1986," *Social and Economic Studies*, No. 65 (Oslo: Statistics Norway).

Alfsen, Knut H., D. Hanson, and L. Lorentsen, 1987, "Tax on SO_2 Emissions From Fuel Combustion: Policy Analysis on a Norwegian General Equilibrium Growth Model," unpublished study (Oslo: Statistics Norway).

Bjerkholt, O., S. Longva, Ø. Olsen, and S. Strøm, eds., 1983, "Analysis of Supply and Demand for Electricity in the Norwegian Economy," *Samfunnsøkonomiske studier No. 53* (Oslo: Statistics Norway).

Brendemoen, A., S. Glomsrød, and M. Aaserud, 1992, "Miljøkostnader i makroperspektiv," *Rapporter 92/17* (Oslo: Statistics Norway).

Burniaux, J.-M., and others, 1992, "The Cost of Reducing CO_2 Emissions: Evidence from GREEN," Economic Department Working Papers, No. 115 (Paris: OECD).

Bye, B., T. Bye, and L. Lorentsen, 1989, "SIMEN, Studies of Industry, Environment and Energy Towards 2000," *Discussion paper No. 44* (Oslo: Statistics Norway).

Cline, William, 1992, *The Economics of Global Warming* (Washington: Institute for International Economics).

Holmøy, E., G. Nordén, and B. Strøm, 1994, *MSG-5. A Complete Description of the System of Equations*, Reports 94/19 (Oslo: Statistics Norway).

Johansen, L., 1974, *A Multi-Sectoral Study of Economic Growth*, second enlarged edition (Amsterdam: North-Holland).

Lone, Ø., 1987, "Economics and Ecology in Natural Resource Management," unpublished note.

————, 1988, "Natural Resource Accounting and Budgeting: A Short History of and Some Critical Reflections on the Norwegian Experience 1975–1987," unpublished note.

Longva, S., L. Lorentsen, and Ø. Olsen, 1985, "The Multi-Sectoral Growth Model MSG-4. Formal Structure and Empirical Characteristics," in *Planning, Multi-Sectoral Growth and Production. Essays in Honour of Professor Leif Johansen,* Contribution to Economic Analysis No. 154, ed. by F. R. Førsund, M. Hoel, and S. Longva (Amsterdam: North-Holland).

Moum, K., ed., 1992, "Klima. økonomi og tiltak (KLØKT)," (Climate, Economy and Control Policies), *Rapporter 92/3* (Olso: Statistics Norway).

Nordhaus, W., 1991a, "A Sketch of the Economics of the Greenhouse Effect," *American Journal of Economics,* Vol. 81(2), pp. 146–50.

————, 1991b, "To Slow or not to Slow: The Economics of the Greenhouse Effect," *The Economic Journal,* Vol. 101(6), pp. 920–37.

Norges Offentlige Utedninger (NOU), 1988, "Norsk økonomi i forandring" (Norwegian Economy in Transition), *NOU* 1988:21, Oslo.

————, 1992, "Mot en mer kostnadseffektiv miljøpolitikk i 1990–årene" (Toward a More Cost-Efficient Environmental Policy in the 1990s), *NOU* 1992:3, Oslo.

Norwegian Ministry of Finance, 1972, "Spesialanalyse I: Forurensninger" (Special Analysis No. 1: Pollution), Annex to the Long-Term Program 1974–77 (Oslo: Ministry of Finance).

————, 1993, "Langtidsprogrammet 1994–1997" (Long-Term Program 1994–97), No. 4, 1992–93 (Oslo: Ministry of Finance).

Offerdal, Erik, K. Thonstad, and H. Vennemo, 1987, "MSG-4. A Complete Description of the System of Equations," *Rapporter 87/14* (Oslo: Statistics Norway).

Pearce, David W., 1992, "Secondary Benefits of Greenhouse Gas Control," *CSERGE Working Paper* No. 92–12, Centre for Social and Economic Research on the Global Environment, University College, London.

Statistics Norway, 1981, "Ressursregnskaper" (Resource Accounting), *Statistiske analyser,* No. 46 (Oslo: Statistics Norway).

————, various years, "Natural resources and the environment," *Statistiske analyser* (Oslo: Statistics Norway).

Sæbø, H. V., 1994, "Natural Resource Accounting. The Norwegian Approach," *Notater 94/9* (Oslo: Statistics Norway).

Discussion

Discussant's Comments

Peter Clark

Alfsen's paper provides an excellent discussion of Norway's pioneering role in integrating macroeconomic analysis with environmental policy issues. As an old modeler myself and a current consumer of the results from econometric models, I find the depth and breadth of the technical modeling efforts described in the paper truly astonishing. Equally impressive is the sensible and sensitive way in which the entire modeling exercise is used as a mechanism for dealing with a major economic and social problem—the degradation of the environment—and in resolving conflicts over how to deal with this problem.

My more specific comments on the paper will cover (1) the lessons of the Norwegian experience and the extent to which these lessons are transferable to other countries, and (2) specific comments and questions on the results of the modeling exercise reported in the paper.

Other countries can glean many lessons from the application of economic models in Norway to the analysis of environmental issues. First, a model-based approach provides a common framework for analysis and a discipline on the debate over the effects of environmental policies. In particular, such a structured approach contributes to rational discourse on the costs and benefits of alternative measures to deal with environmental degradation. This technical analysis gives essential information on the relevant trade-offs by providing rough estimates of the magnitude of the changes in the level and structure of output associated with alternative environmental control policies.

Moreover, in Norway, the process of using model results constitutes an integrating social and political consensus-building mechanism that brings together different parts of the government as well as different social, political, and economic groups. The common frame of reference provides a means for the various constituencies to resolve differences in views on the appropriate policies to deal with environmental pollution.

Second, the Norwegian experience highlights the importance of integrating resource and environmental issues and analysis directly into existing macroeconomic policymaking and planning tools. This makes

---

Note: The discussion was chaired and moderated by Margaret Kelly.

the environment front and center of macroeconomic analysis. If environmental policies are dealt with in a separate exercise, they necessarily receive less prominence, and there would be a tendency to ignore the links between macroeconomic and environmental objectives.

Third, the basic positive finding of the extensive macroeconometric analysis undertaken by the Norwegians is that a major shock to the system—roughly a 40-fold increase in a carbon tax—does not necessarily have major adverse effects on total output. Of course, the estimated effects, reported in the paper, show there will be major changes in the structure of production, as energy-intensive sectors will be more adversely affected than others. But the careful attention to modeling the existing substitution possibilities and the reallocation of resources in a highly developed country, such as Norway, show that it is quite resilient in the face of a major government intervention to deal with environmental degradation.

Finally, the model shows the need to include estimates of the local benefits resulting from reduced pollution, that is, those directly affecting the Norwegian economy through a reduction in damage to forests and lakes, health (a point also emphasized by the Pearce and Hamilton paper), and reduced traffic congestion and accidents. Making estimates of these benefits is an essential part of the analysis; one must put a value on the benefits of measures to protect the environment in making a welfare judgment, as one needs to compare the loss of measured output with the gain associated with a cleaner environment. Presumably, there must be a net welfare gain from measures to enhance the environment if such measures are to be viewed as economically defensible.

While there is much in the Norwegian experience that other countries can emulate, three factors discussed at the end of the paper are likely to limit the transferability of the Norwegian approach. First, Norway is a nature-dependent economy, which appears to imply a greater sensitivity to the environment than would otherwise be the case. Japan may be a counter-example to this connection, as its lack of raw materials has made it sensitive to its dependence on them, and by taking measures to limit this dependence it has become a very energy-efficient economy. Second, the political tradition in Norway has involved the inclusion of different constituencies, especially NGOs, in the discussion of environmental issues. They are all part of a political process that generates a consensus. Finally, there is a long tradition in Norway of using operational models in policymaking. Countries that are lacking these traditions may find it difficult to duplicate the successful experience of Norway in integrating macroeconomic and environmental policymaking.

I would now like to turn to some specific comments and questions on the results of the modeling exercise reported in the paper. First, in the discussion of the historical experience and the projection of emissions, it is noteworthy that Figure 5 shows a decline in SO_2 of over two thirds during 1970–90. This was accomplished by administrative control over, and the closing down of, polluting industries. It would be interesting to know whether this massive reduction had any significant negative macroeconomic effects. In the discussion of NO_x emissions, it is noted in the paper that a carbon tax is an inefficient means to reduce these pollutants. The question that naturally arises is what would be a more efficient tax or set of measures that would reduce these emissions. With regard to CO_2 emissions, the relevant figure shows little net change between 1980 and 1990, that is, before the simulation experiment. However, these emissions are projected to increase dramatically in the future. What accounts for this pause in the growth of these emissions?

Turning now to the simulation results themselves, it is extremely useful to show the sensitivity of these results to alternative assumptions, as is done in Table 1 and Figure 9. The results of these different simulation experiments clearly indicate an incredibly wide range of estimates of the net benefits of environmental taxes. The problem with these reported results is that they are not that comparable because different models were used and the effects are reported over different time periods. It would have been better to use one model over the same time period, for example, to 2030, and then vary the policies and the exogenous assumptions. In this way one would get a much better sense of what accounts for the differences in the results.

In all these results reported by Knut Alfsen, there are reasons to believe that the output losses may in fact have been overestimated. As technology is assumed to be exogenous, there is a clear limit to substitution possibilities. In particular, the decline in output relative to baseline as a result of the carbon tax appears fundamentally to be due to capital/energy complementarity. Thus a tax on energy is a tax on capital, and therefore the long-run effect of a CO_2 tax, implies a decline in the capital-labor ratio and in output per worker. An important question is whether this result is unavoidable. Are environmental damages necessarily related to capital, so that a reduction in CO_2 must entail a reduction in the capital stock relative to baseline? Over a 30- or 40-year period, it might well be possible for improvements in technology to lead to a decline in pollution per unit of capital so as to achieve environmental targets at the same time that output returns to its long-run value. It is of course beyond the scope of the paper to endogenize technological progress, but we do know that energy consumption per unit of output can respond strongly to relative prices over the long run, as the effects of the two oil price shocks of the 1970s have amply demonstrated.

It is unfortunate that employment effects are not analyzed in the paper by Alfsen, who simply states, "a particularly difficult topic here has been the relationship between employment and environmental policy." First of all, some reduction in the real wage will be needed to achieve full employment, as well as flexibility in real wages across sectors of the economy. More generally, a key issue is the need for a labor market policy that encourages the reallocation of labor to accommodate the changes in the structure of production that will result from the carbon tax. Flexibility and mobility on the part of labor are clearly needed to minimize the adjustment costs generated by the environmental taxes being contemplated in Norway.

Finally, it is worth pointing out that the calculated macroeconomic effects of a carbon tax obviously depend on at least two key features of the Norwegian economy: first, power is produced mainly via hydroelectricity, which does not generate pollution, and second, Norway is a net oil exporter. Hydroelectric power puts Norway in a better position in terms of pollution per unit of output relative to a country such as Japan, which is dependent mainly on oil for power generation. However, Japan may for this very reason be able to reduce pollution at the margin more easily than Norway. The second characteristic makes Norway vulnerable to a decline in the world price of oil that may result from the worldwide adoption of pollution control policies. Perhaps in further work and papers, the importance of these particular features of the Norwegian economy could be explored to shed light on the applicability of the results in this paper to other countries.

Other Discussion

Wilfrido Cruz: I have two questions. First, I found the comparison between environmental benefits and income losses interesting. From your perspective, especially for developing countries, where would you say the cushion lies for absorbing conventional income losses? Perhaps in technological changes? Have there been any simulations of environmental policies that you carried out that have been in the nature of output-neutral experiments or revenue-neutral experiments? Second, have you looked at the incidence of carbon taxes and other green taxes? Do they always affect capital or labor more?

Salah El Serafy: I was fascinated by Peter Clark's arguments, which opened up some of the assumptions underlying Knut Alfsen's presentation. I always think that in richer countries when we think of environment we think of pollution. I wanted very much to know how Norway's

CGE model dealt with oil and gas, and how natural resources are integrated in the macroeconomy.

Peter Bartelmus: I think the introductory remarks by Knut Alfsen contain a message for international organizations, such as the IMF, that might still be reluctant to embrace environmental concerns in their economic policy framework. It is his reference to a problem of the integration of environment and economy being due not to the lack of data, but rather to the lack of communication and awareness. I think that here the experience of industrial countries is similar to that of many developing countries. Surprisingly, large amounts of data are available in such countries, but the data are obviously not comparable, they are disparate; the environmental data and economic data do not relate easily to each other. For this reason I feel that there is an urgent need to better connect the data, not necessarily by just putting them in a common framework and juxtaposing them, but by connecting them more intensively in other ways. There are two approaches: the first is to put monetary values on their costs and benefits and arriving at net benefits to evaluate any actions, and the other is to ask specific integrated questions through analysis and modeling. I think that both approaches have their raisons d'être.

I believe that an advantage of integrated data bases like that provided through green accounting is standardization. And for international organizations, it seems important to have comparability. So that would be an argument for green accounting. On the other hand, accounting is, as we all know, backward looking; it does not answer specific questions and, being multipurpose in nature, sometimes its purpose is not quite clear. Hence, the advantage of particular modeling approaches, as are done in Norway. On the other hand, can we really standardize CGE models for broader applications?

Ian Johnson: I would like to ask two questions. First, I am glad that the model developed by Statistics Norway provides an excellent tool for communication. But like any monopoly, a monopoly of knowledge or monopoly of modeling can be hazardous. I want to know if there have been any other alternative models to help broaden the dialogue. For example, your model is driven by your assumptions about expected energy growth, which assumes a transmission mechanism through energy intensity. If you have a pattern of demand, that remains unchanged because of the historical antecedents, you essentially have static emission intensities and elasticities. This can yield very wrong policy conclusions.

Second, the NGOs are always skeptical about the sustainability of the level of economic activity. Have you been able to persuade your NGOs that there is a possibility of maintaining and sustaining the level of economic activity, by introducing some kind of sensible economic policy measures of the kind you have described in Norway?

Response

Knut Alfsen: Peter Clark has asked about the decline in SO_2, and whether it had macroeconomic effects. Yes, there have been macroeconomic effects. In the mid-1970s, it guided the cleanup of the old industries of Norway. As a consequence, a number of the most polluting and least-efficient firms were shut down. The interesting part was that many of these firms had previously been subsidized with very cheap power. So, there was also a macroeconomic gain in shutting them down. Similarly, mining, which was a very good source for sulphur emissions in Norway, was also a loss-making activity. This, too, was kept alive by the government because it was in a remote and backward area of Norway. Only when environmental policy of reducing sulphur emissions was adopted, were we able to close the mining company. Unfortunately, all these sulphur reductions by industries and mining companies were achieved through regulations, and there were negotiations with each firm on how they should reduce their emissions.

One could ask the question with hindsight: What would have happened if CO_2 had been a concern before the sulphur emissions became a concern? If we had introduced a sensible carbon policy, or a sensible CO_2 policy, perhaps some of these sulphur emission regulations would have been unnecessary. So, there certainly have been costs of attacking a specific problem and imposing environmental regulations on the industry.

Willi Cruz asked about the output loss effect and whether technological changes can be expected to reduce the output losses. We are looking at this through sensitivity analysis, that is, building in various assumptions regarding technological change under various policy scenarios. Unfortunately, there is very little empirical knowledge of how technological change will be affected by policy changes. Historically, there is a complementarity between energy and capital in the Norwegian economy, with the result that an energy tax is in fact a tax on capital and enhances the losses of income. That may change over time. However, I am a little bit reluctant in discussing modeling details too much, because as everybody knows, these models are unreliable for the longer term. When we are making projections 40 years into the future, we are talking about a completely different world, with different commodities and different technologies all over the place. What we are doing through our models is simply bringing today's links to the attention of the government and the policymakers rather than giving precise results about how we think the future would look like.

About the incidence of environmental taxes and how they affect the labor is difficult to say, even based on historical data. For that reason it is difficult to predict their future effects as well. David Reed's earlier comment that institutional changes are likely to have a far larger impact on labor market than all these changes in relative prices (or taxes), is worth remembering here.

Willi Cruz also asked about whether we could find revenue-neutral environmental policies in developing countries. Perhaps I should explain that. In Norway, we are also doing work for the World Bank and other agencies with this kind of concept in the context of developing countries, that is, general equilibrium models incorporating various environmental and natural resource issues, mining, soil erosion, and deforestation. Often the data are not good, the behavioral relations are seldom econometrically estimated, and one has to make all kinds of assumptions. But within this shaky foundation, it is possible to find revenue-neutral policies, that enhance or benefit the environment without crushing the economies of the developing countries. The study we did on Ghana recently had such an orientation: when the subsidy for fertilizer was reduced in order to reduce soil erosion, it increased the productivity of the agricultural sector, and the government could tax the agricultural sector. The end result was an increase in GDP at the same time as the reduction in soil erosion. So it is possible to make these kinds of studies.

Cruz also raised questions about distributional issues, for example, the question of whether you hit labor or the capital more through environmental taxes. This will depend on how you use the revenue from a green tax. Do you transfer it back to the people through a lump-sum transfer? Is it the labor tax that you reduce? Or is it capital tax that you reduce? It is possible to deal with such issues, and we are developing these kinds of alternative scenarios. In Norway, which is a relatively homogeneous society, broad-based taxes, like an environmental tax, are seldom biased against certain classes. In developing countries, however, the results can be very different.

Salah El Serafy asked how we are modeling oil and gas in Norway. The oil and gas industry in Norway is large, and we are treating it largely exogenously. It is very difficult to have sensible economic modeling of these sectors, as everybody knows. Our models are not optimizing models, so we do not answer the question how we should optimally manage our oil and gas resources.

I agree with Peter Bartelmus that there are arguments in favor of green accounting, particularly at the international level. The international comparability is important, but I think that the greening of national accounts and natural resource accounting have sometimes been oversold at a national level as a sort of important policy tool. I do not think that is the case. What is important for the politicians is to get answers to the policy questions, and you need the relevant data for answering those questions. Those data could be in the form of natural resource accounting, green accounts, or in other forms.

An important point was raised concerning the monopoly of the Statistics Norway of modeling for the Norwegian Government and whether that gives excessive political power. In a small country like Norway, we could very easily develop into that kind of modeling monopoly. However, there is a Model Forum in Norway, based in the Ministry of Finance, where all economic institutions are present and where they continuously discuss the shortcomings and disadvantages of the available models. The Ministry of Finance in Norway does have its choice of models, but has chosen so far to base most of its analysis on our models.

Have we been able finally to sell to the NGOs the idea that it is possible for the economy to grow and yet be sustainable? I think what we have managed, at least, is to tell the NGOs that economic activity per se is not what you should attack—pollution and its environmental impact should be the target. So we have avoided falling in the trap that we should stop economic growth in order to save the environment. We have convinced them that there is not necessarily a one-to-one negative relationship between economic activity and environmental impact. So the NGOs are more concerned about how we manage the economy than the growth rate of GDP. I would say that the NGOs in Norway are willing to accept the proposition that positive growth in GDP can be sustainable.

Peter Clark: I just wanted to reenforce a point that Knut Alfsen made regarding the possibility of substituting environmental taxes for other taxes. I think there is by now considerable evidence that distortions introduced by existing taxes on capital and labor can have significant macroeconomic effects. We have just done some analysis on this subject, using a macroeconomic model, and have found that fiscal consolidation or reducing fiscal deficits, achieved through raising distortionary taxes, is not necessarily first best and may not even be second best. So, I believe that when you are raising taxes of one kind, say, emission taxes, then as a part of the package you might want to consider reducing distortionary taxes and therefore get a fringe benefit in the form of positive output resulting from a reduction of tax-related economic distortions.

9

Economy-Wide Policies and the Environment: Developing Countries

Mohan Munasinghe and Wilfrido Cruz

D uring the 1980s, economic crises in many developing countries resulted in economic hardship, characterized by severe internal and
external imbalances. Stabilization and adjustment reforms were designed to address these problems and redirect economies toward
growth and development, but these policies often required the adoption of stringent economic and fiscal reform measures. Very broadly,
stabilization measures were implemented to reduce domestic demand
and the pressure on foreign reserves, while structural adjustment policies focused on improving the efficiency of resource allocation and
competitiveness of markets.

Note: Mohan Munasinghe is Division Chief, Environmental Economics and Pollution
Division, Environment Department, and Wilfrido Cruz is Environmental Economist, Environment and Natural Resources Division, Environment Department, World Bank. This
paper draws from the results of recently completed studies coordinated by the Environment Department of the World Bank. The overall study was managed by the authors, together with Jeremy Warford. The country case studies were carried out by Robin Bates,
Jan Bojo, Wilfrido Cruz, Robert Cunliffe, Gunnar Eskeland, Boguslaw Fiedor, Herminia
Francisco, Ian Goldin, Shreekant Gupta, David-Roland Host, Ramon Lopez, Paul Martin,
Peter Meier, Stephen Mink, Kay Muir-Leresche, Mohan Munasinghe, Zeinab Partow, An-
nika Persson, Tilak Siyambalapitiya, Adriaan Ten-Kate, Hu Tao, Jeremy Warford, and
David Wheeler—as cited in the text. Additional background studies and research inputs
were contributed by Noreen Beg, Adelaida Schwab, Shreekant Gupta, and Sanath
Ranawana. An advisory panel of external experts, consisting of Partha Dasgupta, Stein
Hansen, Karl-Goran Maler, Jorn Rattsoe, and Hirofumi Uzawa, provided helpful advice
and guidance. Many others, too numerous to list, gave valuable comments. This work was
supported in part by generous contributions from the governments of Norway and Sweden. Opinions expressed herein are those of the authors and do not necessarily represent
the views of the World Bank Group.

In spite of the economic gains achieved through these reforms, other problems have persisted, especially in natural resource and environmental management. Thus, there is a growing concern that environmental and sustainable development issues have not been sufficiently integrated into the mainstream of economic policymaking. Traditionally, conventional economic reform efforts (including structural adjustment programs) have been guided by the objectives of efficiency and income distribution. These policies are not directed toward influencing the quality of the natural environment, but to the extent that they have a major impact on relative prices or on incomes, such reforms can either help or harm the environment.

Ongoing initiatives both within the World Bank and in other development agencies have emphasized project-level environmental issues. Because of the significance of broad economic policies for the environment and the relative paucity of knowledge regarding the links involved, this paper focuses on the environmental implications of economy-wide policy reforms—that is, measures undertaken at the sectoral or macroeconomic level. Economy-wide policies primarily involve economic instruments ranging from pricing in key sectors (for example, energy or water) and broad sectoral taxation or subsidy programs (for example, agricultural production subsidies, industrial investment incentives) to macroeconomic policies and strategies (exchange rate, interest rate, wage policies, trade liberalization, privatization, and so forth). Economy-wide policies are often packaged within programs of structural adjustment or sectoral reform aimed at promoting economic stability, efficiency and growth, and ultimately human welfare.

In this paper, we will address three related questions.

- What are the implications of economy-wide policy reforms on the environmental concerns of developing countries?
- How do existing policy distortions or market imperfections undermine environmental objectives and subsequently affect prospects for improving economic performance?
- What role can environmentally oriented policies potentially play in conjunction with programs of economy-wide policy reforms?

Although the emphasis of the discussion is on economic policies, other noneconomic measures required to achieve environmental and sustainable development objectives are also relevant, such as social, institutional, and legal actions (see Box 1). Thus, while the focus of this paper is on economic-environmental links, it also includes a discussion of associated social issues like poverty, income distribution, and property rights. However, because of the complexity of the subject, other key social objectives, such as popular participation, empowerment, and the rights of indigenous peoples, fall outside the scope of this paper.

Case Studies

Based on a comprehensive review of recently completed World Bank case studies as well as outside research, this paper uses examples that reflect a wide range of country conditions and environmental problems. The findings are grouped according to the ways in which economy-wide policies tend to interact with the environment.

- First, many economic reforms initiated to promote more efficient resource allocation and use are also environmentally beneficial, but residual imperfections often give rise to environmental harm.
- Second, stabilization measures meant to restore macroeconomic stability are necessary for sustainable development, but short-term contractionary aspects of these programs also may harm the environment.
- Finally, economy-wide policies have longer term implications for economic growth and income distribution that may also lead to environmental changes.

These broad findings are illustrated below with the help of World Bank country studies and other studies.

Efficiency-Oriented Reforms

Consolidating Environmental Gains

Economic liberalization programs that address price-related distortions (getting prices right) can contribute to both economic and environmental goals by promoting efficiency and reducing waste.

In many developing countries, misplaced efforts to promote specific regional or sectoral growth and general economic development have created complex webs of commodity, sectoral, and macroeconomic price distortions, resulting in economic inefficiency and stagnation. Often these economic distortions also lead to unanticipated changes in production and input-use that promote resource overexploitation or pollution. Such economic distortions may arise from a macroeconomic policy (such as the overvaluation of the local currency) or from a sectoral policy with economy-wide implications (such as subsidized energy prices).

In either case, economy-wide policies that correct such price-related distortions will also result in environmental gains. Among the broadest

Box 1. Approaches to Sustainable Development

Current approaches to the concept of sustainable development draw on the experience of several decades of development efforts. Historically, the development of the industrialized world focused on production. Not surprisingly, therefore, the model followed by the developing nations in the 1950s and the 1960s was dominated by output and growth, based mainly on the concept of economic efficiency. By the early 1970s the large and growing numbers of poor in the developing world and the lack of "trickle-down" benefits to them led to greater efforts to improve income distribution. The development paradigm shifted towards equitable growth, where social (distributional) objectives, especially poverty alleviation, were recognized as distinct from, and as important as, economic efficiency.

Protection of the environment has now become the third major objective of development. By the early 1980s, a large body of evidence had accumulated that environmental degradation was a major barrier to development. The concept of sustainable development has, therefore, evolved to encompass three major points of view: economic, social, and environmental (see the figure in Munasinghe, 1993a).

The *economic* approach to sustainability is based on the Hicks-Lindahl concept of the maximum flow of income that could be generated while at least maintaining the stock of assets (or capital) that yield these benefits. There is an underlying concept of optimality and economic efficiency applied to the use of scarce resources. Problems of interpretation arise in identifying the kinds of capital to be maintained (for example, manufactured, natural, and human capital) and their substitutability, as well as in valuing these assets, particularly ecological resources. The issues of uncer-

---

are macroeconomic remedies to correct the foreign exchange rate and taxes that distort trade. More sector-specific reforms seek to shift relative prices, for example, by setting efficient prices for energy or water (which have pervasive effects) or removing taxes or subsidies on commodities or factors of production.

The environmental benefits of macroeconomic reforms were observed in Zimbabwe (Muir-Leresche, Bojo, and Cunliffe, 1994). From an environmental perspective, wildlife-based economic activities (including ecotourism, safaris, hunting, and specialized meat and hide production) are better suited to that country's semiarid climate and poor soils than cattle ranching, which competes for the same limited land resources. The former also constitute some of the fastest growing sectors—wildlife-based tourism alone grew at the rate of 13 percent in 1991, accounting for 5 percent of the GDP. Despite its economic and tainty, irreversibility, and catastrophic collapse pose additional difficulties (Pearce and Turner, 1990).

The *social* concept of sustainability is people oriented, and seeks to maintain the stability of social and cultural systems, including the reduction of destructive conflicts. Equity is an important aspect of this approach. Preservation of social diversity and cultural capital are desirable. Modern society would need to encourage and incorporate pluralism and grass-roots participation into a more effective decision-making framework for socially sustainable development.

The *environmental* view of sustainable development focuses on the stability of biological and physical systems. Of particular importance is the viability of subsystems critical to the global stability of the overall ecosystem. The emphasis is on preserving the resilience and dynamic ability of such systems to adapt to change, rather than conservation of some ideal static state. Natural resource degradation, pollution, and loss of biodiversity reduce system resilience.

Reconciling these various concepts and operationalizing them as a means to achieve sustainable development is a formidable task, since all three elements of sustainable development must be given balanced consideration. The interfaces among the three approaches are also important. Thus, the economic and social elements interact to give rise to issues such as intragenerational equity (income distribution) and targeted relief for the poor. The economic-environmental interface has yielded new ideas on valuation and internalization of environmental impacts. Finally, the social-environmental linkage has led to renewed interest in areas like intergenerational equity (rights of future generations) and popular participation.

environmental advantages, sectoral land policies have generally discouraged wildlife activities since these are perceived as "underutilizing" land. Livestock marketing and price policies have traditionally subsidized cattle ranching.

More important, for many years, the government's foreign exchange and trade policies indirectly penalized the wildlife sector. The Zimbabwean dollar was overvalued by 50 to 80 percent during 1981–90. This meant that export-oriented sectors were implicitly taxed, among them wildlife and nature tourism. Foreign exchange earnings were diverted to other sectors, depressing incomes and investment in wildlife. In the early 1990s, the government introduced an adjustment package, including measures aimed at boosting the level of exports. The currency was devalued by 25 percent and more liberal access to foreign exchange was allowed. These moves were beneficial on both economic and ecological grounds. Although the economy still has a long way to go, exports have improved. At the same time, the wildlife sector had become more profitable, leading to an expansion of land allocated to wildlife, which is also environmentally more desirable.

The environmental implications of sectoral reforms in energy pricing were studied in Sri Lanka and in rangeland management in Tunisia. The Sri Lanka study demonstrates that energy sector reforms can contribute to both economic and environmental goals (Meier and others, forthcoming). As in most developing countries, electricity prices in Sri Lanka have been well below the incremental cost of future supplies. Many studies show that eliminating power subsidies by raising tariffs closer to the long-run marginal cost of power generation, will encourage more efficient use of electricity.

In projecting future electricity requirements, the study found that the economic benefits of setting electricity prices to reflect long-run marginal cost is supplemented by an unambiguously favorable impact on the environment (including local air quality, less biodiversity loss, and fewer greenhouse gas emissions). In addition, pricing reforms were found to have better economic and environmental impacts than purely technical approaches to demand-side management, such as promoting the use of energy-saving fluorescent lights.

The negative effects of underpricing resources in the agricultural sector is illustrated in the Tunisia study. The government's concern with ensuring sufficient supply and affordability of livestock products in Tunisia has resulted in a web of pricing and subsidy interventions. A variety of subsidies has intensified livestock production in certain parts of Tunisia, while in other regions it has encouraged herd maintenance at levels beyond rangelands' carrying capacity. Particularly during dry years, subsidized feed imports have substituted for natural pasture and have averted herd contraction. This failure of herds to respond to diminished feed availability in natural pastures has contributed to significant rangeland degradation primarily in the central and southern regions of the country. Reversing such environmental damage will require policy reforms relating especially to subsidies to the livestock sector (Partow and Mink, forthcoming).

A recent World Bank study suggests that trade policies that encourage greater openness in Latin America have tended to be associated with better environment, primarily owing to environmentally benign characteristics of modern technologies.[1] The nature of the environmental impact of adjustment reforms (such as the exchange rate changes and

---

[1]Birdsall and Wheeler, 1992.

trade liberalization examples above) has been questioned for some time. The broader issues raised by links between trade and environment are summarized in the Annex.

In Zambia, foreign exchange reforms have had a positive impact on wildlife populations, particularly of large mammals—by reducing the incentives for illegal trophy hunting to obtain scarce foreign currency (Mupimpila and others, 1994). In Tanzania, a case study of structural adjustment policies and the impact on the environment suggests that exchange-rate adjustment could provide greater incentives to protect national parks, game reserves, and nature conservation areas (Bagachwa and others, 1994). In Vietnam, a computable general equilibrium (CGE) model simulation of forest-policy reforms indicates a significant increase in forest area and the creation of 24,000 new jobs, as well as benefits from avoiding land degradation and loss of property and lives owing to flooding (DSI and HIID, 1994).

Avoiding Environmental Harm

While liberalizing policies typically help both the economy and the environment, other unaddressed policy, market, and institutional imperfections may cause environmental harm unless they are addressed through specific additional measures that complement the broader reform programs.

Reform is typically undertaken in stages, with the initial adjustment package aimed at the most important macroeconomic issues. Existing distortions that policymakers intend to address later in the adjustment process or other constraints that have been overlooked may cause environmental harm. Paralleling the way in which the social consequences of adjustment should be handled, such potential adverse environmental consequences owing to remaining inefficiencies or inequities in the economic system may therefore require additional measures to complement the original reform program.

In Morocco, low water charges constitute a prevailing policy distortion that have artificially promoted production of water intensive crops, such as sugarcane. Thus, rural irrigation water accounts for 92 percent of the country's marketed water use, while charges cover less than 10 percent of the long-run marginal cost of irrigation (Goldin and David-Host, 1993). Going beyond the traditional sectoral remedy of proposing an increase in water tariffs, the study employed a computable general equilibrium (CGE) model to link sectoral policy reforms with the macroeconomic adjustment program, focusing on trade liberalization.

In the CGE simulation, removal of nominal trade tariffs led to a small rise in real GDP. Household incomes and consumption grew as import barriers were reduced, exports became more competitive, domestic purchasing power rose, and resources were allocated more efficiently across the economy. However, environmental implications were negative, as domestic water use increased substantially owing to the expansionary effects of liberalization. To remedy the environmental harm, water-price increases need to be combined with trade liberalization, so that the beneficial expansionary economic effects of the latter may be largely retained, but now with substantial reductions in water use as well.

Aside from existing policy distortions, the absence of price signals for environmental services can undermine the contribution of efficiency- and growth-promoting reforms. The specific role of *market failure* in influencing the environmental implications of economic reforms is illustrated in the case of liberalization policies and industrial promotion in Indonesia (Wheeler and Martin, forthcoming). In this case, adjustment reforms successful in the traditional sense of stimulating industrial growth may cause pollution because of market failure—no price signals prevent excessive buildup of pollution.

The study identifies growth patterns that can help control pollution. In terms of emissions per unit of output, or pollution intensity, the study found that processing industries (for example, food products, pulp, and paper) tend to be dirtier than assembly industries (garments, furniture). Liberalization in the 1980s promoted a surge in assembly industries, thereby reversing the 1970s pattern of more rapid growth in dirty processing sectors. Projections indicate that the share of basic processing industries in total industrial output will fall from 72 percent in 1993 to about 60 percent by 2020. In addition, industry expanded rapidly outside densely populated Java, reducing the health impact of industrial concentration. However, industrial output growth has been so rapid that general pollution levels have nevertheless increased. Thus, while decreases in pollution intensity and industrial decentralization have helped to limit pollution, formal regulations will also need strengthening to avoid health and environmental damage in the future.

The nature of macroeconomic effects on the environment is also contingent upon prevailing regulations or institutions governing resource use. Thus, *institutional constraints* that are pervasive may undermine the potential contribution of policy reforms. For example, the eventual impact of economy-wide reforms (such as those affecting international and domestic terms of trade) on the incentives facing farm households will be influenced by intervening institutional factors, especially those affecting access and use rights over agricultural resources, such as land and water.

The role of institutional constraints in macroeconomic reform programs is examined in the Ghana case study (Lopez, forthcoming). In this example, trade liberalization, by reducing the taxation of agricultural exports, encourages production, while efforts to reduce the government wage bill tend to increase the pool of unemployed. Thus, adjustment helps to stimulate production of export crops and combines with rapid population growth and lack of employment outside the rural sector to increase pressure on land resources, encroachment onto marginal lands, and soil erosion. This effect on resource use is influenced by the allocation of property rights. Whether in relation to the security of land tenure of peasant farmers or to the right to extract timber by logging companies, uncertainty normally results in environmental degradation. In Ghana, as in many regions of Africa, agricultural lands are governed by traditional land-use institutions, and farms are communally owned by the village or tribe. These common property regimes may have allowed sustainable use of agricultural lands, when the population was much smaller and sufficient fallow periods could allow land to regain its fertility. However, such traditional arrangements have been overwhelmed by economy-wide forces, resulting in reduced fallowing, loss of soil fertility, and environmental decline.

Another common institutional problem relates not to the rules and regulations themselves, but rather to the government's capacity to establish and enforce such rules. Regulating large numbers of potentially environmentally degrading activities is especially difficult, even for industrial country governments. Substantial reductions in institutional monitoring may be achieved with the use of indirect measures or modified pricing-regulation approaches. This is illustrated in Mexico by the Mexico City air pollution study, which shows that while, in principle, pollution taxes are the most desirable means of achieving reductions in pollutants, in practice, administrative feasibility demands that less-refined instruments, such as taxes on consumption of fuels, may have to be used (Eskeland and Ten-Kate, forthcoming). While recourse to blunt instruments will help, the magnitude of the institutional capacity-building challenge nevertheless remains clear. Building the relevant institutional capacity in developing countries should therefore be underscored, and appropriate resources should be made available early in the adjustment process to assist country governments in this task.

A study of energy prices in Poland concludes that energy intensity and excessive pollution are due not only to the undervaluation of coal in the centralized price system, but, more important, to institutional problems rooted in state ownership that encourage output maximization rather than cost minimization (Bates and others, 1994). This means that price responsiveness is blunted, since financial losses are simply absorbed by the public budget or passed on to consumers in the form of higher output prices. Thus, energy restructuring efforts have recognized the need to create a new institutional and legal framework that will facilitate competition and greater private participation. Coupled with aggressive energy pricing reforms, this strategy appears to be making some headway.

The need for *complementary environmental reforms* is illustrated also in the case of forestry in Tanzania, where specific reforms in forest sector pricing and regulation are needed to ensure that the incentives from currency devaluation and trade liberalization do not lead to increased timber exports and unsustainable forest exploitation (Bagachwa and others, 1994). Similarly, in Jamaica, an ongoing study shows how foreign exchange reforms have increased the revenue generated by tourism (Alleyne and others, 1994). However, the increasing pressure of associated economic activity has caused considerable degradation of natural habitats and increased urban pollution—thus calling for complementary environmental protection measures.

Macroeconomic Stabilization Measures

Consolidating Environmental Gains

Measures aimed at restoring macroeconomic stability will generally yield environmental benefits since instability undermines sustainable resource use.

The relationship between environmental issues and policy reforms is fairly straightforward at a general level. Macroeconomic instability is not only disastrous for the economy, but also frequently detrimental to the environment. For example, high interest rates associated with economic crises can severely undermine incentives for sustainable management of resources, as producers seek to maximize current yields at the expense of future output.

Thus, to the extent that policy reforms can help restore macroeconomic stability, their impact will be unambiguously beneficial for long-term natural resource management and environmental concerns. This link is illustrated in a Costa Rica case study, which used a macroeconomic model incorporating timber harvesting activities to examine the deforestation implications of various macroeconomic factors (Persson and Munasinghe, 1995). Simulation results demonstrate that lower interest rates associated with a stable economy allow the logging sector to anticipate correctly benefits from future returns to forestry, thereby leading to a decline in current logging activities.[2] In Brazil, a recent Bank study found that if interest rates are very high, farmers would choose farming practices that have initially high returns but lead to significant subsequent declines in productivity (Schneider, May 1994). Thus, to the extent that adjustment policies can help restore macroeconomic stability, their impact will be unambiguously beneficial for long-term natural resource management and environmental concerns.

The issue of high debt levels (often associated with sustained periods of government budget deficits and macroeconomic instability) and its implications for environmental degradation were also raised some time ago. However, the available evidence indicates that the linkage is neither clear cut nor significant, as summarized in Box 2.

Avoiding Environmental Harm

While restoring economic stability is needed for sustainable development, specific measures to promote stabilization may have an unforeseen adverse impact on the environment, and compensating environmental measures will be needed.

To the extent that economy-wide policy reforms promote new economic opportunities and employment, in the long term they will clearly alleviate poverty and reduce unsustainable exploitation of fragile resources by the unemployed. However, in the transition period, when fiscal austerity is required to arrest deteriorating economic conditions, short-term distributional problems may arise, linked to the recessionary aspects of reforms.

Apprehension over the short-term environmental impact of adjustment-related reforms parallels concerns regarding the social impacts of adjustment. With austerity measures, it was feared that the poor, who would be most vulnerable to the effects of macroeconomic contraction, would also be adversely affected as social services were cut. Indirectly, short-term negative effects on poverty may have environmental implications (see Box 3). However, the main source of concern regarding environmental impacts was that government budgetary restrictions might disproportionately affect environmental protection programs.

In a study by ECLAC, 1989, it was concluded that adjustment policies pursued in Latin America during the 1980s led to cutbacks in current

---

[2]The effect of inadequate tenurial security over the resource (and future benefits from it) parallel the results for high discount rates. This corresponds to the well-known result in renewable resource exploitation models that the effects on economic behavior of open-access resource conditions are formally equivalent to those of having secure property rights with infinitely high discount rates.

Box 2. Debt and the Environment

One of the early antecedents of the concern about the relationship between economy-wide policies and the environment was the debt and degradation link noted by the Brundtland Report, 1987: *debt that cannot be amortized forces raw material-dependent countries in Africa to deplete their fragile soils, with the result that good land is turned into desert.* The perception was that many countries reacted to the external shocks during the economic crisis years of the early 1980s by exploiting natural resources unsustainably. However, evidence from country case studies and from cross-country statistical exercises does not support this view.

For example, a World Wildlife Fund report, based on case studies for Côte d'Ivoire, Mexico, and Thailand, concluded that there is no simple relationship between external debt levels and environmental degradation. In the case of Côte d'Ivoire the research team found that although the country's deforestation rate was one of the highest in the world, external debt did not affect environmental degradation in general or the forestry sector in particular (Reed, 1992). In another study, using econometric models with cross-country deforestation data, no consistent statistical relationship was found between debt and forest depletion (Capistrano and Kiker, 1990).

In fact, many factors are at work, and the export of primary commoditie, such as timbe, do not exhibit any simple trend during the debt crisis and adjustment periods. For example, in the early 1980s, primary commodity exports were subject to falling international commodity prices. Thus, production, domestic absorption, and price effects need to be assessed for specific commodities and countries (Reisen and Van Trotsenburg, 1988). Indeed, since the debt crisis was associated with falling export prices and domestic economic contraction for many developing countries, it would not be unreasonable to expect that in some countries the rate of resource extraction, instead of increasing, would have actually declined during this period.

Ideally, countries go into debt with the expectation that the benefits from the productive activities to be funded will more than pay for the loan. In practice, debt is often incurred to support balance of payments deficits. In the environmental context, debt-for-nature projects represent an effort to directly channel debt (or in this case its converse, debt-relief) to beneficial environmental activities. Such debt-relief efforts have enabled environmental organizations to leverage their available funds significantly. In countries, such as Costa Rica, debt relief programs have allowed environmental agencies to fund forest or biodiversity protection initiatives.

expenditure allotments for managing and supervising investment in sectors such as energy, irrigation, infrastructure, and mining.[3] This limited the funds available for environmental impact assessments and the supervision of projects to control their environmental impacts. Muzondo and Miranda, 1991, in an IMF survey, recognized this problem and suggested that high levels of government expenditure in other areas may lead to reduced funding of environmental activities.[4] Recent case studies attributed increases in air pollution problems in Thailand and Mexico to reductions in expenditures for adequate infrastructure.[5]

While the argument sounds reasonable enough that government cutbacks undertaken as part of adjustment austerity efforts may undermine the funding for environmental initiatives, empirical assessment of its true importance is difficult. Usually only general categories of expenditures can be identified in most government budgets, so that detailed assessments of environmental programs usually cannot be initiated. In one effort undertaken to assess the social consequences of adjustment lending in Africa, it was found that despite a decline in government expenditure, the budget proportion going to social expenditures and agriculture actually increased during the adjustment period.[6]

The results of studies focusing on social safety nets during adjustment programs confirm that pursuing fiscal discipline and macroeconomic stability need not take place at the cost of increased hardship for the poor. In much the same way, specific environmental programs could be protected when stabilization efforts are being pursued. For example, it has been reported that in many countries in sub-Saharan Africa, forestry departments and their activities have always been severely underfunded.[7] Thus, targeted efforts to support forestry management activities could, with modest costs, be included in reform packages as part of a proactive environmental response.

In Cameroon (Tchoungui and others, 1994), government retrenchment measures eliminated successful village extension programs (thereby causing a major setback in rural development), and also cut back on forest services, (affecting the monitoring of logging and collecting of stumpage fees). Similarly, in Zambia, because of adjustment-related budget cutbacks, urban water pollution problems have worsened, in part owing to the shrinking budget of the Water Affairs Department (Mupimpila and others, 1994). Indirect, recessionary effects are being

---

[3]ECLAC, 1989.
[4]Muzando and Miranda, 1991.
[5]Reed, 1992.
[6]World Bank, 1994b.
[7]Stryker and others, 1989.

Box 3. Poverty and the Environment

It is no accident that assessments of the impact of pollution invariably bring up concerns about poverty. In many cases, the worst effects of environmental pollution and resource degradation are borne by the poor, especially health problems and reduced productivity. In both urban and rural areas and in various occupations, the poor can least afford to protect themselves from environmental degradation: they spend long hours in polluted factories; they are exposed to agricultural chemicals; and services, such as clean water and trash disposal, which are usually taken for granted by the better-off, are normally unavailable in slums and rural areas.

Environmental degradation is also systematically linked to the problem of access to productive resources. The rural poor and landless workers often depend on the exploitation of fragile, open-access resources to supplement their meager livelihood. For example, agricultural plantation workers may depend on seasonal fishing or slash-and-burn agriculture for subsistence. In addition, if poverty and unemployment are pervasive, the poor may be forced to migrate to environmentally vulnerable areas, such as hilly lands or coastal fisheries, where there is open access.

Such open-access conditions in the face of increasing population and unemployment result in overexploitation. The situation in many coastal fisheries illustrates this problem of the "tragedy of the commons." As long as there is a surplus to be gained from fishing, more households will migrate to the coastal fishery areas, until eventually output declines and everyone is relegated to equally poor levels of subsistence. Population pressure on hilly lands lead to similar results for shifting cultivators. In both cases, the landless poor are driven to overexploit open-access resources and, in the process, degrade their source of livelihood. In brief, the very poor, struggling at subsistence levels of consumption and preoccupied with day-to-day survival, have limited scope to plan ahead and make natural resource investments (for example, soil conservation) that give positive returns only after a number of years. Such short time horizons are not innate characteristics, but rather the outcome of policy, institutional, and social failures. The poor's use of natural resources is also

---

studied in Tanzania, where the government has sought to control inflation by restricting the money supply, and also abolished government controlled rural cooperatives (Bagachwa and others, 1994). The impact of these policies has reduced farmers' access to credit, and the overall economic and environmental impacts are likely to be negative—owing to an increase in deterioration of irrigation networks and depletion of soil fertility, as well as greater pressure to clear new land.

affected by their facing greater risks, with fewer means to cope. These risks range from misguided policy interventions in input and output markets to changing land tenure systems that favor those with greater political clout. This means that the poor will have little choice but to overexploit any available natural resources.

How can policy reforms help alleviate the problem? From an individual decision-making perspective, policies that alter relative prices will affect current production and consumption activities of farming households as well as their future use of available resources. Thus, price policy reforms could promote environmentally benign crops and farming practices or discourage excessive water or pesticide use. Land improvement and soil conservation could also be encouraged if increased income and welfare allowed farmers to invest more in land and water management. Clearly, this "resource endowment" effect owing to the increased valuation of the household's resources would be sensitive to whether or not access to such resources is secured, for example, through well defined land-tenure arrangements.

Beyond the microeconomic aspects of poverty-oriented reforms, broad sectoral price changes and macroeconomic prices, that alter factor flows and change the structure of the economy, will also affect conditions of poverty and the environment. Thus, to the extent that economy-wide policy distortions have contributed to population pressure on fragile resources, adjustment-related reforms should also help. Import-substitution, industrial protection, and regressive taxation have historically been associated with lagging employment generation, income inequality, and poverty. These reforms, including those that promote export growth, will lead to higher incomes for sectors producing exportable crops and manufactured goods, generally reducing poverty among rural and industrial workers. Better economic conditions in agriculture and industry would also reduce the problem of frontier migration that has been associated with agricultural extensification. Because of their economy-wide impacts, the potential contribution of such policies to alleviating poverty and reducing environmental degradation could be substantial.

Longer-Term Poverty and Income Effects

In addition to the short- to medium-term concerns discussed earlier, economy-wide policies will have significant longer-term environmental impacts—both positive and negative.

The crucial long-term links between poverty and environmental degradation in developing countries are recognized (Dasgupta and

Maler, 1990). For example, the *World Development Report 1992* noted that the growing evidence of the relationship between reducing poverty and addressing environmental goals points to the need to undertake poverty and population programs as part of environmental efforts.[8] The need to break the cycle of poverty, population growth, and environmental degradation has also been identified by the International Development Association as a challenge to sustainable development.[9]

An important result of examining the general equilibrium effects of macroeconomic policy is that indirect resource allocation effects are important and may dominate the more direct effects of some price or income policy changes. In the Costa Rica study, the economic and environmental implications of wage restraints in structural adjustment are examined with the use of a computable general equilibrium model, which highlights the economic activities and factors affecting deforestation in Costa Rica (Persson and Munasinghe, 1995). The model differs from standard approaches in two important respects. First, it can simulate the effect of introducing property rights on forest resources, thus allowing the private valuation of future forestry returns to contribute to sustainable management. Second, it includes markets for logs and cleared land—loggers deforest to sell timber to the forest industry and squatters clear land for agricultural production and for sale as agriculture expands and requires more land.

The importance of indirect effects in Costa Rica is demonstrated in the analysis of economy-wide policy changes, such as an increase in the wage rate. Because the role of intersectoral resource flows is incorporated in the CGE model, the effects of changes in wages differ from partial equilibrium results. If the wage of unskilled labor were increased owing to, say, minimum wage legislation, the model predicts that deforestation could expand rather than shrink. Although logging declines because of increased direct costs, this is more than made up by the indirect effect of intersectoral flows since the industrial sector (where minimum wage legislation is more binding) is much more adversely affected by the higher labor costs. Labor and capital thus tend to flow from industry to agriculture, leading to greater conversion of forest land for farming.

This simulation exercise suggests the need for caution in attempting to legislate income improvements by increasing minimum wages. Introducing higher wages initially improves labor incomes, but the resulting contraction of industrial and agricultural employment leads not only to

---

[8]World Bank, 1992a.
[9]IDA, 1992.

higher unemployment but to environmental degradation as well. Higher unemployment leads to cultivation in forest lands.

Beyond pricing and intersectoral environmental links that can be identified in general equilibrium approaches, policies addressing rural poverty and unemployment would also affect the environment. This link occurs within the broader context of the social and demographic problems of inequitable land access and rapid population growth.[10] Import substitution, industrial protection, and regressive taxation have historically been associated with lagging employment generation, income inequality, and poverty. Unequal distribution of resources and inappropriate tenure also contribute to the problem. Inequitable assignment of endowments and rapid population growth result in unemployment and income inequality, which force the poor to depend on marginal resources for their livelihood, with consequent pressure on fragile environments. This effect can be analyzed in conjunction with the assessment of migration, which may occur as part of resettlement programs or may be induced by inappropriate policies, such as land colonization programs.

With regard to sustainable agriculture concerns, a World Bank study entitled *Population, Environment and Agriculture Nexus in Sub-Saharan Africa* explicitly links the related problems of rapid population growth, agricultural stagnation, and land degradation in Africa.[11] The study found that shifting cultivation and grazing in the context of limited capital and technical change cannot cope with rapid population growth. At the same time, the traditional technological solution of relying on high yielding crop varieties is not available. Thus, the study identified the need for a mix of reforms to remove subsidies for inappropriate land uses, improve land-use planning, recognize property rights, provide better education, and construct appropriate rural infrastructure to promote production.

Regarding economy-wide factors affecting deforestation, the Philippines case study evaluates the policy determinants of long-term changes in rural poverty and unemployment that have motivated increasing lowland to upland migration (Cruz and Francisco, forthcoming). This process has led to the conversion of forest lands to unsustainable agriculture and has contributed to deforestation. The inability of the government to manage forest resources is a direct cause of deforestation, but economic policies, both sectoral and economy-wide, also significantly contribute to the problem. The study links lowland poverty to

[10]Feder and others, 1988; Cruz and Gibbs, 1990; Lele and Stone, 1989.
[11]Cleaver and Schreiber, 1991.

agricultural taxation, price controls, and marketing restrictions, and uses an econometric model to demonstrate that poverty contributes to migration to forest lands.

Trade and exchange rate policies have also played important roles in the Philippines, but have been biased toward the urban consumer and industrial sector. The agricultural sector was implicitly taxed by an average of about 20 percent for most of the 1970s and early 1980s. Because the industrial sector did not provide an alternative source of growth, poverty generally has worsened and rural incomes in particular have suffered. The study indicates that these economic problems affect the environment mainly through migration and the conversion of forest lands to unsustainable agriculture. Population pressure already evident in the 1970s grew during the 1980s. The net upland migration rate grew from 3.4 percent in 1970 to 9.4 percent in 1975, and increased substantially to 14.5 percent by 1985. Consequently, upland cropped area grew at annual rates exceeding 7 percent from 1971 to 1987. These results suggest that while forestry conservation programs are needed, economy-wide policy reforms could be as important in arresting deforestation.

The environmental impact of reform policies depends largely on how the benefits are distributed among society. Several current studies point out that the benefits accruing to the poor, especially the rural poor, are disproportionately low. Based on a review of five structural adjustment programs (Côte d'Ivoire, Ghana, Indonesia, Philippines, and Jamaica), a World Bank study showed that the poor benefited most through an increase in demand for their services. Although incomes of farmers may increase owing to higher prices for crops, the net effect of reform policies depends on whether they are net buyers or sellers. Price liberalization, elimination of subsidies on food products, and high inflation often result in lowering the purchasing power of the poor in real terms.

A pattern of disproportionate distribution of benefits is illustrated in Zambia. The study contends that adjustment policies (elimination of government subsidies on food products, price liberalization measures, higher real interest rates, and fiscal contractionary policies) will have a greater impact on the poor. Although a social program targeting services most crucial to the poor (health, nutrition, and education) was developed, it received minimal funding.

In the case of Cameroon, the study explains that rural farmers were adversely affected by the reform policies. The overvalued exchange rate, combined with Cameroon's deteriorating terms of trade, created unfavorable conditions for the country's major export crops, such as coffee and cocoa. The government was forced to reduce support prices by about 50 percent, which amounted to a direct reduction of farmers' incomes. Between 1983 and 1993 the percentage of rural households living below poverty increased to 71 percent from 49 percent. Many farmers were forced to curtail investments on improving the land. Perennial cash crop cultivations were abandoned or converted into cultivation of subsistence food crops, which generally implied more erosive and environmentally unsound practices. Farmers expanded cultivated areas and civil servants undertook farming on the side to supplement their incomes. The overall result was increased pressure on forests and marginal lands.

The persistence of other economic distortions not addressed in reform programs may also have a constraining effect on the environmental contribution of reforms. This is illustrated by several Western African countries in the CFA franc zone. The CFA franc, which remained firmly linked to the French franc until January 1994, was highly overvalued throughout the duration of adjustment programs in such countries as Cameroon. In spite of extensive stabilization and structural adjustment policies adopted by these countries, the overall economic impact was limited. Thus, in Cameroon budgetary problems remained unresolved in spite of drastic measures to reduce public expenditure.[12] The tradable goods sector suffered a major setback owing to the overvaluation of the currency. As the formal sector declined, the informal sector expanded, particularly in cities. Along with a deterioration of social services in health and education, these trends had a negative impact on poverty alleviation and on the environment.

Links Between Economy-Wide Policies and the Environment—Conclusions

Evidence from the studies discussed above allows an answer to the three questions posed in the introduction. As to the first question, do economy-wide policy reforms have significant implications for the environment, the studies indicate that they have important effects, but in the less-than-perfect economic and policy conditions in which they are being undertaken, there is no assurance that efficiency-oriented reforms will also be environmentally beneficial.

In relation to the second question on the role of existing environmental policy imperfections and their subsequent (feedback) implications for the economy, recent studies show that these preexisting policy distortions or externalities have a crucial role in the environmental sec-

---

[12]Tchoungui and others, 1994.

tor. When policy reforms are undertaken elsewhere to stimulate the economy, perverse incentive signals may be transmitted to environmentally sensitive sectors, owing to intervening imperfections. These could lead to overexploitation of resources and environmental degradation. In most such cases, mitigating this harm will require the introduction of additional and more specific measures to complement (rather than halt) economy-wide reforms.

There is much less evidence, however, regarding the feedback effect of continuing environmental problems on the economy. Resource accounting studies in the past few years suggest that the depletion of productive natural resources has been significant and that conventional measures of economic performance may be inflated. For developing countries, the first such study was done for Indonesia, and estimates of the "depreciation" of forest, agricultural land, and petroleum resources were made for the period 1971–87 (Repetto and others, 1989). The main purpose of the exercise was to value the depreciation of "natural capital" in generating economic activity and to use this resource depreciation to adjust estimates of GDP. Other resource accounting exercises followed in Costa Rica (Solorzano and others, 1991), Philippines (Cruz and Repetto, 1992), and Mexico (Lutz, 1993).

From such studies, the rate of economic growth has been adjusted downwards, but environmental and resource accounting studies, being primarily accounting exercises, cannot shed light on the interaction between current depletion and future economic performance. The review of studies above provides some limited information on this interaction. On a sectoral basis, the Ghana study represents one of very few attempts in the developing world to quantify the implications for agricultural productivity of deforestation and land degradation. At the country-wide level, the CGE studies (e.g., on Costa Rica) suggest that environmental degradation could constrain growth, but more work needs to be done to better understand the mechanisms involved.

On the third and last question posed at the beginning of this paper, the potential contribution of improved environmental policies, the studies indicate substantial scope for undertaking such complementary policy actions in coordination with economy-wide reform efforts. The following section describes in detail the practical implementation of this approach.

Integrating the Environment in Economic Policy Reform

The challenge posed by these findings on economy-environment interactions is the need explicitly to incorporate environmental components in economic reform programs. Traditionally, economic development initiatives and environmental management efforts have followed separate tracks. On the economic planning side, ministries of finance or economic planning often formulate development plans or initiate growth-oriented reforms without serious consideration of resource use and environmental implications. On the environmental side, ministries of environment or environmental protection agencies have proposed national environmental action plans that have rarely incorporated analysis of the underlying economic causes of environmental problems.

The economy-environment links identified in the country studies described above indicate that a coordinated analysis of the economic policies and priority environmental problems can be undertaken. While the relationships between economy-wide policies and the environment are complex, and involve many economic and noneconomic variables, the main concerns may often be limited to a small subset of priority environmental problems. Specific steps for addressing these concerns are presented below, together with a framework for undertaking integrated economy-environment analysis at the country level.

- *Problem Identification.* Decision-makers could be more systematic in *monitoring environmental trends and anticipating emerging problems* when policy reform proposals are being prepared. Currently available environmental information should be analyzed to identify pre-existing or emerging environmental problems and their sensitivity to policy measures.
- *Analysis.* The potential environmental impact of proposed economy-wide reforms identified in the problem identification stage could then be subjected to *careful environmental analysis*—to the extent that data and resources permit. Many techniques and examples presented in this paper will be helpful in tracing the simpler and more obvious links between economy-wide policies and the environment.
- *Remedies.* Where potential adverse impacts of economy-wide reforms can be identified, *targeted complementary environmental policies or investments* should be implemented as soon as feasible to mitigate predicted environmental damage and enhance beneficial effects. Where links are difficult to trace ex ante, greater reliance will need to be placed on *preparing contingency plans* to be invoked expost (see below).
- *Monitoring and Follow-Up.* A follow-up system for monitoring the impacts of economic reform programs on environmentally sensitive areas (identified earlier) should be designed, and resources made available to address environmental problems during implementation.

- *Economic-Environmental Coordination.* Beyond analyzing specific reforms or programs, there should be an effort to institutionalize a
  synergistic approach in planning and management. Economic
  planning exercises (represented by economic development plans
  or economic strategy papers) should more systematically discuss
  environmental issues. Similarly, environmental documents should
  strengthen their analyses of economic linkages.

Action Impact Matrix

To implement systematically the steps described above, an Action Impact Matrix (AIM) approach may be utilized. This approach introduces
a framework for identifying the thrust of policy *actions* in government
reform programs and their potential environmental *impact*. A simple example is shown in Table 1, although an actual AIM would be larger and
more detailed. Such a matrix helps to promote an integrated view,
meshing economic decisions with priority environmental and social impacts. The first column of Table 1 lists examples of the main development interventions (both policies and projects), while the first row indicates some sustainable development issues. Thus the elements or cells
in the matrix help to (1) identify explicitly the key links, (2) focus attention on valuation and other methods of analyzing the most important impacts, and (3) suggest action priorities. At the same time, the organization of the overall matrix facilitates tracing impacts, as well as the
coherent articulation of the links between a range of development actions, that is, policies and projects.

An objective of the AIM-based process would be to help *in problem
identification*—by preparing a preliminary matrix that identifies broad
relationships without necessarily specifying with any accuracy the magnitudes of the impacts or their relative priorities. For example
(Table 1), a currency devaluation may make timber exports more profitable and lead to destruction of open-access forest. The appropriate
remedy might be to strengthen property rights or restrict access to the
forest. A second example might involve equating energy prices with
marginal costs to improve energy efficiency and decrease pollution.
Adding pollution taxes to marginal energy costs will further reduce pollution. Increasing public accountability will reinforce favorable responses to these price incentives by reducing the ability of inefficient
firms to pass on cost increases to consumers or to transfer their losses to
the government. In the same vein, a major hydroelectric project is
shown in Table 1 as having two adverse impacts—inundation of forested
areas and inundation of villages, as well as one positive impact—the replacement of thermal power generation (thereby reducing air pollu-

Table 1. *Action Impact Matrix (AIM)*

Activity/Policy	Main Objective	Matrix of Other Impacts on Key Sustainable Development Issues			
		Land degradation	Air pollution	Resettlement	Others
1. Macroeconomic and sectoral policies	Macroeconomic and sectoral improvements	Positive impacts owing to removal of distortions Negative impacts mainly owing to pre-existing constraints			
Exchange rate	Improve trade balance and economic growth	(−H) (deforest open-access areas)			
Energy pricing	Improve economic and energy use efficiency		(+M) (improve energy efficiency)		
2. Complementary measures	Specific or local social and environmental improvements	Enhance positive impacts and mitigate negative impacts (above) of broader macroeconomic and sectoral policies			
Market-based	Reverse negative impacts of market failures and policy distortions		(+M) (pollution tax)		
Nonmarket-based		(+H) (property rights)	(+M) (public sector accountability)		
3. Investment projects (examples)	Improve efficiency of investments	Investment decisions made more consistently with broader policy and institutional framework			
Project 1 (Hydro dam)	Use of project evaluation (cost-benefit analysis, environmental assessments, multi-criteria analysis)	(−H) (inundation)	(+M) (displace fossil fuel use)	(−M) (displace people)	
Project 2 (Reforestation)					

Note: A few examples of typical policies and projects as well as key environmental and social issues are shown. Some illustrative but qualitative impact assessments are also indicated; thus, + and − signify beneficial and harmful impacts, while H and M indicate high and moderate severity. The AIM process focuses on the highest priority environmental issues and related social concerns.

tion). An afforestation project coupled with adequate resettlement efforts may help address the negative impacts. The matrix-based approach therefore encourages the systematic articulation and coordination of policies and projects to achieve sustainable development goals. Based on readily available data, such an initial matrix could be developed for individual countries.

This process may be developed further to assist in *analysis* and *remediation*. For example, more detailed analyses may be carried out for the subset of main economy-wide policies and environmental impact links identified in the cells of the preliminary matrix. This in turn would lead to a more refined final matrix, which would help to quantify impacts and formulate additional measures to enhance positive links and mitigate negative ones. The more detailed analyses that could help to determine the final matrix would depend on planning goals and on available data and resources. They may range from the application of conventional sectoral economic analysis methods (appropriately modified to incorporate environmental impacts) to fairly comprehensive system or multi-sector modeling efforts.

The difficulties of analyzing the potential environmental impacts of proposed economy-wide reforms should not be underestimated. Linking specific causes with particular effects is especially problematic in countries where many conditions are simultaneously changing. Nevertheless, this paper indicates the many direct links that may be traced using existing methods, and the potential gains from integrating environmental aspects into policy reform discussion could be substantial.

World Bank Work and Future Directions

An outreach program has already been initiated in the World Bank to integrate environmental issues into country economic and sector work. The preparation of AIMs is already being initiated in Bolivia, Ghana, Philippines, and Sri Lanka, and more country examples are being planned. Training workshops have been held to disseminate the results of the case studies reported in this paper.

Concurrent with dissemination, more work is required in tracing the environmental implications of economy-wide policies. A broad collaborative program, including several specific initiatives and country case studies, is being implemented in the Bank and this is being complemented by collaboration with researchers undertaking related work in development institutions, nongovernmental organizations, and the academic community. The next round will rely on studies that relate comprehensive packages of economy-wide policy reforms to the full range of priority environmental concerns in a variety of countries. Current research interest, such as development of environmental indicators and environmental analysis of trade reform and privatization policies, will receive early attention.

In addition to these topics, distributional, political economy, and institutional issues need to be emphasized in future work. Greater attention needs to be paid to the identification, evaluation, and mitigation of the social impacts of economy-wide policies. The nature of environmental and social problems depends on the allocation of political and institutional power, and policy reforms may have substantial implications for the distribution of income and wealth. Thus, implementation problems, such as asymmetries in the incidence of environmental costs and benefits (especially health impacts), consultation and empowerment of disadvantaged groups, timing of reforms, and the role of environmental conditionalities, will have to be studied.

Annex

Trade and the Environment

As noted by the *World Development Report 1992: Development and the Environment*, concern with environmental implications of trade involves both the domestic implications of policy reforms as well as the global environmental dimension of international trade agreements. Although liberalizing reforms generally promote more efficient resource use (including use of environmental resources), in practice there is no clear-cut reason to expect that trade liberalization will be either good or bad for the environment, because trade reforms may be undertaken, but the presence of preexisting market, policy, or institutional imperfections in the environment sector may lead to adverse environmental impacts. The following discussion illustrates various environmental initiatives that will be needed to complement reforms in the trade sector.

Regarding national or domestic trade reforms, early concerns about negative effects were raised regarding the North American Free Trade Agreement (NAFTA) and pollution in Mexico. Similar concerns involved cassava exports and soil erosion in Thailand, and exchange rate depreciation and deforestation in Ghana. However, more recently there has been increased recognition that the links between trade and the environment are much more complex since economic expansion from trade is characterized not only by growth but also by changes in the intersectoral composition of output, in production techniques and input-use, and in location of economic activity.

For example, if liberalized trade fosters greater efficiency and higher productivity, it may also reduce pollution intensity by encouraging the growth of less-polluting industries and the adoption of cleaner technologies. In Mexico, as Grossman and Krueger, 1991, conclude, increased specialization owing to NAFTA-related trade liberalization would result in a shift to labor-intensive and agricultural activities that require less energy input and generate less hazardous waste per unit of output than more capital-intensive activities. Similarly, in the Indonesia case study (cited in the text), both pollution and energy intensity declined owing to such shifts. Pollution impacts probably declined as well, because of the dispersion of industry away from Java. However, the rapid growth of the industrial sector in recent years has also meant an increase in total pollution in spite of reduced pollution intensities. As more countries succeed in attaining rapid and sustained growth, there will be an increasing need to examine more carefully the relationship between the changing structure of high growth economies and the danger of excessive pollution. In such cases, the pollution problem may need to be addressed aggressively, with a combination of regulations and economic incentives.

On agriculture and forestry, contrary to popular perceptions, a shift in cropping patterns towards export crops expansion does not necessarily imply increased erosion. Repetto, 1989, using examples for sub-Saharan Africa, concludes that many export crops tend to be less harmful to soils. In West Africa, tree and bush crops are grown with grasses, and erosion rates are two to three times less than similar areas planted for locally used food crops, such as cassava, yams, maize, sorghum, and millet. In Malawi, Cromwell and Winpenny, 1991, found that adjustment led to changes in product mix and production intensity instead of changes in cultivated area or production techniques. Soil improving crops were adopted and agricultural intensification helped absorb a rapidly growing population on less land. Also, contrary to popular belief, export crop expansion has not generally occurred at the cost of reduced food crop output, with subsequent potentially negative social and environmental effects. However, in a study of 11 developing countries, it was found that rapid expansion of cash crops, in fact, does not tend to reduce food production (Braun and Kennedy, 1986). This complementarity rather than competition has been observed in countries where initial productivity is low and is partly explained by technology spillovers from cash crop activities that also enhance food crop production.

The more pressing question is whether these export crops displace forests. In Sudan, Stryker and others, 1989, found that trade and other adjustment-related reforms resulted in significant deforestation because increased producer prices encouraged woodland clearing for crop cultivation. However, recent studies have shown that in such cases, deforestation pressures are due to prevailing distortions within the forestry sector, such as very low stumpage prices or poor forest management capacity that are not corrected with the trade reforms. Inadequate land tenure and land clearing, as a requirement for tenure, prevent more efficient exploitation of existing agricultural lands, and have also contributed to the problem. For example, in Côte d'Ivoire, the effects of price-related policies were believed to have led to deforestation, but to a lesser extent than the lack of a consistent and secure land tenure system (Reed, 1992). The Ghana study (cited in the main text) also analyzed the interaction between effects of price changes and the institutional factors governing resource ownership and management. Using both household data and remote sensing information on agricultural and forest resources, the study found that increased crop incentives have contributed to pressures for deforestation. However, if producers had secure tenure and could internalize the implications of excessive land exploitation, these pressures would have been reduced significantly.

With regard to the global environmental dimension of international trade, the debate has revolved around the issue of whether freer trade is beneficial to global and national environmental conditions and whether it should be used to influence national and international environmental standards and agreements. Studies arising from a General Agreement on Tariffs and Trade (GATT) symposium have concluded that expanding global production and consumption does not necessarily cause greater environmental degradation (Anderson and Blackhurst, 1992). Indeed, with appropriate national policy reforms, greater trade would generally contribute to environmental gains. In the case of coal, trade liberalization and the removal of price supports in richer countries would reduce coal output, lead to higher international prices, and consequently decrease coal consumption. This would be beneficial for the environment. In the case of food production, the reduction of agricultural trade protection in rich countries would lead to a relocation of production to poorer countries, leading to greater incomes, and reduced agricultural pollution in developed countries. In poorer countries, it is recognized that the incentive to produce more will probably increase fertilizer and pesticide use. However, maintaining high levels of agricultural protection in rich countries is not an effective way of protecting the environment.

Domestic tax incentives and regulations would be a better way of limiting environmental degradation (Anderson and Blackhurst, 1992; Lutz, 1993). The same general conclusion is reached in recent studies on biodiversity and forestry. For example, the overexploitation of biodiversity and wildlife for international trade plays a minor role in species extinction since the major cause is habitat destruction (Burgess, 1991). Thus, attempts to ban wildlife trade will have limited benefit plus large cost; proper trade mechanisms, such as taxes and subsidies, would be better at encouraging conservation.

With respect to global deforestation, Barbier and others, 1991, found that the timber trade has not been the major source of deforestation. The domestic factors (distorted prices, subsidies, tax regimes, regulations, management capacity) leading to conversion of forest land to agriculture has played the larger role. In general, an appropriate combination of domestic environmental and agricultural policy measures, combined with trade reforms, will result in both welfare gains and in better environmental quality (Harold and Runge, 1993). On the international front, however, the challenge is to initiate coordinated international action on domestic reform measures to counter the environmentally negative effects of scale—any country attempting to implement domestic reforms in isolation will lose income and jobs to its neighbors.

An early view on the effect of freer trade given different national environmental standards between North and South, was that dirty industries would migrate to poor countries, where environmental standards were either less strict or nonexistent (Leonard, 1989). Recent work indicates that pollution abatement and control expenditures by firms do not appear to have had a significant effect on competitiveness in most industries since these expenditures represent a modest share of total costs. For example, environmental costs generally comprise only 0.5 percent of the value of output and only 3 percent for the most polluting industry (Low, 1992). Thus, environmental costs are not a dominating factor in decisions for locating new industrial investments. In fact, trade openness, which may promote newer technologies, may tend to have positive environmental effects since most new technologies are also cleaner (Birdsall and Wheeler, 1992; Huq and Wheeler, 1993).

These findings also suggest that there is no pressing reason for requiring national environmental standards to be made identical. Patterns of resource exploitation and pollution are primarily affected by economic and social conditions, with environmental regulations or standards (especially in poor countries) playing a minor role. Promoting acceptance of similar environmental principles, such as requiring that polluters pay for the damage they inflict, or incorporating environmental values in cost-benefit analysis, will probably be more effective as well as politically more acceptable.

Further work in this field should include efforts to establish more clearly (a) the environmental implications of liberalized trade flows, (b) the extent to which pollution from industrial growth may undermine declining pollution-intensity effects from trade reforms, and (c) whether trade measures should be resorted to as "second best" policies when international coordination fails to remove domestic distortions (for example, green labeling in the timber trade when the timber resource is underpriced in exporting countries).

Bibliography

Alfsen, Knut H.,1991, *Use of Macroeconomic Models in Analysis of Environmental Problems in Norway and Consequences for Environmental Statistics*, Discussion Paper (Oslo: Central Bureau of Statistics).

Alleyne, Dillon, and others, 1994, "Economic Reforms and Sustainable Development in Jamaica," World Wide Fund for Nature (unpublished).

Anderson, Kim, and Richard Blackhurst, 1992, *The Greening of World Trade Issues* (New York: Harvester Wheatsheaf).

Anderson, R.J., and others, 1994, *Economy-Wide and Regional Policies in Forest Degradation: Loggers and Migrants in Bolivia* (Washington: World Bank).

Bagachawa, M., and others, 1994, "Structural Adjustment and Sustainable Development in Tanzania: A World Wide Fund for Nature Study," Overseas Development Institute (unpublished).

Barbier, E.B., 1988, "The Economics of Farm-Level Adoption of Soil Conservation Measures in the Uplands of Java." Working Paper No. 11, Environment Department (Washington: World Bank).

———, B.A. Aylward, J.C. Burgess, and J.T. Bishop, 1991, "Environmental Effects of Trade in the Forestry Sector," Paper prepared for the Joint Session of Trade and Environment Experts. OECD Paris, London Environmental Economics Centre (London: International Institute for Environment and Development).

Bates, Robin, Janusz Cofala, and Michael Toman, 1994, *Alternative Policies for the Control of Air Pollution in Poland* Environment Paper No. 6 (Washington: World Bank).

Bates, Robin, S. Gupta, and F. Boguslaw, 1994, "Economy-Wide Policies and the Environment: A Case Study of Poland," Environment Working Paper No. 63, Environment Department (Washington: World Bank).

Binswanger, Hans P., 1989, "Brazilian Policies that Encourage Deforestation in the Amazon," Environment Working Paper No. 16, Environment Department (Washington: World Bank).

Birdsall, Nancy, and David Wheeler, 1992, "Trade Policy and Industrial Pollution in Latin America: Where Are the Pollution Havens?" in *International Trade and the Environment*, ed. by P. Low, Discussion Paper No. 159 (Washington: World Bank).

Braun, J. von, and E. Kennedy, 1986, *Commercialization of Subsistence Agriculture: Income and Nutritional Effects in Developing Countries* (Washington: International Food Policy Research Institute).

Burgess, J.C., 1991, "Environmental Effects of Trade on Endangered Species and Biodiversity," Paper prepared for the Joint Session of Trade and Environment Experts. OECD Paris, London Environmental Economics Centre (London: International Institute for Environment and Development).

Capistrano, Ana Doris, and C. Kiker, 1990, "Global Economic Influences on Tropical Closed Broadleaved Forest Depletion, 1967–85," Paper presented at the International Society for Ecological Economics Conference (Washington: World Bank).

Committee of International Development Institutions on the Environment (CIDIE), 1993, *Environmental Economics and Natural Resource Management in Developing Countries* (Washington: CIDIE).

Cleaver, Kevin M., and Gotz A. Schreiber, 1991, "The Population, Environment and Agriculture Nexus in Sub-Saharan Africa," Africa Region Technical Paper (Washington: World Bank).

Cooper Weil, Diana E., and others, 1990, *The Impact of Development Policies on Health* (Geneva: World Health Organization).

Cromwell, C., and J. Winpenny, 1991, *Has Economic Reform Harmed the Environment? A Review of Structural Adjustment in Malawi* (London: Overseas Development Institute).

Cruz, M.C., C. Meyer, R. Repetto, and R. Woodward, 1992, *Population Growth, Poverty, and Environmental Stress: Frontier Migration in the Philippines and Costa Rica* (Washington: World Resources Institute).

Cruz, Wilfrido, and Robert Repetto, 1992, *The Environmental Effects of Stabilization and Structural Adjustment Programs: The Philippines Case* (Washington: World Resources Institute).

Cruz, Wilfrido, and C. Gibbs, December 1990, "Resource Policy Reform in the Context of Population Pressure: The Philippines and Nepal," *American Journal of Agricultural Economics* (Vol. 72), No. 5.

Cruz, Wilfrido, and H. Francisco, forthcoming, "Poverty, Population Pressure, and Deforestation in the Philippines," in *Environmental Impacts of Economy-Wide Policies*, ed. by M. Munasinghe and others (Washington: World Bank).

Daly, Herman, and J. Cobb, 1989, *For the Common Good* (Boston: Beacon Press).

Dasgupta, P., and K.G. Maler, 1990, "The Environment and Emerging Development Issues," Proceedings of the World Bank Annual Conference on Development Economics, Supplement to *The World Bank Economic Review* and *The World Bank Research Observer* (Washington: World Bank).

Devarajan, S., September 1990, "Can Computable General Equilibrium Models Shed Light on the Environmental Problems of Developing Countries," unpublished paper prepared for WIDER Conference on the Environment and Emerging Development Issues, Helsinki.

Dixon, J.A., and others, 1986, *Economic Analysis of the Environmental Impacts of Development Projects* (Manila: Asian Development Bank).

Dobson, P.A., R.E. Bernier, and A.H. Sarris, 1990, *Macroeconomic Adjustment and the Poor—The Case of Madagascar*, Cornell Food and Nutrition Policy Program, Monograph 9 (Ithaca, New York: Cornell).

Development Strategy Institute (DSI) and Harvard Institute for International Development (HIID), 1994, unpublished, "Structural Adjustment, the Environment, and Sustainable Development in Vietnam."

Economic Commission for Latin America and the Caribbean (ECLAC), 1989, *Crisis, External Debt, Macroeconomic Policies and Their Relation to the Environment in Latin America and the Caribbean,* Paper prepared for the Meeting of High-Level Government Experts on Regional Co-Operation in Environmental Matters in Latin America and the Caribbean (Brasilia: United Nations Environmental Program).

Eskeland, G., December 1992, "Attacking Air Pollution in Mexico City," *Finance and Development* (Vol. 29), No. 4, pp. 28–30.

———, and E. Jimenez, 1991, "Choosing Policy Instruments for Pollution Control: A Review," PRE Working Paper No. 624, Country Economics Department (Washington: World Bank).

Eskeland, G., and A. Ten-Kate, forthcoming, "Environmental Protection and Economic Development: Selected Findings from Mexico," in *Environmental Impacts of Economy-Wide Policies,* ed. by M. Munasinghe and others (Washington: World Bank).

Feder, G., T. Onchan, Y. Chalamwong, and C. Hongladarom, 1988, *Land Policies and Farm Productivity in Thailand* (Baltimore: Johns Hopkins University Press).

Freeman III, A. Myrick, 1993, *The Measurement of Environmental and Resource Values: Theory and Methods* (Washington: Resources for the Future).

Glickman, J., and D. Teter, 1991, *Debt, Structural Adjustment, and Deforestation: Examining the Links—A Policy Exercise for the Sierra Club* (Cambridge, Massachusetts: Harvard University).

Goldin, I., and R. David-Host, 1993, "Economic Policies for Sustainable Resource Use in Morocco," unpublished paper prepared for the Joint Meeting on Sustainable Economic Development: Domestic and International Policy, sponsored by the OECD Development Center and CEPR, Paris, 24–25 May 1993.

Grossman, G.M., and Anne B. Krueger, November 1991, "Environmental Impacts of a North American Free Trade Agreement," Discussion Papers in Economics (Princeton: Princeton University).

Hamilton, Kirk, and J. O'Connor, 1994, "Genuine Saving and the Financing of Investment," Environment Department (Washington: World Bank).

Hansen, Stein, February 1988, "Debt for Nature Swaps: Overview and Discussion of Key Issues," Environment Working Paper No. 1 (Washington: World Bank).

———, October 1990, "Macroeconomic Policies and Sustainable Development in the Third World," *Journal of International Development,* Vol. 2, No. 4.

———, 1990, "Macroeconomic Policies: Influence on the Environment," in *Development Research: The Environmental Challenge,* ed. by J.T. Winpenny (London: Overseas Development Institute).

Harold, C., and C.F. Runge, 1993, "GATT and the Environment: Policy Research Needs," Staff Paper P93-5, Department of Agricultural and Applied Economics (St. Paul, Minnesota: University of Minnesota).

Holmberg, J., 1991, *Poverty, Environment and Development—Proposals for Action,* (Stockholm: Swedish International Development Authority).

Hufschmidt, M.M., and others, 1983, *Natural Systems and Development: An Economic Valuation Guide* (Baltimore: Johns Hopkins University Press).

Hughes, G., September 1992, "Cleaning Up Eastern Europe," *Finance and Development,* Vol. 29, No. 3.

Huq, M., and David Wheeler, 1993, "Pollution Reduction Without Formal Regulation: Evidence from Bangladesh," Environment Department Divisional Paper No. 1993–39 (Washington: World Bank).

Hyde, W.F., D.H. Newman, and R.A. Sedjo, 1991, "Forest Economics and Policy Analysis: An Overview," World Bank Discussion Papers No. 134 (Washington: World Bank).

International Development Association (IDA), 1992, *IDA's Policies, Operations, and Finance in the Second Year of the Ninth Replenishment (FY92)* (Washington: World Bank).

Kahn, J., and J. McDonald, 1991, "Third World Debt and Tropical Deforestation," Unpublished paper prepared by the Oak Ridge National Laboratory (Oak Ridge, Tennessee: U.S. Department of Energy).

Larson, B., and D. Bromley, October 1991, "Natural Resource Prices, Export Policies, and Deforestation: The Case of Sudan," *World Development* (Washington: World Bank).

Lele, U., and S. Stone, 1989, "Population Pressure, the Environment and Agricultural Intensification: Variations on the Boserup Hypothesis," World Bank MADIA Discussion Paper No. 4.

Leonard, H.J., ed., 1989, *Environment and the Poor: Development Strategies for a Common Agenda* (Rutgers: Transaction Books).

———, 1988, *Pollution and the Struggle for the World Product: Multinational Corporations, Environment, and International Comparative Advantage* (New York: Cambridge University Press).

Lopez, R., 1991, "Trade Policy, Economic Growth and Environmental Degradation," Unpublished paper, Symposium on International Trade and the Environment (Washington: World Bank).

———, 1992, "Resource Degradation, Community Controls and Agricultural Productivity in Tropical Areas," unpublished paper (College Park, Maryland: University of Maryland).

———, forthcoming, "Economy-Wide Policies, Agricultural Productivity, and Environmental Factors: The Case of Ghana," in *Environmental Impacts of Economy-Wide Policies,* ed. by M. Munasinghe and others (Washington: World Bank).

Low, P., ed., 1992, "International Trade and the Environment," World Bank Discussion Papers No. 159 (Washington: World Bank).

Lutz, Ernst, ed., 1993, *Toward Improved Accounting for the Environment* (Washington: World Bank).

Lutz, Ernst, and Mohan Munasinghe, March 1991, "Accounting for the Environment," *Finance and Development*, Vol. 28, No. 1, pp. 19–21.

Mahar, D., June 1988, "Government Policies and Deforestation in Brazil's Amazon Region," Environment Working Paper No. 7, Environment Department (Washington: World Bank).

Meier, P., and Mohan Munasinghe, 1993, "Incorporating Environmental Costs into Power Development Planning: A Case Study of Sri Lanka," in *Environmental Economics and Natural Resource Management in Developing Countries*, ed. by Mohan Munasinghe (Washington: World Bank/CIDIE).

Meier, P., M. Munasinghe, and T. Siyambalapitiya, forthcoming, "Energy Sector Policy and the Environment: A Case Study of Sri Lanka," Environment Working Paper, World Bank Environment Department (Washington: World Bank).

Muir-Leresche, K., J. Bojo, and R. Cunliffe, 1994, "Economic Policy, Wildlife and Land Use in Zimbabwe," Environment Working Paper No. 68, World Bank Environment Department, September (Washington: World Bank).

Munasinghe, Mohan, 1990, *Electric Power Economics* (London: Butterworths Press).

———, 1992, *Water Supply and Environmental Management* (Boulder, Colorado: Westview Press).

———, 1993a, *Environmental Economics and Sustainable Development*, World Bank Environment Paper No. 3 (Washington: World Bank).

———, 1993b, "The Economist's Approach to Sustainable Development," *Finance and Development*, Vol. 30, No. 4, pp. 16–19.

———, and Jeremy Warford, 1982, *Electricity Pricing—Theory and Case Studies* (Baltimore: Johns Hopkins University Press).

Munasinghe, Mphan, Wilfrido Cruz, and Jeremy Warford, September 1993, "Are Economy-Wide Policies Good for the Environment?," *Finance and Development*, Vol. 30, No. 3, pp. 40–43.

———, eds., forthcoming, *Environmental Impacts of Economy-Wide Policies* (Washington: World Bank).

Mupimpila, C., and others, 1994, "Structural Adjustment and Sustainable Development in Zambia: A World Wide Fund for Nature Study," ODI draft working paper, London.

Muzondo, Timothy, and Kenneth Miranda, June 1991, "Public Policy and the Environment," *Finance and Development*, Vol. 28, No. 2, pp. 25–27.

Panayotou, T., and C. Sussangkarn, October 1991, "The Debt Crisis, Structural Adjustment and the Environment: The Case of Thailand," Paper prepared for the World Wildlife Fund Project on the Impact of Macroeconomic Adjustment on the Environment.

Partow, Z., and S. Mink, forthcoming, "Tunisia: Livestock Policies and Environmental Impacts During Economic Adjustment," in *Environmental Economics and Natural Resource Management in Developing Countries*, ed. by M. Munasinghe (Washington: World Bank).

Pearce, David W., and K. Turner, 1990, *Economics of Natural Resources and the Environment* (Baltimore: Johns Hopkins University).

Pearce, David W., and Jeremy J. Warford, 1993, *World Without End: Economics, Environment and Sustainable Development* (Washington and New York: World Bank and Oxford University Press).

Perrings, C., February 1993, "Pastoral Strategies in Sub-Saharan Africa: The Economic and Ecological Sustainability of Dryland Range Management," Environment Working Paper No. 57, Environment Department (Washington: World Bank).

Persson, A., and Mohan Munasinghe, 1995, "Natural Resource Management and Economy-Wide Policies in Costa Rica: A CGE Modeling Approach," *World Bank Economic Review*, May 1995.

Reisen, H., and A. von Trotsenburg, 1988, *Developing Country Debt: The Budgetary and Transfer Problem* (Paris: Organization for Economic Cooperation and Development).

Reed, D., ed., 1992, *Structural Adjustment and the Environment* (Boulder, Colorado: Westview Press).

Repetto, Robert, 1989, "Economic Incentives for Sustainable Production," in *Environmental Management and Economic Development*, ed. by Gunter Schramm and Jeremy J. Warford (Baltimore: Johns Hopkins University).

Repetto, Robert, and others, 1989, *Wasting Assets: Natural Resources in the National Income Accounts* (Washington: World Resources Institute).

Robinson, S., 1990, "Pollution, Market Failure, and Optimal Policy in an Economy-Wide Framework," Working Paper No. 559, Department of Agricultural and Resource Economics, University of California at Berkeley.

Schneider, R., April 1993, "Land Abandonment, Property Rights, and Agricultural Sustainability in the Amazon," LATEN Dissemination Note No. 3 (Washington: World Bank).

———, May 1994, "Government and the Economy on the Amazon Frontier," Latin America and the Caribbean Technical Department, Regional Studies Program, Report No. 34 (Washington: World Bank).

Sebastian, Iona, and A. Alicbusan, October 1986, "Sustainable Development: Issues in Adjustment Lending Policies," Environment Department Divisional Paper No. 1989-6 (Washington: World Bank).

Shilling, J.D., June 1992, "Reflections on Debt and the Environment," *Finance and Development*, Vol. 29, No. 2, pp. 28–30.

Solorzano, R., and others, 1991, *Accounts Overdue: Natural Resource Depreciation in Costa Rica* (Washington and San Jose, Costa Rica: World Resources Institute and Tropical Science Center).

Southgate, D., and D.W. Pearce, October 1988, "Agricultural Colonization and Environmental Degradation in Frontier Developing Economies," Environment Working Paper No. 9, Environment Department (Washington: World Bank).

Steer, Andrew, and Ernst Lutz, December 1993, "Measuring Environmentally Sustainable Development," *Finance and Development*, Vol. 30, No. 4, pp. 20–23.

Stryker, J.D., and others, June 1989, "Linkages Between Policy Reform and Natural Resource Management in Sub-Saharan Africa," unpublished paper, Fletcher School, Tufts University, and Associates for International Resources and Development.

Tchoungui, Roger, and others, 1994, "Structural Adjustment and Sustainable Development in Cameroon: A World Wide Fund for Nature Study," ODI draft working paper, London.

Ten-Kate, A., April 1993, "Industrial Development and the Environment in Mexico," PRE Working Paper No. 1125 (Washington: World Bank).

Torfs, M., 1991, "Effects of the IMF Structural Adjustment Programs on Social Sectors of Third World Countries," unpublished discussion paper (Washington: Friends of the Earth).

United Nations Statistics Office (UNSO), 1993, *System of National Accounts 1993* (New York: United Nations).

Warford, Jeremy J., A. Schwab, Wilfrido Cruz, and Stein Hansen, 1993, "The Evolution of Environmental Concerns in Adjustment Lending: A Review," Paper presented during the CIDIE Workshop on Environmental Impacts of Economy-Wide Policies in Developing Countries, 23–25 February 1993 (Washington: World Bank).

Wheeler, David, and P. Martin, forthcoming, "National Economic Policy and Industrial Pollution: The Case of Indonesia, 1975–89," in *Environmental Economics and Natural Resource Management in Developing Countries*, ed. by M. Munasinghe (Washington: World Bank).

World Bank, 1986, *World Bank Lending Conditionality: A Review of Cost Recovery in Irrigation Projects*, Report No. 6283 (Washington: OED).

———, 1987, "Environment, Growth, and Development," Development Committee Paper No. 14, Washington, D.C.

———, September 1989, "World Bank Support of the Environment—A Progress Report," Development Committee Paper No. 22, Washington, D.C.

———, 1989a, *Sub-Saharan Africa: From Crisis to Sustainable Growth* (Washington: World Bank).

———, 1989b, "Philippines: Environment and Natural Resource Management Study" (Washington: World Bank).

———, 1990, "Towards the Development of an Environmental Action Plan for Nigeria," Report No. 9002-UNI.

———, 1991, *Environmental Assessment Sourcebook*, Environment Department (Washington: World Bank).

———, October 1991, "Environmental Assessment Operational Directive."

———, 1992a, *World Development Report 1992: Development and the Environment* (New York: Oxford University Press).

———, 1992b, "World Bank Structural and Sectoral Adjustment Operations: The Second OED Review," Operations and Evaluation Department.

———, 1992c, *Poverty Reduction Handbook* (Washington: World Bank).

———, 1992d, "The Welfare Consequences of Selling Public Enterprises: Case Studies from Malaysia, Mexico, Chile, and the U.K.," Country Economics Department Working Paper.

———, 1992e, "China Environmental Strategy Paper," Report No. 9669-CHA.

———, 1992f, "Economic Report on Environmental Policy—Malawi," Report No. 9888-MAI.

———, 1992g, "Water Supply and Sanitation Projects, The Bank's Experience: 1967–89," Report No. 10789, OED.

———, 1992h, "Operational Directive on Environmental Action Plans."

———, 1992i, "Adjustment Lending Policy."

———, 1993a, "Indonesia Environment and Development: Challenges for the Future," Report No. 12083-IND.

———, 1993b, "Environmental Action Program for Central and Eastern Europe," Report No. 10603-ECA.

———, 1993c, "Setting Environmental Priorities in Central and Eastern Europe," Report No. 11099.

———, 1993d, "Indonesia Environment and Development: Challenges for the Future," Report No. 12083-IND.

———, 1993e, "Jamaica Economic Issues for Environmental Management," Report No. 11239-JM.

———, 1993f, "Democratic Republic of São Tomé and Príncipe: Country Economic Memorandum and Key Elements of an Environmental Strategy," Report No. 10383-STP.

———, 1993g, *The World Bank and the Environment: FY 1993* (Washington: World Bank).

———, 1993h, "Energy Efficiency and Conservation in the Developing World," World Bank Policy Paper (Washington: World Bank).

———, 1993i, "The World Bank's Role in the Electric Power Sector," World Bank Policy Paper (Washington: World Bank).

———, 1993j, "Peru: Privatization Adjustment Loan," Report No. P-5929-PE.

———, 1993k, "Towards an Environmental Strategy for Asia," Asia Technical Department (Washington: World Bank).

———, 1994a, "Sierra Leone: Initial Assessment of Environmental Problems," Report No. 11920-SL.

———, 1994b, "Adjustment in Africa: Reforms, Results and the Road Ahead," World Bank Policy Research Report.

———, 1994c, "Thailand: Mitigating Pollution and Congestion Impacts in a High-Growth Economy," Report No. 11770-TH.

————, 1994d, "Environmental Action Programme for Central and Eastern Europe." Pre-publication draft, Lucerne, Switzerland.

World Commission on Environment and Development, 1987, *Our Common Future* (Oxford: Oxford University).

World Resources Institute, 1989, *Natural Endowments: Financing Resource Conservation for Development* (Washington: World Resources Institute).

Discussion

Discussant's Comments

Cielito Habito

It was not very long ago that structural adjustment programs (SAPs) were being roundly indicted by various people as having done great harm to the environment wherever they were implemented, leading to the outright condemnation of such programs and of the institutions that were seen as their main purveyors, the World Bank and the IMF. Having headed our country's ministerial delegations to some recent international meetings on social development and sustainable development, including the Cairo population conference, the Copenhagen World Summit on Social Development, and the recent Third Session of the UN Commission on Sustainable Development, I could not help notice a change in the language now being used by the critics from the NGO circles and representatives from the developing countries (i.e., that SAPs are important, but that they must also integrate sustainable development concerns). This is in marked contrast to the messages I heard about three years ago in an international conference on the topic held in Berlin, for example, where I recall Ved Gandhi almost single-handedly defending the Bretton Woods institutions on this matter before a predominantly hostile group. Most recently, in New York, the language used by the Group of Seventy-Seven in calling on the multilaterals to address this issue—which I had expressed in behalf of the Philippines as chair of the Group of Seventy-Seven this year—was to call on these institutions to "reorient their mandates to integrate sustainable development concerns" in their work.

All this tends to affirm what Munasinghe and Cruz conclude in their paper, that is, the environment would have been worse off if these structural reforms had not been undertaken. We all agree that macroeconomic reform programs are not inherently bad for the environment; in fact, in many, if not most cases, they have actually been beneficial to the environment. Admittedly, they could have detrimental short-, medium-, or even long-term effects that must be guarded against, or mitigated. I like the way the authors have systematically summarized the circumstances under which these negative effects can arise, which has provided

---

Note: The discussion was chaired and moderated by Naheed Kirmani.

a good basis for organizing their paper, that is, (1) when residual imperfections give rise to environmental harm, (2) when short-term contractionary aspects of such programs may have adverse implications on the environment, and (3) when negative long-term changes in the environment could result from such reforms.

While the paper steers clear of issues on displacement of indigenous peoples and resettlement of communities, unfortunately these issues have consistently provoked strong public emotions among the critics of policies and projects that promote sustained economic growth. However, these issues normally arise not as a result of economy-wide policies, but more in connection with specific development projects, especially the large infrastructure projects that the World Bank has often been associated with. Nonetheless, these have tended to be associated by the critics with structural adjustment programs because of the usual thrust toward industrialization embodied in these SAPs, which in turn entails public investment in infrastructure that often give rise to such issues. It is for this reason that we still have strident critics in the Philippines who condemn our Medium-Term Development Plan, and our vision for Philippines 2000, on the misplaced notion that it is based on a strategy that displaces or penalizes poor communities, a perception coming out of the development projects that are part of the concrete implementation of the Plan.

Looking at the Philippines, excessive industrial protection and a concomitant bias against agriculture in past decades contributed significantly to our environmental degradation, and this has been cited by the authors. The overall economic policy regime led to a weak industrial base, a high degree of geographical concentration in economic activities in the national capital region, at the expense of the countryside, pervasive rural unemployment and underemployment, and a high incidence of poverty.

Perhaps the best way to examine the links between economy-wide policies and environmental degradation in the Philippines is to work back from the main environmental problems besetting the country today. These are (1) forest degradation, (2) soil erosion and siltation of major waterways, (3) depletion of coastal and inland fishery resources, (4) water and air pollution, and (5) urban congestion.

The severe degradation and depletion of forest resources of the Philippines has been the result both of indiscriminate logging owing to past liberal licensing rules and unduly low stumpage charges and of encroachment on the uplands by poor rural folk practicing unsustainable agriculture. Some analysts claim that the latter has been the more telling factor in the destruction of our upland environment. In turn, this has resulted from widespread rural poverty that traces its origins from macroeconomic policies biased against agriculture, lack of access to land because of a highly inequitable asset distribution, and lack of nonagricultural employment. Soil erosion and siltation problems likewise arise from forest degradation.

The depletion of coastal and inland fishery resources is likewise the result of the dearth of employment in rural areas, which has driven too many to rely on fishing as a livelihood and driven fisherfolk to overfish their fishing grounds. Again, this ultimately traces back to an overall economic policy environment that inhibited growth of economic activity in the Philippines countryside.

Air pollution is the result of the excessive industrial protection of the past, which appeared to have had the effect, among other things, of weakening the incentive to invest in newer, more efficient, and cleaner equipment and technologies. Coupled with the lack of appropriate regulatory or market-based instruments to check pollutive practices of firms, the atmosphere in the major cities has deteriorated to alarming proportions. It has been noteworthy that the economic reforms we have recently undertaken toward an open, competitive economy are now leading to a surge in new investments by existing enterprises in newer, more productive and more environmentally friendly technologies.

It has been established that the greater part of our water pollution comes more from domestic sources than from industries, because of lack of sanitary sewerage facilities and garbage collection services, especially with the congestion in the cities resulting from migration from the countryside. As I have already cited above, the past economic policy regime that favored the traditional cities led to this situation, which is now being addressed under the government of President Ramos through a regional development strategy that expects to stem the tide of urban migration by providing job opportunities in the countryside.

The authors suggest a framework for analyzing and addressing the links between economy-wide policies and the environment through the Action Impact Matrix, or AIM. The value of the matrix is enhanced by the fact that there appears to be wide diversity in circumstances in different countries, leaving little scope for drawing standard lessons. The various case studies cited by the authors attest to this. But while the AIM does appear to be a useful tool for a more systematic approach to the issues, drawing one up would be more complicated than it initially appears. The authors themselves admit that linking specific causes with particular effects on the environment is especially problematic when many conditions are simultaneously changing, and the Philippines is one such case, where several factors and policies at once impact on a particular environmental system. Furthermore, the relative magnitudes of the effect of economy-wide policies on particular elements of the environment are difficult to isolate from more direct policies impinging on the environment (e.g., logging license regulations or lack thereof, lack of enforcement of municipal fishing laws).

Thus, appropriate corrective adjustments cannot be defined with any degree of precision, a situation that can be dangerous when the level or magnitude of a policy instrument (e.g., exchange rate, tax policy) can have profound implications on other variables in the system (e.g., inflation, employment, interest rates). Thus, I agree with the Gandhi and McMorran paper that macroeconomic policies are not the best instruments for improving the environment. Mohan also indicated this by saying that appropriate complementary measures need to be relied on to address the environmental "side effects," if you will, of macroeconomic policies. I may be too much of a pessimist, but it seems to me that the usefulness of the AIM for analysis and remediation, as suggested by the authors, would be extremely limited given these constraints and the reality of scarce data and quantitative tools needed for the purpose. I am a CGE modeler myself and I am only too familiar with the constraints on the usefulness of such models.

Nonetheless, I see the construction of such a matrix as a useful exercise even if only to provide a tool for problem identification, thereby providing policymakers a better understanding of the environmental problem, and for providing some general indications of policy implications. Thus, I keenly await the AIM for the Philippines that the authors indicate is being constructed. For such a matrix for the Philippines, I would include in the list of economy-wide policies

- trade liberalization/tariff reform policies
- investment liberalization
- anti-monopoly policy
- fiscal reforms
- privatization program (including Board of Trade for public infrastructure)
- Key Production Areas program of the Department of Agriculture
- Regional Industrial Centers program.

On the list of investment projects, the matrix should highlight the so-called Flagship Projects of the Ramos administration, of which there are about 18, and should proceed with the other projects in the Medium-Term Public Investment Program for 1993–98.

On the list of key sustainable development issues, I would include

- land degradation
- forest degradation

- indiscriminate land conversions
- water pollution
- air pollution
- fisheries depletion
- soil erosion/siltation
- resettlement.

Finally, I would just like to address an issue mentioned by the authors that is relevant to economies like that of the Philippines, which are seeking a transformation toward a more industrialized structure from one in which the agricultural and other primary industries dominate. Under our circumstances, an industrialization strategy that initially stresses processing industries is deemed desirable on the basis of stronger links with the rural (and predominantly agricultural) economy, thereby promoting more equitable growth. But as indicated by the authors, these types of industries also tend to be more pollutive than assembly-type industries, which usually do not lend themselves to location in the countryside, but are more attractively located at or near cities where the ports are. Thus we seem to encounter a situation where there is a trade-off between equity and environmental concerns. This suggests the crucial need for newly industrializing countries to adopt the necessary complementary measures that will address the higher levels of pollution that would otherwise occur in successfully industrializing economies.

I have not dealt at all with the feedback effects of environmental protection or lack thereof on economic growth, for which the authors admit there remains lack of more systematic evidence. But the value of environmental protection as a goal that goes hand in hand with economic development should no longer be in question in a world where people have become more forward looking, caring not only for the welfare of the current generation, but also for that of our children and grandchildren to come.

Other Discussion

Peter Bartelmus: The sounds that I hear from Mohan Munasinghe on remedial actions appear to me a bit like the add-on policies to deal with the environment after the effects on the environment have occurred. The proposal of complementary actions seems to be nothing more than improved environmental impact assessments, which is no different from previous approaches at the World Bank when environment was added to economic policy reform, as an afterthought.

I also hear sounds like let us not touch our well-established macroeconomic policies, which are producing the required necessary benefits. Have we examined the possibilities of revising macroeconomic policies, which, after all, are the enabling conditions—both for the success of project implementation and for environmental outcomes. It looks to me that we are still marginalizing environmental objectives when we use an add-on approach.

Salah El Serafy: I am delighted to hear that there is now an active process in the Bank to integrate the national environmental action plans (NEAPs) and strategies into the economic work. I hope now, in addition to meaningful NEAPs and strategies, it has been mandated for the country economists in the World Bank to think about the long term, which is the essence of environmental issues.

Ved Gandhi: Given the importance of complementary environmental policies, such as appropriate environmental taxes, proper user charges, removal of subsidies, removal of price distortions, raising energy prices, and raising water charges, I have a question essentially for Cielito Habito. What, as a technocrat-politician, does he see to be the probability that the policymakers of any country can be pushed into adopting such environmental policies in the short run? Or, must we all take a longer-term perspective until the politicians themselves have realized the urgency of implementing environmental policies, when these policies will be adopted? We in the Fund can pursue environmental objectives as a part and parcel of our work only if there is some probability of appropriate environmental policies being adopted. Without an assessment of the political feasibility, we may well be wasting our time in talking about environmental policies on our missions.

Ian Johnson: I have a question about the supply responses in response to the removal of subsidies. I do not believe that the removal of subsidies alone would be enough to ensure sustainability. Consider the price of water, which is highly subsidized in a country such as Morocco. Its true efficiency price is certainly far above the price that people would be required to pay after the water subsidies have been removed. The latter will only mean that actual costs are being met. If the full efficiency prices were charged, there would be a strong negative supply response, and these will affect the country's agricultural programs. Given that the World Bank is in the business of economic development as well as sustainability, it will be interesting to know whether the Bank staff really considers water subsidy removal as a first step or the only step toward sustainable agricultural water policy.

David Reed: Both the Fund and the Bank staff have emphasized that there are a number of situations in which the "win-win" opportunities exist. Indeed, we all recognize that price changes can lead to economic efficiency, which can also have positive environmental effects. I am not quite sure, however, what proportion of adjustment policies actually do result in win-win outcomes and how broad and comprehensive they are.

My broader concern is with the impact of macroeconomic reforms on social structures, and it is unclear to me how the IMF staff deals with them. We have an ongoing debate about this issue based on the latest WWF studies relating to the impact of the adjustment programs on the environment of nine countries. I am very concerned with the response I got yesterday when I raised this issue, the response to which was that the Fund is basically a monetary organization and does not have any sociologists and does not plan to get any soon. I think it is important to point out the Fund has done extensive work on the impact of macroeconomic policies on the breadth and depth of poverty as well as on the delivery of social services, on the efficiency of that delivery, and alternatives to it. The Fund staff could easily continue exploring the impacts of stabilization programs on the environment, for example, through the impacts of fiscal reductions on poverty. Ignoring the environment, in my opinion, will be really shortsighted.

From our WWF studies it is clear to us that it is not the price changes—whether expenditure switching or expenditure changing policies—that have an impact, it is the social dimension that has the most direct and enduring impact on the environment. For the Fund staff to simply argue that they have no capacity will be very short-sighted.

Ganga Ramdas: Is it correct to prescribe taxes that should be proportional to the physical emissions? How will they be designed and implemented?

Responses

Wilfrido Cruz: In responding to some of the comments, let me say that there is no real counterpart to the use of benefit-cost analysis in calculating the environmental impact of the projects. If you want to think of the methodological counterpart, perhaps domestic resource costs is the closest counterpart of a benefit-cost ratio. Unfortunately, the complex analysis of macroeconomic policy-environment links does not fit neatly into these analytical frameworks.

Regarding the effects of macroeconomic policies on social structures pointed out by David Reed, without doubt, these are some of the thorniest issues. The whole idea of social safety nets and complementary social policies and initiatives to accompany the need for macroeconomic adjustment or stabilization is in response to these effects.

I fully agree with David Reed that social issues are closely related to environmental ones. But I do not think that the social scientists and the environmentalists have invested the kind of time and analytical efforts required to make progress on these questions, which, among other things, cover subjects as diverse as indigenous people, resettlements, gender issues, and so forth. In fact, in these areas, one sees somewhat of a disturbing trend of anecdotal statements being made such as, I went to a World Bank project and I saw this thing happening, which is terrible. I have nothing against first-hand experience and information—those are very important inputs—but the problem is that we need much more evidence and analytical work. We in the World Bank are starting to feel that just as macroeconomy-environment links are too important to be left to environmentalists alone, social issues-environment links, too, are just too important to be left solely to social scientists!

Mohan Munasinghe: The point Ian Johnson has made that subsidies can be important in causing environmental damage is absolutely correct. If you look at the extent to which energy and water prices are subsidized in many countries, they are large and, in my opinion, it is important to deal with them first before we deal with environmental externality, to get to a full sustainability price. I fully agree with Ian that it usually will involve a two-step process; however, the efficiency prices are easily calculable while the externalities are far more difficult to calculate.

I also agree with Salah El Serafy that we do need to bring the economic and the environmental tracks together, at least within the World Bank, if not in our member countries. One way is really to make sure that the National Environmental Action Plans and the Country Assistance Strategy documents are consistent with each other or, at least, are not at cross purposes from each other. I realize fully that this is easier said than done. We have to prove to the Bank staff that this kind of cross-fertilization is actually helpful to both—that the economic arguments are helpful on the environmental side and the environmental arguments are helpful on the economic side, and that they are not necessarily at cross purposes.

On the question that Peter Bartelmus raised, yes, we have talked about environmental measures in tandem with economy-wide reforms. Ideally, before you get into major dialogue with member countries, you have to identify what the environmental issues might be and build their solutions into the overall package, as an articulated set. Once again, easier said than done. We are trying this in four countries, and it is very hard going. For example, if you want to introduce property rights, which may be difficult because of legal factors or the entrenched interests and you cannot easily move on that front, the question is, should we hold off the devaluation of currency? The obvious answer is no. Thus, you must identify where remediation should take place, but whether or not you can implement it in time is something else. So that the intent is to anticipate rather than put a band-aid after the damage.

In response to the question raised by Ganga Ramdas, take something like air pollution and let us say we are considering fuel prices and taxes. Is it really a complicated process to design the right measures or to implement them? You first have to determine where you want to apply your tax—whether at the point of generation of electricity, somewhere along the chain, or at the consumer level—and whether or not it is going to be passed along. You also need to calculate the extent of the damage and decide on what exactly is causing the damage. Suppose it is the ambient concentration of particulate matter, then we have to look at the exposure of population, which, in turn, will depend on the location of population, how much people inhale, and how well nourished they are, and the amount of health care they actually receive. So, it is a very tangled problem and it is not very easy for us to either calculate the emission and tax, or to be able to evaluate its effects.

Let me reassure David Reed on social issues. The mandate we received from the organizers of this seminar was to explore the macroeconomics-environment links, but we do know that the third leg of the sustainability pyramid is social. How seriously would the economy-wide reforms work through the social side into the environment is an important question, and the Bank staff is working on it.

Peter Bartelmus: In connection with the question by Ganga Ramdas on how emissions should be taxed, I would like to flag something we encounter in green accounting. Indeed, there we would have to follow, on theoretical ground, the chain from emission to ultimate damages, and the principle is that marginal costs should equalize marginal benefits in the form of reduction of damages through environmental action, so that we have a marginal cost-benefit ratio for internalization purposes. There are two reasons why that is not possible. First, it is very difficult to measure benefits or damages or reduced benefits from environmental action. Second, in order to link the different costs generated to those that cause them, we have to apply the polluter-pays principle and it is not easy to decide on the incidence issues. That is why we continue to have this very crucial problem in environment cost accounting.

Further Discussion

Cielito Habito: I would also like to comment on the need to revise, if not overhaul, macroeconomic policies to truly integrate environmental concerns. I would be the first one to accept that macroeconomic policies are not the best instrument to achieve environmental objectives. But this is not to deny that there is some scope for adjusting macroeconomic policies, or, at least, redesigning the timing and phasing of some of these policies that could have important impacts on the environment, through their social impacts. I guess the problem here is that there is a difference between the short-term social impacts and the long-term social impacts of such policies. I would readily agree that the long-term social impacts may well be positively served by the reform of macroeconomic policies, while in the short term there may be negative social impacts. This is the reason why the phrase social safety net came into vogue—the idea was to do something about the short term while the longer-term positive impacts are not yet forthcoming.

There is an urgent need for continuing information and explanation to the outside world by the authorities on the benefits of macroeconomic policy reform or structural adjustment policies, because the agreement that these are necessary is not yet universal. Of course, economists are already convinced, that in the long term, both in the interest of sustained economic growth and to be able sustainably to address social and environmental concerns, we need macroeconomic stability and macroeconomic policy reforms. Others, including the environmentalists and sociologists, need to be educated.

In response to Ved Gandhi's question, regarding the prospects of implementation of environmental policies in the short run, I can only speak for the Philippines, where the NGOs now enjoy a strong role in policymaking. They have a very active participation in most consultative and recommendatory bodies and there is a great willingness on the part of the government to listen to what nongovernment advocacy groups have to say about how we should be handling overall development problems. It is for this reason that I am quite optimistic that the kinds of adjustments in policies, whether it is the macroeconomic policies themselves or the complementary environmental policies, are going to be very positively received, at least in our context. The politicians in the Philippines also have been won over to the need for structural adjustment or macroeconomic reforms (it was an uphill battle over the last few years), but we now have a very supportive Congress. It should be easy, given the background of these debates that we are having here, to convince them that we do need many complementary measures in environmental policies to address the short-term negative impacts of macroeconomic adjustment. I am therefore quite optimistic that all these discussions we are having today are not going to come to naught.

Stein Hansen: Have there been any detailed and concerted studies on how the levels and patterns of environmental expenditures have been affected in countries that have gone through sustained periods of severe fiscal stringency?

Mohan Munasinghe: Some of the very early reviews in the World Bank of structural adjustment programs looked not only at the extent of environmental policies that were incorporated in those programs, but also at the expenditure side. However, the best systematic study we have seen is one done in Latin America and the Caribbean Regional Office of the World Bank, which looked at this. There is enough evidence in a number of our other ongoing studies that can help answer your question whether or not environmental expenditures are being badly slashed in the belt-tightening process of structural adjustment.

Ved Gandhi: The critics of structural adjustments keep on pointing out that social expenditures are being curtailed as a part of adjustment effort under the Bank and Fund structural adjustment programs. In this connection, we have recently completed a study covering eight countries that shows that during the adjustment period public expenditures on health and education as proportions of GDP did not decline in any of them.

Vito Tanzi: One aspect worries me. Whenever I meet ministers of the environment, they always castigate the Fund staff for not doing more in this area. Very often I remind them that the person who represents their countries on the Executive Board of the Fund does not wish the staff to get deeply involved in the environment. Perhaps he believes that one should use an organization for one main objective and that the Fund should remain the main instrument of macroeconomic adjustment and related monetary issues. I would like to point out that the Fund has a very powerful Executive Directors body, which represents all member countries and which gives specific instructions to the staff.

I have, of course, always argued that we cannot ignore environmental concerns, even if they are the side effects of our policy recommendations. We therefore try to encourage more involvement of the staff in the environment, but always emphasizing that we should not lose sight of the main objective of the Fund.

So, the point I would like to make is that very often the coordination between economic and environmental objectives must occur within a country. If one day we were to receive instructions from our Board that we should spend far more time on the environment than we are spending, there are lots of people in the Fund who would be perfectly willing to do that.

Session 4

Looking Ahead

Issues of Interest

Session 4 consisted of luncheon remarks by Stanley Fischer on "What Is Reasonable to Expect of the IMF on the Environment?" followed by panel discussions in which panelists were asked to deal with specific questions to help the Fund staff look ahead and lay the groundwork for integrating environment into their macroeconomic policy advice.

David Pearce was asked the following questions.
- Do you see taking environment into account to be consistent with the Fund's mandate as set out in Article I of its Articles of Agreement?
- Can the Fund staff, with its specialization in macroeconomics, deal with the complexities of environment? What aspects of the work on the environment should the Fund staff itself undertake and what aspects should it leave to the staff of the World Bank and other specialized institutions?

Cielito Habito was asked the following questions.
- Are the authorities of developing countries really ready to integrate environment into macroeconomic policymaking?
- What steps must the Fund take and what steps must developing country authorities take to pursue the aims of environmental protection?

Andrew Steer was asked the following questions.
- Do we know enough about interrelationships between macroeconomics and the environment to act now?
- Where is further research needed in the near future and where should we hope to be five years from now?
- What can the World Bank and the IMF working together do to help member countries correct macroeconomic policy failures with serious environmental impacts?

Ved Gandhi was asked the following questions.
- What has the Fund staff learnt from the seminar and how this knowledge can be used in Fund operational work?
- Are there any questions that are still unanswered, and what are the respective roles of international financial organizations (IMF and World Bank) and academics in answering them?

10

What Is Reasonable to Expect of the IMF on the Environment?

Stanley Fischer

To a remarkable extent, the work of the IMF is still guided by its original mandate, as spelled out in the Articles of Agreement. In 1944, the founding fathers charged the IMF with, among other things, facilitating "the expansion and balanced growth of international trade and to contribute thereby . . . to the development of productive resources" and helping member countries with temporary balance of payments problems so that they do not have to adjust by "resorting to measures destructive of national or international prosperity." These goals are pursued primarily through balance of payments assistance and what has come to be called surveillance.

Although the Articles of Agreement do not refer to the environment, it is clear that environmental issues must be taken into account in trying to attain what the Managing Director often refers to as "high-quality growth"—that is, growth that is sustainable, that improves living standards, and that does not mortgage the future for short-lived gain. As the Managing Director pointed out when he addressed the Earth Summit in Rio in 1992, IMF member countries, themselves, are redefining and expanding the concept of sustainable economic growth to encompass social and environmental objectives. In turn, the IMF is adapting its views on economic development and thus the advice it gives. For instance, the IMF is acutely aware that natural resource degradation that threatens growth cannot be ignored. But why should it be otherwise? Taking account of such environmental concerns is just good economics.

Note: These remarks were made at a luncheon talk during the seminar.

What are the links between macroeconomics and the environment? This seminar has explored the question at great length. The consensus seems to be that the causality is two-way, giving rise to three broad themes.

- First, macroeconomic stability is good, indeed essential, for environmental protection.
- Second, macroeconomic policies might, under certain circumstances, have an adverse impact on environmental conditions.
- Third, environmental conditions themselves can have an adverse impact on economic growth and macroeconomic balances.

I would like to elaborate briefly on each theme and then conclude with some thoughts on what I believe the IMF can reasonably be expected to do with respect to the environment.

Why are stable macroeconomic conditions considered a necessary requirement for preserving the environment? Research efforts so far suggest that in the absence of economic stability, the critical incentives to preserve environmental resources or undertake investment in environmental protection are distorted. For example, high and variable rates of inflation—which frequently distort intertemporal choices, including those relating to the use of forests, mines, and other natural resources—reduce the incentive to preserve resources, as producers and consumers act as though they were facing high discount rates, thus ignoring the future.

Numerous country studies and our own experience suggest that when economic stability is restored, the necessary incentives are reintroduced. For example, a study of Costa Rica undertaken by the World Bank showed that lower and less volatile interest rates, brought about by macroeconomic stability, helped reduce the high rates of deforestation. This happened because logging firms were able to make better intertemporal choices—that is, they could more easily determine future benefits.

But do the results of these studies mean that good macroeconomic policies are always good for the environment? The answer appears to be a qualified no. That is, there are cases in which macroeconomic policy reforms might have an undesirable impact on the environment—but these cases occur only when appropriate environmental policies are lacking.

Let me give a few examples:

- An exchange rate depreciation may raise the value of a natural resource that generates export earnings and it may encourage excessive exploitation. Of course, expectations of an exchange rate appreciation may also lead to the same outcome. Both cases, however, can only occur when the fiscal system does not adequately capture resource rents or reflect the country's opportunity cost of extracting the resource.

- Similarly, when governments raise taxes on petroleum products—such as kerosene—to improve fiscal balances, they may encourage the use of wood as fuel, leading to increased deforestation. While this will occur only when charges for the exploitation of forestry resources are inadequate and are not appropriately adjusted, it has to be recognized that charging for the use of forests may be difficult.

Thus, wherever environmental policies are lacking, there is a possibility that macroeconomic reforms may run counter to environmental preservation. But even then, the solution is not to give up on macroeconomic stability. Rather, countries should be encouraged to tackle the root causes of environmental degradation—the market, policy, and institutional failures—to ensure that households and businesses adequately internalize the costs of environmental damage.

How about the reverse causality? Studies increasingly confirm that the environment itself may affect macroeconomic conditions. Indeed, research shows that environmental degradation and depletion can give rise to structural balance of payments problems and can reduce economic growth prospects.

Take the case of exhaustion of both nonrenewable natural resources (such as mines) and renewable natural resources (such as forests and fisheries) through exports. Without adequate replacement and renewal, the future export base of resource-dependent economies can be seriously curtailed. Similarly, soil erosion can seriously diminish a country's domestic food supply and curtail its agricultural exports.

The Fund's Role

What do these findings mean for the IMF? The confirmation of the two-way links suggests that environmental issues could show up in our dealings with member countries in a number of ways.

First, *developing countries.* The economic growth strategy of a developing country that relies on depletable resources for current economic activity has to be different from that of other countries. Resources need to be used at an optimal rate, and provision needs to be made—through saving and investment—for the time when economic activity cannot rely to such an extent on raw materials. Most obviously, these considerations are paramount in the oil-exporting countries, but they are also important in other natural resource-exporting countries. For example, Kiribati built up a reserve fund as it used up its stock of guano.

Next, the *economies in transition.* For countries switching to a market-oriented economy, the opportunities for efficiency gains—through realigning prices, removing subsidies, and ending soft budget constraints for state-owned enterprises—are enormous. The IMF can encourage these countries to adopt policies that would serve both the economy and the environment. These might include, as a first step, adjusting energy prices to their market value, which the World Bank has estimated could reduce atmospheric emissions of sulfur by up to 60 percent in Central and Eastern Europe.

Finally, the *industrial countries.* In countries where IMF efforts focus largely on surveillance, the Fund can draw on the work by national governments, international organizations, and academics on country-specific studies of the impact of environmental policies and conditions on the macroeconomy (for example, proposed carbon taxes and common environmental policies in the European Union), and bring these to bear, where pertinent, on our policy discussions.

There is no question, however, that environmental issues tend to be sectoral and require special analytical expertise. For this reason, we in the Fund look to the World Bank—our sister organization—to take the lead on these issues. At the same time, though, we cooperate closely with the Bank in two key ways.

- First, in connection with some of the IMF's longer-term lending programs, we work closely with the Bank to help countries prepare Policy Framework Papers, which often include medium-term plans for addressing environmental problems. For example, as part of Burkina Faso's Policy Framework paper the medium-term (1995–97) macroeconomic and structural program includes the implementation of the National Environmental Action Plan, the reform of environmental institutional and regulatory structures, and the strengthening of the water management sector.
- Second, together we assist countries in designing public policy reforms supportive of the environment.

Finally, environmental or "green" accounting can help policymakers fashion better environmental *and* economic policies. For that reason, the IMF has been supporting the work of the World Bank, the United Nations, and others that have more direct mandates to develop methodologies for environmental accounts that augment conventional national accounts. Although the recently completed version of the System of National Accounts does not fully integrate environmental concerns into the core accounts, it does recommend the compilation of satellite accounts, denominated in both physical and monetary units, that record the depletion, degradation, and other changes in the environment. Already, several countries are experimenting with variants of the satellite account approach—notably Costa Rica, Mexico, the Netherlands, Norway, and Papua New Guinea.

The work being carried out on green accounting promises to be important in practice, particularly in providing a framework for thinking through the two-way interactions: the ramifications of environmental problems on production and consumption, and the ramifications of production and consumption on the environment. Moreover, some of the early results are showing just how significant environmental factors may be for long-term growth, with indicative estimates suggesting that conventionally measured GDP may, in some circumstances, exceed GDP adjusted for natural resource depletion and environmental degradation by an appreciable margin. The cost of depleting petroleum reserves in Indonesia, for example, has been estimated to have averaged approximately 2 percent of GDP between 1971 and 1984. For Mexico, the cost of oil depletion, deforestation and soil erosion has been estimated at between 6 and 13 percent of net domestic product in 1985. For Italy, net domestic product was estimated to have been reduced by about 1.6 percent in 1986 owing to environmental degradation.

11

Panel Discussion

David Pearce, Cielito Habito, Andrew Steer, and Ved P. Gandhi

Vito Tanzi: This panel discussion is the most informal part of the seminar. Certain questions were given to individual speakers, in the hope that they would spend a few minutes and give answers. The four speakers are David Pearce, Cielito Habito, Andrew Steer, and Ved Gandhi, and we will go in that order.

The question posed to David Pearce concerned the extent to which the Fund can take into account the environment within its current mandate as set out in Article I of the Articles of Agreement and with its staff specialization in macroeconomics. (Actually, this macroeconomics part is slightly misleading, because there are lots of people in the Fund who do not have a macroeconomic background, while others have a much broader background.) The second question given to David was, given that the environment is a multifaceted and complex subject, whether the Fund staff should limit itself to only certain aspects of work on the environment, leaving others to the World Bank and other specialized institutions. And, if so, what aspects should the Fund staff focus on?

David Pearce: I had the privilege of being a consultant for the World Bank when the Bank decided that environment was an issue it would come to terms with. It was entirely understandable at the time to find many people who resisted taking the environment on board, partly because at that time it was thought to be the flavor of the month (something that might soon pass away) and partly because in some ways it was an unsatisfying subject (it was not clear what you were trying to grasp

---

Note: The panel discussion was chaired by Vito Tanzi.

hold of when you are trying to grasp hold of environmental issues). I believe that the concern that I detect here is similar. Once you start on environment you might find yourself muddled up with all types of sociological issues about poverty, gender, participation, and so forth. Looking back at the Bank in the mid-1980s, one detected very much the same kind of concerns among professional staff that can be seen in the Fund now, or for that matter in the GATT when the GATT was being asked to account for the relationships between trade and the environment.

So, one should look at the way environment entered into the Bank's operations. If one did that, one would find that environmental skills were acquired by staff who were trained in something entirely different. Maybe one begins by bringing a few specialists in, but eventually you end up effectively training existing staff in environmental skills.

The question put to me refers to the environment as a multifaceted and complex subject, implying that somehow it is going to involve a huge amount of work for Fund staff to acquire those environmental skills. I do not think that is quite the case. It is certainly difficult, but it is not so difficult for people who are well trained in economics in the way that Fund staff are trained. So the first observation I will make with respect to this question is that there is not really a lot to be afraid of. It has already happened in the World Bank, it has already happened in GATT and the new World Trade Organization, and I see no particular reason why there should be a serious obstacle to the acquisition of environmental skills by the Fund staff.

The more important issue, however, is whether the Fund should be concerned with the environment. I suggested some answers yesterday. Let me just summarize those again. I put on my legal hat and suggested yesterday that the Fund's Article I does, in fact, invite the staff to be concerned with sustainability. The words are not there, but the sustainability issue is fundamental. It does not make sense to talk about the reform of an economic system or the adjustment of an economy to achieve growth, if that growth is not going to be sustainable. It would hardly make any sense to talk about revitalizing an economy to achieve growth over a three- or four-year period, if that growth comes, in fact, at the expense of the resource base on which it ultimately depends. In my opinion, there is enough now in environmental economics—enough experience and enough case material—to demonstrate that in fact economies cannot be sustainable unless that natural resource base is itself conserved. I do not wish to imply that you must never sacrifice environmental assets. And I take that environmental resource base to include not just natural resources (oil, gas, and so on) but also what I would call the assimilative capacity of the environment, its capacity to absorb the waste products that essentially go with the economic process. Putting it another way, if sustainable growth simply depends on net investment, then the crucial word is "net." We must be sure that what we are looking at is a process whereby we are fully accounting for the depreciation, not just of existing conventional assets, but also of environmental assets.

The last observation I would like to make is the one I drew attention to yesterday when we had what I thought was the most interesting intervention from the floor, pointing out that the Fund already looks at some elements of the resource base, for example, by looking at what is happening to the mineral resource base in economies dependent on minerals, and the energy base for economies dependent on energy, and the forests for economies dependent on timber. I would urge that one just needs to go a bit further and say the Fund also needs to be looking at the soil base for an economy dependent upon agriculture and look carefully at rates of soil erosion. If you are looking at economies where the value of human capital is of fundamental importance, then it is logically incumbent to start looking at the situation with respect to air pollution and water pollution, because, as I demonstrated yesterday, the cost to human capital of ignoring this environmental damage can be enormous.

So my response to the question whether the Fund staff can do it is yes. I do not think it is a major issue. In 30 years of trying to do interdisciplinary research, the one lesson I have learned is that you cannot have interdisciplinary research unless it is embodied in one person. It simply amounts to saying that if you are an economist, you have to acquire these other skills, and if you are a sociologist, you have to acquire the economic skills, and so on. I see no reason why the Fund staff should not be in a position to develop the necessary skills.

Should the Fund take the environment into account, I am absolutely clear in my mind that, because of the fundamental importance of the Fund to developing economies, it is essential that the Fund takes the environment on board.

Vito Tanzi: Thank you very much. The second speaker is Cielito Habito. The questions posed to him were how can developing countries and the Fund work together on integrating macroeconomics and the environment, what steps must the Fund take, and what steps must developing countries take.

Cielito Habito: In addressing these questions, I bring today the perspective of a developing country that continues to have an IMF program (in the form of an extended fund facility) that involves the usual monitoring of economic policy performance indicators or what some like to call "conditionalities."

In this connection, in fact, let me share with you first the apprehension expressed by my own colleagues in the government, particularly in my own agency, the National Economic and Development Authority, almost as a knee-jerk reaction when they found out that the Fund was holding this seminar and that I was going to be participating in it. Many said that if this was going to lead to new conditionalities, then we do not want to have anything to do with it.

Well, I would like to think that this is too simplistic a view. I would like to think that the IMF is indeed beginning to have an environmental conscience, if you like, or a social conscience, perhaps in the face of the strident criticisms from various advocacy groups and the traditional detractors of the Fund. I would like to think that the Fund is moving away from its traditional hard-nosed monetarism in dealing with developing countries' economic problems and is willing to recognize that perhaps the tightening of the monetary reins and lowering inflation as quickly as possible and at all costs are not necessarily in the best interests of the people in the countries under Fund programs. And so, notwithstanding my colleagues' apprehensions, I decided to come all the way here to participate in these discussions, which, I trust, will lead to an IMF much more responsive to the needs of people, not only of our generation but of succeeding generations as well.

I mentioned this morning about the Group of Seventy-Seven's call to both the World Bank and the IMF to reorient their mandates to integrate sustainable development concerns. I see this seminar as indicative of a willingness to consider this call seriously. I do not know whether we will see the establishment of a full environment department here in the IMF in the near future, as has already been done at the Bank. This would be a notable step indeed if it was to happen and one that would certainly be welcomed by the Fund's traditional critics.

On the part of developing countries, it appears that progress is being made toward the goal of mainstreaming environmental considerations in overall economic policymaking. I am reminded of the constant clamor that had been expressed in the United Nations Commission on Sustainable Development (UNCSD), since its first session two years ago, for economic and finance ministers to become more directly involved in its affairs and that the UNCSD should not just be limited to environment ministers. In this year's session, held less than two weeks ago, we welcomed about a third of the ministers who were non-environment ministers, while last year I was one of only two economic ministers who came (the other one was Minister Pronk of the Netherlands). This development perhaps signals the recognition by the country representatives of the UNCSD that the environment is much too important to be left to environmentalists alone.

In fact, in the Philippines, it was I, as Economics Minister, whom President Ramos appointed to head our multisectoral Philippine Council for Sustainable Development (PCSD), while our Environment Minister sits as vice-chair. And it was our Department of Environment and Natural Resources that had recommended this setup from the very beginning. This is in recognition that the country's environmental concerns must be fully integrated in overall socioeconomic planning and not be treated as a mere sectoral concern. I am therefore forced to give environmental concerns their due importance in the fulfillment of my work, which, among other things, includes negotiating with the IMF missions on our economic program. As the PCSD includes representatives of the nongovernment organizations and people's organizations, as full members, I am also better able to appreciate the nongovernment viewpoint in dealing with sustainable development issues than would perhaps be possible otherwise.

Now, how can we in developing countries, on the one hand, and the Fund staff, on the other hand, work together toward integrating macroeconomics and the environment? This question is best addressed in the design of the economic programs associated with the various facilities of the Fund with its member countries. In these programs, fiscal and monetary policies and reform measures in these areas tend to dominate. Between the two, the more obvious entry point for environmental concerns appears to be in the design of the fiscal program. On the public expenditure side, it has been said that budgetary cutbacks as part of austerity measures required for macroeconomic stabilization have impacted on environmental programs of governments in a somewhat disproportionate way, although Ved Gandhi cited evidence to the contrary this morning. In our own experience, in the Philippines, I took a quick look at the budget releases for the projects of the Department of Environment and Natural Resources during 1991–93 when we had an active Fund program. I found out that as much as 30 percent was withheld by our Budget Department from the budgetary expenditures already appropriated by our Congress for environment projects. I would, however, have to express the caveat that this is not really very conclusive because other factors may have impinged on the ability of the Budget Department to make these releases. Anyway, my view is that perhaps the fiscal program should have a way to "insulate" environmental programs and projects from such budgetary cutbacks, or at least provide some flexibility to prevent the environmental projects from being the first to suffer as a result of austerity measures.

In the Philippines, in fact, we adopted a concept of a core public investment program, two years ago, in which we identified a set of priority public investment activities for which budgetary appropriations had been made for the year and for which full budget releases were guaranteed in accordance with the congressional appropriations even in the face of revenue shortfalls that normally would require cutbacks in actual government releases. In my opinion, government programs and projects of environmental protection should be part of such a core public investment program. Given the relatively small magnitude of these expenditures, as compared with the much larger numbers involved in infrastructure projects, it should not be too hard to do this.

On the revenue side, fiscal reform programs typically involve commitments to adopt measures that would raise additional revenues for the government. Again, given our discussions here, it would be desirable to highlight environment-friendly tax measures, such as taxes on petroleum products, pollution taxes (the so-called Pigouvian taxes), and forestry charges, in these fiscal reform programs.

These taxes, however, are never popular, especially the taxes on petroleum products. You may be aware of our own experience with what we officially called an Energy Conservation and Environmental Levy (which everybody insisted on calling the "oil levy" anyway) that we attempted to impose on petroleum products in early 1994, only to be forced to roll back, after very strong public resistance threatened to destabilize the otherwise hospitable political environment for the rest of our economic reform program. Thus, I guess stronger education and advocacy work are still needed to improve the acceptability of such tax and revenue measures that are demonstrably advantageous to the environment.

Incidentally, we had also expected this additional levy on oil products to provide benefits to both consumers and the drivers and operators of public transport vehicles, owing to the improvement of traffic flows that was expected to result from the more expensive transport fuel. We had an empirical basis for this expectation: our own Energy Regulatory Board had cited previous studies on gasoline-price increases showing that the turnaround time of public transport vehicles became faster and permitted more trips per day and therefore led to higher net earnings for the transport operators and drivers (especially the famous "Jeepneys" plying the Metro-Manila routes). This is not to mention the added convenience to commuters, time savings, and reduced emissions owing to less idling time.

In general, structural adjustment programs ought to incorporate more market-based incentive measures for environmentally sound practices in the production sectors of the economy. Appropriate pricing of natural resources, tradable pollution permits, and environmental charges that force firms to internalize external costs inflicted on the environment should figure more prominently in the overall programs entered into by developing countries with the Fund.

It is clear that Fund programs have been aimed at macroeconomic stability in member countries, which is a vital prerequisite to sustainability of economic growth. Indeed, the debates that I have had with Fund missions coming to Manila have tended to center on determining the limits of sustainability, in terms of tolerable money supply growth and inflation, without questioning the desirability of controlling these. But, sustainable development not only calls for sustainable economic growth or getting out of the "boom and bust" cycle that our economy had been prone to in past decades. Equally important, as indicated by David Pearce, is environmental sustainability, which is what will ensure sustainability of economic growth in the longer run. And, if short-term stabilization measures begin to impair government initiatives to address this aspect of sustainability, then the situation certainly requires some serious rethinking. After all, we must not lose sight of the fact that the ultimate objective of structural adjustment programs is to improve the lives of people, both now and in the future. To undertake structural adjustment at the expense of people's welfare and the protection of the environment is to miss the whole point of it all.

Vito Tanzi: Thank you very much. The next speaker is Andrew Steer, who was asked to tell us where we stand in terms of research, in terms of knowledge, and in terms of what is feasible and what is not feasible, and where we should be five years from now.

Andrew Steer: The past three or four years have witnessed important first steps in the effort to disentangle the interactions between macroeconomic policy reforms and the environment and the state of knowledge on this issue has been presented in the papers in this volume. But where should we go from here? We in the World Bank have been giving some thought to this question as we plan our own work programs for the coming years. I believe there are five items on the agenda that will need priority attention.

First, we need to assess first-order impacts of macroeconomic policy reforms on the environment in a more systematic manner. To date some good efforts have been made, but largely on a pilot basis. We now know enough to make such exercises routine. In some instances, it will be worthwhile to construct more sophisticated general equilibrium models to enable assessment of second- and third-order indirect impacts. But I believe that the biggest bang for the buck will come from more modest exercises.

These would involve, in the first instance, figuring out the three or four impacts most likely to be important. In the case of a comprehensive macroeconomic reform package, these may involve, for example, the impact of devaluation and trade liberalization on the exportable extractive sector and on cropping patterns in the agricultural sector, the potential impact of budget cutbacks on public expenditures on environmental protection, and the potential impact of recession on activity patterns among the poor. To do a full assessment of even these "paths of influence" would require a general equilibrium approach. But in many instances, in my experience, the effort would be best spent in deepening our understanding of the individual, albeit partial impacts.

Second, having undertaken the first-order analysis, it will be necessary to utilize the findings in designing environmental policies that will mitigate any potentially adverse impacts. Ideally, such "first-best" environmental policies should be embedded in the macroeconomic and structural adjustment program itself. This has the advantage of giving clout to the environmental reforms inasmuch as they too, like the macroeconomic reforms, would be subject to careful scrutiny and monitoring.

We are starting to see examples of this approach. The recent World Bank-supported private sector adjustment program in Peru is an example. Here the authorities and the Bank recognized that the economic liberalization that was an essential element of the program would likely place additional pressure on the already-stressed offshore fish stocks (which were fished largely for export). It became clear therefore that a substantially strengthened fishing law would be required to ensure that the benefits from the program would be sustainable. A new fishing law (involving, incidentally, tradable permits in allowable fish offtakes) was thus designed and implemented as an integral part of the overall program and is monitored along with all the other elements of the program for tranche release.

Sometimes it will not be possible to incorporate such environmental policy strengthening in the core of the reform program itself (governments may choose a parallel track, or the phasing of the programs may not correspond closely enough). This is less important than the fact that both tasks (macroeconomic and environmental reforms) get implemented effectively, and in a manner that ensures that the environmental policies do not lag behind the shift in incentives that is the essence of the structural adjustment program.

Third, if we are to succeed at integrating environmental concerns into the way we do our economic analysis, it will be necessary to incorporate environmental concerns into calculations of macroeconomic aggregates. This is now commonly accepted at the project level. In calculating the economic rate of return of an investment it is clearly desirable to build in any negative impacts of environmental damage stemming from the investment into the calculations. So too at the aggregate level, it will be necessary to treat depletion of natural capital in a manner analogous to man-made capital. Macroeconomic policy is, at root, all about ensuring that economies save and invest appropriately to ensure long-term benefits to their citizens. But it will be of little use to a nation to ensure adequate financial saving to finance the continued growth of the fabricated capital stock if at the same time other equally valuable aspects of the natural capital stock are eroding in an unsustainable manner.

It is for this reason that the World Bank has recently published (World Bank, 1995, *Monitoring Environmental Progress*) revised aggregate savings rates for all of our member countries. By factoring in the depreciation of the natural capital stock we are able to ask the question, "are nations saving enough for the future?"—surely a question of vital interest for macroeconomics. These calculations are very rough and preliminary, and we see them as only the first tentative step toward a more fundamental shift in the way we measure progress. We would not support the view of some environmentalists that GDP measures should be replaced entirely. Clearly there are policy choices that need to be made (such as monetary policy) for which an accurate measure of the monetized transactions in an economy will be essential. But the current national accounts are obviously poor indicators of the long-term sustainability of a nation's development path.

Fourth, we will need to make progress in our understanding of the indirect influence of structural economic reforms on the environment via their effects on institutional and social structures. To date the common criticism of austerity measures for the environment has been couched in terms of the impact of public cutbacks on the capacity of formal public agencies to carry out their task of environmental protection. But I believe that probably more important is the potential impact on informal traditional mechanisms. We are all slowly recognizing that often the most effective measures to protect the environment are not undertaken by governments but by a set of rich traditional and modern mechanisms that, while sometimes receiving support from the public sector, are essentially independent. These range from water and forest users associations, traditional communal management mechanisms, and even business-led self-enforcement schemes, to voluntary conservation organizations.

These informal mechanisms work for a variety of reasons associated with group self-interest and (occasionally) altruism. How vulnerable they are to substantial shifts in the economic policy structure of an economy is not clear. But there is plenty of evidence from the rich literature on common-property regimes that once lost these mechanisms are very hard to recreate. For this reason it is vital that we improve our understanding of these important impacts. The broad concepts have been laid out (see David Reed, forthcoming, *Structural Adjustment, the Environment, and Sustainable Development*). It is now necessary to take a tough empirical look at this issue.

Finally, it will be necessary to deepen the dialogue and partnership between macroeconomists and the environmental community. To date in the discussion between environmental experts and macroeconomists, the flow of wisdom has generally been from the former to the latter. For the future it will be necessary for learning to occur on both sides. Many of the impacts of economic reform will be positive for the environment, and while macroeconomic stability will not guarantee a sustainable future, instability will guarantee an unsustainable future.

It has been surprisingly hard to mobilize enthusiastic support from the environmental community even for those aspects of economic adjustment programs—such as the elimination of subsidies on energy and other inputs—that are unambiguously in favor of the environment. Support for the broader objective creating a stable investment climate that will encourage a longer-term perspective on the part of investors (an essential ingredient for sustainability) has been even more half-hearted. When it comes to macroeconomics, the environmental community still tends to emphasize what it is against (such as cutbacks in environmental expenditures owing to the need to balance the budget) than what it is for (which surely includes macroeconomic stability and the removal of perverse incentives). If environmental groups, which are gaining in influence in many of the countries in need of improved economic policies, were to take a position as aggressively in favor of pro-environment economic reform as they have taken against many other measures, this could help mobilize support for these much needed policies among a constituency that has traditionally been highly suspicious of such policy reforms. This is one of the reasons why we need to build deeper partnerships with those serious environmental groups who are willing to engage in these important issues.

Vito Tanzi: Thank you very much, Andrew. Now Ved Gandhi is going to draw the main conclusions and lessons of the seminar.

Ved Gandhi: Our purpose in holding this seminar was to learn from experts and professionals in the field of environment, and the seminar has been a tremendous success in that respect.

To begin with, I must say it was good to hear from Andrew Steer that our own conclusions on relationships between macroeconomics and the environment were not wrong, but that more needs to be done and can be done.

So what have we learned over the last one and a half days? Let me list a few things.

From David Pearce we learned why the Fund must pay greater attention to environmental degradation, whether or not it is caused by macroeconomic policy reform, because of its effects on human capital, natural capital, and loss of output, and therefore on the sustainability of economic growth.

From Stein Hansen we learned that environmental targets (even though not all but only a few crucial ones can be integrated into economic policymaking) should be taken into account and economic policymakers should be shown the possible trade-offs, if any, through a computable general equilibrium model and in a country-specific context. Doing this will require commitment of policymakers and advisors to this activity, but it will also require substantial allocation of resources.

From Bartelmus, Bloem and Weisman, El Serafy, and Ward we learned that while developing comprehensive "green accounting" is desirable, and should be our first choice, the Fund does not need to wait till these accounts are ready. For short- and medium-term financial purposes, present national accounts may be sufficient, but important physical environmental indicators and targets, especially relating to the basic social services, must be borne in mind and actively woven into the design of structural adjustment programs.

From Knut Alfsen we learnt that there are countries, especially in the industrial world, where work is being done in integrating macroeconomics with environmental concerns and this work can help enhance the breadth and depth of policy dialogue. The Fund staff could benefit from it, if they diligently sought out this work and brought it to bear on their policy dialogue with the authorities. This will help us develop policies to benefit macroeconomic stability as well as environmental objectives of the country.

From Munasinghe and Cruz and Habito we learned that macroeconomic policy reform is essential and often results in win-win outcomes, for the economy as well as for the environment, and that the removal of price distortions, removal of subsidies, adjusting utility and energy prices, levying or raising stumpage fees, protecting some crucial and essential environmental expenditures and environmental investments from budgetary discipline, levying or increasing environmental taxes, user charges, and so forth, can be and should be pursued with additional vigor by Fund staff. Some of these can also provide finances for strengthening social safety nets, which will be welcome from an equity point of view as well as from an environmental point of view. The Fund staff could also start thinking of making assessments of whether we are encouraging any form of environmental degradation through macro-economic policies and thinking about what remedial measures can be put in place.

We have also learned many things from various speakers and floor discussions. Here I will list three.

- Environmental conditions, including resource depletion and pollution can affect the level and growth of output significantly. Sustainability of balance of payments and macroeconomy, which is a main mandate of the Fund, cannot be ensured in our member countries unless these environmental conditions are taken into account.
- Environmentalists and economists need to work together, instead of following independent tracks and separate objectives (hidden or open). As Mohan Munasinghe and Knut Alfsen put it, they need to be brought into one room and made to listen to each other's needs, constraints, objectives, and the resultant implications. The Fund staff can perhaps do its part in bringing them together in its member countries—this is because there are many win-win policies that are not being considered seriously at this stage as these two groups are not talking to each other. If these groups could be brought together, you have the potential of raising environmental taxes, levying appropriate resource user charges, reducing environmental damaging subsidies, and institutionalizing property rights, all of which will be win-win policies.
- First-best conditions, neither in the environmental policy field nor in the economic policy field, exist or are likely to exist in many member countries of the Fund. Both sets of policies, environmental policies as well as economic policies, would therefore continue to be made in a second-best world. There is no need to be disheartened, we were told, as long as we push ahead on both fronts, the best we know how. As one speaker mentioned yesterday, even modest progress on basic environmental objectives will be progress!

So, we have learned a great deal about what the Fund can do, but this audience must recognize that others have to play their part in helping us do it, and do it well. The academics must keep on working on the country-specific computable general equilibrium models, their development, as well as their uses. Statisticians must keep on working on greening the national accounts. Country authorities must themselves start paying sufficient attention to environmental objectives, both national and international, encourage a closer dialogue between their environment policymakers and economic policymakers, and make use of two Bretton Woods Institutions toward the development and implementation of environmentally friendly and environmentally sustaining economic policies. NGOs can do their part in keeping the environment and related agendas on the table and in helping keep the country authorities, academics, statisticians, and policy advisors, like us, on our toes, but in ways that are helpful, supportive, and constructive.

Vito Tanzi: Thank you very much. We can now have general interventions, which can be either in the form of questions directed to the speakers or in the form of statements, as long as the statements are not too long.

Other Discussion

Emilio Sacerdoti: Dealing with small or medium-size African countries, sometimes we find ourselves in impasses and contradictions. What do you do when you have small countries with populations growing by 3.5 percent per annum, the resources being encroached, fisheries being depleted, soils being eroded with intensive agriculture, forests being cut? You have countries in sub-Saharan Africa where households basically use natural gas, propane bottles, or butane bottles to do their cooking, and these bottles are subsidized. If these subsidies are eliminated, bushes will be cut, and the little remaining forest will be cut, with resulting desertification. In this sense we face some real limits in poor countries with limited natural resources and very large population growth.

It is not the question of doing green accounting or getting taxation right. I assure you that in the poorer countries in Africa, we are very aware of the problems of soil erosion. When we do projection of the balance of payments of countries, in which cotton exports are large, we are concerned about the environment. We know that cotton production is not environment-friendly—it requires a lot of fertilizers—yet the fact is that farmers love cotton production in Western Africa because prices are favorable. The farmers sometimes manage to get fertilizers informally from neighboring countries in order to produce more cotton.

So, we should be realistic. In countries where population continues to grow rapidly, if we do not have environment-friendly industrialization, we will have a serious deterioration of the environment over the next five or ten years, and there will be very little we would be able to do. Where we can use the right taxation measures we should, of course, use them; however, pressures on the environment in many countries remain serious.

Vito Tanzi: Thank you very much. Perhaps Andrew Steer can address this comment.

Andrew Steer: What you say is clearly true. It would take a different conference to talk about what is the right development strategy for Africa, but I will make a couple of points. You are correct in saying that if Africa's environment is going to have any hope whatsoever in the future, there has to be accelerated economic development. And the stability of the macroeconomy in Africa cannot but be profoundly pro-environmental over the long term.

What this seminar is asking, though, is a slightly different question. If what you are doing over the short term might actually hurt the environment, and I think there is some evidence that that may be so, how can we get the long-term benefits of macroeconomic stabilization without some of the short-term costs? I think that is the real question. Addressing the broader issue of what to do when populations are growing at 3 percent a year, and soil fertility and forests are declining by 1 percent a year, urban populations are rising by 6 percent a year, will require another conference.

Salah El Serafy: I am inspired by the last comment. I am puzzled how institutions like the GATT, and even the IMF, do nothing about the dumping of manufactured goods, while dumping of primary products is perfectly acceptable and is encouraged. Have the Fund or the Bank a role in directing attention to the fact that richer countries are exporting primary products at far lower prices than if you internalized their environmental costs. Is there a position on this? This also draws attention of the world that we are really exploiting the poor for the benefit of the rich!

Vito Tanzi: This is very interesting. Actually, I never heard of environmental dumping, but I suppose one could easily build up the concept whereby if you are exploiting the resources and are selling them internationally at a price that does not take into account externalities, that is a form of dumping. Any reaction from the experts? Professor Pearce or Mr. Steer?

David Pearce: Well, I do not know what the Bank or the IMF are doing about that. Just to tell you that in Europe this is actually a very hot issue. We are discussing, probably against all odds, the fundamental reform of the common agricultural policy (CAP). One of the effects of the CAP is to do exactly what Salah El Serafy said, which is to dump surplus production in the developing world to the detriment of the developing world. One of the arguments, and I would confess it is one of the arguments and not the dominant argument, suggests that by not moving toward world prices we are unfairly exploiting the developing world. The dominant arguments for the reform of CAP obviously are based on the sheer size of the budgetary requirement for subsidizing European agriculture and the environmental effects.

Andrew Steer: When a country's exports involve a negative externality that is not being costed, this is different from dumping. Clearly there should be some kind of pricing of that externality. Given the stress they are under to earn foreign exchange, these countries may not want to put a tax on their exports or tax fertilizer or whatever else is destroying their environment. In such cases, you might want some kind of international negotiation. We have suggested that the international trading system and the issues of negative externalities need a thorough examination. If there could be some kind of international agreement on the taxation of externality-causing outputs and inputs, it would be a great idea.

Margaret Kelly: Regarding what the IMF is doing about things like the CAP, we do not have direct responsibility over trade issues. But if you look through what the IMF has been doing, both in its trade policy dialogue with countries and in the reports that have been put out by the Fund on trade policy, as well as in the *World Economic Outlook*, the IMF has certainly taken up these issues. Quite a lot of analyses have been done on the adverse effects of policies such as the CAP.

David Nellor: I think the focus of much of the discussion over the last couple of days has been on what the Fund should or should not do, and that includes issues such as the national accounts and use of CGE models and the like. I think it is worth mentioning that there are some cases in which the Fund has actively taken into account environmental issues. In cases where natural resources are important, we have taken these actively into account and looked at the possibility of a reduction in the major exports of some natural-resource producers. We have analyzed the questions of how macroeconomic adjustment should be undertaken, whether exchange rate adjustments are appropriate, and the like, taking this possibility into account. I think we have also taken into account issues of the social structure that David Reed alluded to. In some cases, the logging companies have given local landowners four-wheel-drive vehicles, resulting in large rent transfers. These had to be taken into account in designing fiscal adjustment strategies. These are the types of issues that we have tried to come to grips with in designing programs, and it is not right to say that we have ignored these issues altogether. I think, in the case of natural resource-rich countries, we do actively take environmental impacts into account.

David Reed: I very much appreciated the comments of Stanley Fischer today and I also appreciated the comments of, I am not sure whether it is a chastised or reformed, Ved Gandhi in his concluding comments. Indeed I think that the challenge that the Fund has before it is to translate the very positive forward-looking orientation both of them suggested more evenly throughout the staff and its operations.

May I suggest that one of the lessons I would hope the Fund would take from this very positive exchange, also derived from the experience of Norway, is the benefits of the partnership formed between economic policymakers and those concerned about environmental sustainability, and the benefits that that society will derive from this partnership in the long run. The benefits are quite demonstrable through the long term. We have come to the Fund a number of times, either to reform the system of national accounts or to review macroeconomic reforms, and have found that there is the embryo of the partnership there. I would encourage you to look at the long-term benefits of developing this partnership.

Ved Gandhi: The Fund staff is a servant of the member countries that are the signatories to the Articles of Agreement of the IMF. We can move in any particular direction, but only at the pace at which the countries themselves move and allow us to move. One of the reasons why I stress this point is that the country authorities themselves have to integrate their environmental objectives with economic objectives and the environmental ministers and the economic ministers must be brought in one room. We can take an active role in facilitating that, but it is absolutely essential that this occurs. Until that happens, to expect the Fund staff to move much more rapidly will be a pious hope. Therefore, my request to the NGOs is to please go back to the countries you deal with, make sure that the environmental ministers and the economic ministers meet, and ask them to bring the Bretton Woods institutions in the same room while they talk. This has not occurred. Until that occurs, the movement toward envirnmental sustainability will be slow.

12

Concluding Remarks

Vito Tanzi

Let me conclude the seminar with two observations that are highly relevant to our discussions of the past two days and then with a few remarks on the future direction of Fund work in the environment area.

My first observation is that, as with any field of enquiry, we need facts before analysis and analysis before prescription and I am not sure that we have all the agreed facts or analytical tools or prescriptions as far as environment is concerned.

Facts. Facts regarding environmental issues are important and in the past few years we have certainly made a lot of progress in this area. The World Bank, together with NGOs and some other specialized institutions, has been instrumental in gathering and generating lots of facts about the environment, which all are essential. However, from time to time, one wonders whether the facts that we have on hand are really final facts or just transitory facts. As an example, we are told that electric cars are a solution for present-day transportation problems, but then we are also being told that electric cars would lead to an environmental disaster, because they would need large lead batteries, whose disposal would create greater problems than the problem the electric cars are trying to solve. We have to be certain about the facts before solutions to environmental problems can be presented with a certain degree of certainty.

Analysis. Except for very few countries like Norway, where serious work has been done, analytical work seems to be lagging behind facts. It may well be that the issues themselves are not precisely defined. As an example, what is the optimal basis for the taxation of environmental inputs? The truth is that, in many cases, we really do not know precisely the base on which we should apply an optimal environmental tax. We may have some broad approximation, which may or may not have much relevance (the United Nations is suggesting, for example, that we tax international airline travel as a way of achieving environmental improvement; however, the relationship between taxing airplane travel and the environment is not very clear). If we do not have a precise base that we should tax, we really do not have an appropriate environmental tax. So, in certain cases, the analysis is still at the very early stages.

Prescription. We should be hesitant to make strong prescriptions unless we are confident that our facts are right and that our analytical tools are correct. In many cases, as I have indicated, we should be hesitant to prescribe because we are unsure of the facts or the analysis. In many other cases, however, the institutions that have to carry out the prescriptions may be nonexistent. You can enact a prescription and pass a law, but if you do not have the institutions to implement the law, you cannot get very far. So, we have to make sure that the institutions are in place and that the rules will be implemented in the intended way.

My second observation relates to the reversibility of environmental damage and the role of technology in bringing it about, both of which we have not discussed in the seminar. After all, things do change over time. What may be an environmental problem at one stage (say, a beach that becomes polluted because construction material is being dumped into it) may reverse itself at a later stage when the government responsible for the beach can afford the cost of cleaning it up. So, if the environmental damage is reversible, and this relates to the sustainability issue, then maybe one can have policies that lead to some environmental degradation in the short run but that can be addressed in the medium to longer run. This, of course, also depends upon the availability of relevant technology to help solve these problems.

Let me now remark on the past and the future work of the Fund in the environmental area. We knew almost nothing about the environment four years ago but know quite a bit today, so there has been a gigantic jump in our knowledge of environmental issues. We had a similar experience when we started dealing with poverty. There was a time when the word poverty was almost unheard of in the Fund. Then we got concerned about it and began to worry about it. As time passed, this concern became quite broadly spread within the institution, so that now almost everyone, who leads a program mission to a member country, worries about the impact of the Fund program on the poorest 10 percent or 20 percent of the country's population. I am sure that progressively, though slowly, we are moving in that same direction with regard to the environment as well.

A point that has been made frequently during this seminar is that the mandate of the Fund limits the Fund's work on the environment as it is not the Fund's main responsibility. In my opinion, there are certain things in the environment that we can do even now without having to go to the IMF Board or changing the mandate of the Fund. As we have discussed over the last two days, we know that environmental degradation and natural resource depletion can have an impact on macroeconomic balances and growth prospects of countries. As Fund staff become aware of these problems in the countries in which they work, I would expect that they, of necessity, would start taking into account the implications of these problems in their assessment of macroeconomic conditions as well as in their policy dialogue with the authorities of the country.

Let me give a few other examples of what we can possibly do. We have discussed today the work being done in Norway on the interplay between macroeconomics and the environment. Certainly, work of this kind could enter into the policy dialogue with our industrial country members where our role is mainly that of surveillance.

In developing countries, and economies in transition as well, where we are providing financial support for macroeconomic policy reform to help countries achieve sustainable external balances, we can encourage countries to take advantage of win-win opportunities for improving macroeconomic balances and the environment, through the adoption of sound economy-wide policies, such as price reform, subsidy reform, and liberalizing markets. We do recognize that such policies may interact with existing market, policy, or institutional failures for environmental resources. In such circumstances, the Fund staff could encourage the country authorities to adopt appropriate complementary environmental policies. Of course, such encouragement cannot and should not lead to "environmental conditionality."

However, all of us must admit that the issues of environmental sustainability extend beyond the timeframe of the Fund-supported programs and it is not something that the Fund staff alone is capable of dealing with. Besides, we must respect the commands of our member countries, represented by their ministries of finance or central banks, that the Fund must remain a monetary institution. With regard to longer-term environmental issues, therefore, we will have to continue to rely on the World Bank and other specialized environmental institutions.

Regarding the role of the countries themselves, the point has been made here as well as in other fora, that the Fund prescribes structural adjustment policies, and, among other things, tells the country to cut its public expenditure on social services or the environment. It is important to stress that our member countries are completely independent and sovereign entities, and while we do negotiate the final objectives of the programs, it is left up to the country authorities to decide on how they wish to achieve those objectives. If they decide that they want to cut the public expenditure on social services or the environment, we can make some noises about it, but there is not much else that we can do. It is, and has to be, an internal political decision of the country as to what is finally done to achieve the program objectives. Incidentally, someone mentioned that a recent study by the Fund staff showed that social spending on education and health was not reduced in eight countries' structural adjustment programs. In fact, a study of African countries, done by David Sahn of Cornell, also shows that structural adjustment programs led to little to no reduction in public expenditure on health and education, quite the contrary from what is normally believed.

In this connection, Cielito Habito suggested earlier that environmental projects should be insulated from cuts in public expenditures under the IMF-supported programs. Quite apart from the fact that this is essentially a decision for the authorities to make, as I said before, I see a possible problem with this approach: you open yourself to equal pressure from other groups. The environmental group is not the only group out there trying to push its objectives, you could get pressures from other groups, say, those who want to protect the spending for certain regions of the country, or for civil servants, for the aged, for defense, for sports and youth welfare, and so forth. So, one has to hope that the authorities themselves would be wise enough to decide upon the best allocation of the country's resources.

Finally, I do not wish to minimize the problems of environmental degradation and resource depletion in many countries and we hope to be able to expand our work in the environment. There are, however, some constraints. The latest constraint is that the Fund has started reducing its staff at a time when a major activity of the Fund, surveillance, has to be expanded.

Participants

Knut Alfsen
Director of Research, Research Department, Statistics Norway, Norway

Philip Bagnoli
Research Associate, Brookings Institution

Peter Bartelmus
Officer-in-Charge, United Nations Statistical Division

Adriaan Bloem
Division Chief, Real Sector Division, Statistics Department, International Monetary Fund

Benedicte Christensen
Division Chief, Development Issues Division, Policy Research and Review Department, International Monetary Fund

Peter Clark
Division Chief, Economic Modeling and External Adjustment Division, Research Department, International Monetary Fund

Paul Cotterell
Deputy Division Chief, Real Sector Division, Statistics Department, International Monetary Fund

Wilfrido Cruz
Environmental Economist, Environment Department, World Bank

Herman Daly
Senior Research Scholar, School of Public Affairs, University of Maryland, Maryland, USA

Mohammed El-Erian
Deputy Director, Middle Eastern Department, International Monetary Fund

Salah El Serafy
Economic Consultant, Arlington, Virginia, USA

Nuri Erbas
Senior Economist, Middle Eastern Department, International Monetary Fund

Stanley Fischer
First Deputy Managing Director, International Monetary Fund

Ved Gandhi
Assistant Director, Fiscal Affairs Department, International Monetary Fund

Cielito Habito
Secretary of Socio-Economic Planning and Director-General, National Economic and Development Authority, Republic of the Philippines

Kirk Hamilton
Senior Fellow, Centre for Social and Economic Research on the Global Environment, University College London and University of East Anglia, UK

Stein Hansen
Director, Project for a Sustainable Economy, Norway; Partner, Nordic Consulting Group A.s.; and Senior Research Fellow, Fridtjof Nansen Institute, Norway

Ian Johnson
Assistant Chief Executive Officer, Global Environment Facility

Margaret Kelly
Deputy Director, External Relations Department, International Monetary Fund

Naheed Kirmani
Division Chief, Trade Policy Division, Policy Development and Review Department, International Monetary Fund

Malcolm Knight
Deputy Director, Middle Eastern Department, International Monetary Fund

Jim MacNeill
Chairman of the Board, The International Institute for Sustainable Development, Winnipeg, Canada

Ronald McMorran
Economist, Fiscal Affairs Department, International Monetary Fund

Mohan Munasinghe
Chief, Pollution and Environmental Economics Division, Environment Department, World Bank

David Nellor
Deputy Division Chief, Fiscal Analysis Division, Fiscal Affairs Department, International Monetary Fund

Kirit Parikh
Director, Indira Gandhi Institute of Development Research, Bombay, India

David Pearce
Director, Centre for Social and Economic Research on the Global Environment, University College London and University of East Anglia, UK

Ganga Ramdas
Assistant to the Executive Director, Office of the Executive Directors, International Monetary Fund

David Reed
Director, International Institutions Policy Program, World Wide Fund for Nature—WWF International

Emilio Sacerdoti
Division Chief, West Africa Division II, African Department, International Monetary Fund

Andrew Steer
Director, Environment Department, World Bank

Vito Tanzi
Director, Fiscal Affairs Department, International Monetary Fund

Michael Ward
Principal Economist, Socio-Economic Data Division, International Economics Department, World Bank

Ethan Weisman
Economist, Statistics Department, International Monetary Fund